THE CULT OF SAINT CATHERINE OF SIENA

The Cult of Saint Catherine of Siena

A Study in Civil Religion

GERALD PARSONS
Open University, UK

Routledge
Taylor & Francis Group
LONDON AND NEW YORK

First published 2008 by Ashgate Publishing

2 Park Square, Milton Park, Abingdon, Oxfordshire OX14 4RN

711 Third Avenue, New York, NY 10017

Routledge is an imprint of the Taylor & Francis Group, an informa business

First issued in paperback 2018

British Library Cataloguing in Publication Data
Parsons, Gerald
The Cult of Saint Catherine of Siena: A Study in Civil Religion
1. Catherine, of Siena, Saint, 1347–1380 – Cult. 2. Civil religion – Italy – Siena – History. 3. Siena (Italy) – Church history.
I. Title.
282.4'558

Library of Congress Cataloging-in-Publication Data
Parsons, Gerald.
The Cult of Saint Catherine of Siena: A Study in Civil Religion / Gerald Parsons.
p. cm.
Includes bibliographical references (p.) and index.
1. Catherine, of Siena, Saint, 1347–1380 – Cult. 2. Civil religion – Italy – Siena.
I. Title.
BX4700.C4P35 2008
282.092–dc22 2008007338

ISBN 978-0-7546-5645-6 (hbk)
ISBN 978-1-138-37600-7 (pbk)

Contents

List of Illustrations

Colour Plates

Placed between pages 86–87

Black and White Plates

Preface

In researching and writing this book I have been fortunate to receive the help and support of a number of institutions and individuals and it is a pleasure to express my thanks to them here.

In Britain, I am grateful to the Research Committee of the Faculty of Arts of the Open University for funding for travel to Siena for periods of research, and to the British Academy for a grant to fund the cost of illustrations. Colleagues in the Religious Studies department of the Open University have offered encouragement and comment. I am also grateful to Carol Richardson for her assistance with photographs, to Callum Brown, Grace Davie and Mike Snape for advice on particular aspects of the book, and to Joanna Cannon for permission to quote from an unpublished paper. Of course, responsibility for whatever shortcomings remain is entirely my own.

In Italy I am once again indebted to the staff of the Biblioteca Comunale degli Intronati in Siena: they have continued, over many years, to offer help and assistance with great courtesy and kindness. I also thank the archivists of the Archivio Arcivescovile di Siena, the Nobile Contrada dell'Oca, and the Associazione Internazionale dei Caterinati for their courtesy and assistance. For permission to publish illustrations of material in their possession, I am grateful to the Archivio di Stato di Siena, the Comune di Siena, the Pinacoteca Nazionale di Siena, the Consorzio per la Tutela del Palio di Siena, the Associazione Internazionale dei Caterinati, the Casa Santuario di Santa Caterina da Siena, and the Ven. Confraternita di Santa Caterina da Siena in Rome.

I owe a particular debt of gratitude to Dottoressa Franca Piccini, the archivist of the Associazione Internazionale dei Caterinati. Not only did she offer me generous assistance with my research in the archives of the Associazione, provide me with a number of the Associazione's publications and photocopies of other materials but, in addition, when she realized the particular focus of my research, she drew my attention to collections of photographs and other documents in the possession of the archive, but not in the published catalogue. She also subsequently sent me copies of a number of the photographs. As several of the illustrations demonstrate, and as the footnotes to Chapter 3 of the book also indicate, her assistance was not only generous but invaluable.

As ever, however, my greatest debt is to my partner, Diana Norman. As always, she has offered the most consistent encouragement to the project and also the most astute criticism of its earlier versions. The book is dedicated to her – and to our continuing Sienese adventure together.

Introduction

Civil Religion and the Cult of Catherine of Siena

Every year, on the weekend of, or following, 29 April – the day on which Catherine of Siena died in Rome in 1380 – her annual festival is celebrated in the city of her birth. Although the celebrations extend over an entire weekend, the principal events occur on the Sunday. In the morning, a procession takes place from the Palazzo Pubblico – the town hall of Siena – to the Sanctuary of Saint Catherine which is located near to San Domenico, the Dominican church in Siena, in the neighbourhood of Siena known as Fontebranda. The Sanctuary – built on the site of the house in which Catherine's family lived – consists principally of a church, the Chiesa del SS. Crocifisso, that houses the wooden crucifix in front of which Catherine claimed to have experienced the stigmata in April 1375, and two oratories, the Oratorio della Cucina and the Oratorio della Camera, as well as a spacious courtyard and portico, the Portico dei Comuni, which acts as an entrance to the complex of buildings.[1]

When the procession from the Palazzo Pubblico – which includes the civic authorities of Siena, representatives of the seventeen districts (known as *contrade*) into which Siena is divided, and other visiting civic and ecclesiastical dignitaries – reaches the courtyard and portico at the Sanctuary, a carefully constructed ceremony takes place. The Mayor of Siena and the Archbishop of Siena both speak in celebration of Catherine and her life and significance, and a gift of oil is donated – by representatives of either another Italian city or an Italian cultural or charitable organization – as a symbolic gift to maintain the flame on a Votive Lamp, dedicated to Saint Catherine, which burns permanently in the nearby Chiesa del SS. Crocifisso. After this ceremony, the civic and religious authorities proceed to the nearby church of San Domenico for the celebration of a solemn high mass, at which the principal celebrant and preacher will be a visiting cardinal, officially representing the Pope and the Vatican. In the afternoon, in the Campo – the central piazza of Siena – in front of the Palazzo Pubblico, the final ceremony of the annual festival takes place. In the presence of representatives of the various branches of Italy's armed forces and of the Red Cross – and following an inspection of these representatives by the visiting cardinal and a speech by a minister representing the Italian government – a blessing is imparted to Siena, to Italy, and to Europe by the cardinal, using the relic

1 Aspects of the history of the Sanctuary will be discussed in greater detail in later chapters. For detailed analyses of the buildings see Torriti (1982); Sabelli (2002).

of the finger of Saint Catherine which has been brought in procession to the Campo from the church of San Domenico.[2]

These annual ceremonies – and in particular the blessing in the Campo at the climax of the day's events – conveniently encapsulate Catherine of Siena's three historical and contemporary roles as, simultaneously, a patron saint of Siena, a patron saint of Italy and a patron saint of Europe. Thus, the participation of the Sienese civic authorities – and the fact that the day begins with a procession from the Palazzo Pubblico and ends with a ceremony and blessing in the piazza in front of this centuries-old symbol of Sienese civic life – serves to demonstrate the continuing strength of Sienese civic devotion to the cult of the most famous of Siena's local saints. At the same time, however, the presence of a representative of the Italian government, of officials from other Italian cities or institutions, and of a representative of the Vatican, draw attention to the national significance of Catherine of Siena as one of the two official patron saints of Italy – a status that she has enjoyed, together with Francis of Assisi, since their official proclamation as *Patroni d'Italia* by Pope Pius XII in June 1939. Finally, the closing blessing – with its benediction not only of Siena and Italy but also of Europe – and the official designation of the contemporary annual festival as a '*Festa Internazionale*' in celebration of Catherine's significance emphasizes the fact that, since the official proclamation by Pope John Paul II in October 1999, Catherine of Siena has also been one of the official co-patron saints of Europe.[3]

The present book analyses the way in which – from the late fourteenth century until the early twenty-first century – the cult of Saint Catherine of Siena developed to encompass these three distinct, yet complementary, roles. The first chapter examines the development of the cult of Saint Catherine – especially, but not exclusively, in Siena – and the way in which she became the pre-eminent '*santa senese*'. It therefore begins by reviewing the history of her cult from her death in 1380, through the process leading to her canonization by Pope Pius II in 1461, showing how, during this time, Catherine's status developed from that of one local *beata* amongst others, to her being one of the principal members of the pantheon of Sienese civic saints and *beati*. The chapter then examines the way in which – after the fall of the Sienese republic in 1555 and the loss of Sienese independence – between the mid sixteenth century and the mid nineteenth century, Catherine's status in Siena continued to

2 The origins and historical development of this annual festival will be examined in detail in Chapters 3 and 4. See also Parsons (2004b).

3 Europe has six official patron saints. The first, Benedict, was proclaimed patron saint of Europe by Pope Paul VI in 1964, in recognition of the contribution of Benedictine monasticism to the creation of a spiritual unity from the Mediterranean to Scandinavia and from Ireland to Poland. Subsequently, Cyril and Methodius were proclaimed additional patron saints of Europe by Pope John Paul II in 1980 because of their role in bringing Christianity to the Slav peoples and to emphasize, alongside Benedict, the unity of Europe, East and West, for which see Walsh (1987, pp. 71, 133); Grygiel (2004). In October 1999 John Paul II then proclaimed Bridget of Sweden, Catherine of Siena and Teresa Benedetta della Croce (Edith Stein) additional female co-patron saints of Europe – for which see also Chapter 4 of the present book.

increase as she became not merely a prominent member of the Sienese pantheon of civic saints but its pre-eminent and predominant figure.

The second chapter examines the beginning of the development of the modern cult of Catherine of Siena, from the mid nineteenth century until the end of the fourth decade of the twentieth century. It thus traces the increasing interest in Catherine as a saint of national as well as Sienese significance, analysing in particular the campaign during the 1920s and 1930s – and thus in the context of Mussolini's Fascist regime – to secure her official proclamation as a patron saint of Italy. Chapter 3 focuses on the crucial and tumultuous years from 1940 to 1945, beginning with the first *Festa Nazionale* in Catherine's honour in 1940, and then exploring the ways in which her cult became the focus for the religious devotion of Italians during the changing fortunes and the turmoil of the Italian experience of the Second World War. Chapter 4 then analyses the successive transformations of the cult of Catherine of Siena in the decades since 1945. It examines, first, the reconstruction of Catherine's cult in the post-war period and her re-interpretation as a patron saint for a post-Fascist and democratic Italy, before then tracing the development of her cult as *Patrona d'Italia* during the 1950s, 1960s and 1970s. Secondly, the chapter analyses the further transformation of Catherine and her cult during the 1980s, the 1990s, and the first years of the twenty-first century as she was increasingly promoted as – and finally formally proclaimed – a co-patron saint of Europe.

In thus examining and analysing the history of the cult of Saint Catherine as patron saint of, respectively, Siena, Italy and Europe, the book will also, necessarily, explore a number of other themes that are central to that history. The central concern of the book will be the role, function and significance of the cult of Saint Catherine of Siena specifically as an expression of 'civil religion'. That is to say, it will examine the various ways in which devotees of Catherine of Siena, and other advocates of her significance, have promoted, deployed and exploited her cult as a means of seeking to cultivate a shared sense of history and destiny – and to promote particular values – as Sienese, as Italians and as Europeans. In so doing it will show how the cult of Catherine of Siena has been used to relate these societies to particular values; to provide a unifying vision which seeks to integrate these communities; to provide a collection of beliefs, values, rites, ceremonies and symbols which give sacred meaning to their lives, and thus to provide an overarching sense of unity that can transcend internal conflicts and differences.[4] In so doing, the book will build upon my previous study of Sienese civil religion, *Siena, Civil Religion and the Sienese*,[5] but it will do so in a way that is at once both narrower in focus in one respect, yet much wider in scope in another. Thus, in so far as the present book is concerned with Sienese civil religion, it focuses not on Sienese civil religion as a whole – with its central and defining devotion to the Virgin and its principal festival of the *Palio* – but on the specific and particular aspect of Sienese civil religion that is expressed through

4 This definition of civil religion is derived from Richard Pierard and Robert Linder's work on civil religion and the American presidency, for which see Pierard and Linder (1988, especially pp. 22–3). I have previously applied this interpretation of civil religion to the Sienese context, for which see Parsons (2002, chs 4–7; 2004a; 2004b; 2006).

5 Parsons (2004a).

Sienese enthusiasm for Catherine of Siena and her cult. In this respect, the focus of the present work is much narrower than its predecessor. Conversely, however, whereas my previous study focused only on Siena and its various expressions of civil religion, the present study, whilst focused on the cult of one Sienese saint, nevertheless carries the study of that cult firmly beyond Siena itself to explore the cult of Saint Catherine as, firstly, an expression of Italian civil religion and, secondly, a potential focus for an emerging sense of a European civil religion.

In exploring the significance of the cult of Catherine of Siena for each of these varieties of civil religion, the present study will also touch upon a number of themes relating to issues of gender, political power and the relationship between secular and religious impulses in the cultivation and exploitation of the cult of this particular saint.

It will therefore include consideration of the relative contributions of secular communities and interest groups (such as the Sienese civic authorities and particular political parties and organizations) and religious ones (such as the Dominican Order, various societies dedicated specifically to Catherine of Siena, the Catholic church in Italy, and particular popes). Thus, in the period leading to Catherine's canonization in 1461, it will be necessary to consider the relative importance of the Sienese government and the Dominican Order in the promotion of her cult and in the presentation of the case for her canonization. Subsequently, in considering the development of Catherine's cult in the twentieth century, a major theme will be the relationship, during the 1920s and 1930s, between the interests and influence of, on the one hand, the Sienese, the Dominican Order and the Italian Catholic church in general in the campaign to have Catherine proclaimed patron saint of Italy, and on the other hand the interest in – and use of – Catherine and her cult on the part of Fascism and its supporters and sympathizers. Similarly, in considering the campaign, in the later twentieth century, to have Catherine proclaimed a patron saint of Europe the balance between specifically Sienese advocacy of this cause and the contributions and influence of both the Dominican Order and the policies of the contemporary papacy will also be examined.

In this way the book aims to address the question of the political uses of Catherine and her cult – a theme which, it has recently been noted, merits serious historical discussion.[6] In seeking to address this hitherto neglected theme the principal aim will be to allow the various contemporary sources to speak for themselves. Thus, especially in Chapters 2, 3 and 4, a variety of often starkly contrasting interpretations of Catherine will be examined in order to understand the ways in which she and her cult were adopted by, and adapted to the particular needs of, a series of contrasting political contexts and ideologies.

The book thus provides a distinctive and innovative approach to the study of Catherine of Siena and her cult. Whilst it does not engage directly with issues such as the nature of her spirituality and theology, her spiritual or theological significance for the contemporary church, the detailed history of her iconography or the debates over the precise historical details of her life – all of which are the subjects of extensive

6 Zaggia (2006, p. 175, note 114).

bibliographies in their own right[7] – it does present a study of the development of her cult and of devotion to it specifically in respect of its relationship to three distinct yet related types of civil religion: Sienese, Italian and European. In pursuing this particular end, however, the book will inevitably touch occasionally on aspects of all of the above themes, and in particular upon specific aspects of Catherine's portrayal in both painting and sculpture – especially where such portrayals were central to the development of her cult as an expression of one or other type of civil religion.[8] Similarly, frequent reference will also be made to various moments in – and traditions concerning – her biography, especially where particular incidents in or aspects of her life have become central to the elaboration and celebration of her cult and its significance for one or other type of civil religion.

It is necessary, therefore, to include here a brief outline of the life of Catherine of Siena, as conventionally understood and interpreted by her followers and devotees, and as exploited by them in the construction and promotion of her cult. The summary that follows is not a carefully considered historical analysis of the sources regarding Catherine, such as would be essential for a thorough and critical historical assessment of her life. Rather, it is an account of her life – and her hagiographical tradition – as it has been understood, interpreted and deployed by those concerned to celebrate Catherine and promote her cult. For it is the potent 'myth' of Catherine of Siena – and the way in which that 'myth' has been exploited and manipulated across the centuries by various interest groups – that is the principal concern of this book. There are, therefore, a number of questions which, although interesting and significant in themselves, nevertheless lie beyond the scope of the present study. These questions include, for example, such issues as the precise nature of Catherine's mystical and 'miraculous' experiences; the exact nature and reality of her claim to have experienced the stigmata; the most appropriate explanation for her practice of extreme fasting and her habitual refusal of food;[9] the actual extent (or not) of her influence upon Pope Gregory XI in his decision to return to Rome from Avignon;[10] and the degree of accuracy in the accounts of Catherine provided by her principal male followers and hagiographers. What is essential in understanding the historical development of the cult of Saint Catherine of Siena and its significance in terms of civil religion – and is therefore central to the present work – is the way in which those who have promoted her cult, especially at key moments in its history, have understood her life. The outline of her 'life' which follows therefore summarizes her biography, as conventionally and traditionally understood by her followers and

---

7 Those wishing to obtain an overview of the immense modern literature on all aspects of Catherine and her cult should consult the five volumes of analytical and annotated bibliography edited by Zanini and Paterna and covering the century from 1901 to 2000. The first two volumes, Zanini (1971, 1985), cover the period 1901–75; the third, fourth and fifth volumes, Paterna (1989; 2000; 2003), cover the period 1976–2000.

8 For an overview of the history of the portrayal and iconography of Catherine of Siena, see, principally, Bianchi and Giunta (1988).

9 For discussion of such issues, see for example Noffke (1980); Bell (1985, pp. 22–53); Walker Bynum (1987, esp. pp. 165–80); Slattery (1989); Scott (1992; 1993; 1994; 1999); Rattazzi Papka (1995); Bornstein (1998).

10 See for example Vauchez (1997, pp. 380–81); Luongo (2006, pp. 165, 167, 175–6).

devotees, before also briefly noting a number of important critical issues concerning this 'life' that have been identified in recent historical scholarship.[11]

Catherine is believed to have been born in 1347, the year before the Black Death struck Siena with brutal and devastating force. She and a twin sister were the 23rd and 24th of the 25 children born to Jacopo Benincasa, a dyer, and Lapa Piagenti. Her family lived in the district of Siena known as Fontebranda, which was the centre of the Sienese wool trade and was located below the hill on which stood the imposing church of San Domenico – the principal Dominican church in Siena. According to her hagiographical tradition, Catherine first manifested a precocious capacity for the mystical and the visionary when, at the age of only six, she experienced a vision of Christ – in the sky above the church of San Domenico – dressed in pontifical vestments and accompanied by the apostles Peter and Paul. The following year, 1354, Catherine is said to have made her first vow of perpetual virginity. In 1359, at the age of twelve, under pressure from her mother and her older sister Bonaventura – who hoped to secure a good marriage for her – she is reputed to have agreed to wear finer clothes and take greater care of her appearance. In 1362, however, Bonaventura died in childbirth – an event that Catherine interpreted as a punishment for her vanity. She therefore reaffirmed her commitment to her vow of perpetual virginity and – on the advice of her Dominican confessor, her cousin Tommaso della Fonte – cut her hair short in explicit defiance of her family's plans for her marriage. In response her mother – according to the conventional account – made Catherine act as a servant to the household and deprived her of the room to which she retired for prayer. In 1363, following the death of her younger sister Nanna, Catherine summoned her entire family and informed them that, although she would act as their servant for the rest of her life, she would never marry. Her father, allegedly, then ordered that she should no longer be prevented from her chosen vocation.

Catherine then began a three-year period of solitude and silence in a room within the family home, which she effectively turned into a contemplative's cell, and also began to eat only bread, water and raw vegetables. During this time she learned to read and underwent an increasing number of mystical experiences and visions, including that of a 'mystical marriage to Christ'. Subsequently, however, Catherine experienced a call from Christ to leave her cell in order to serve the sick and the poor of Siena. She duly devoted herself to nursing the sick in Siena's major city hospitals, thus establishing an association with both the Sienese Misericordia and the Spedale di Santa Maria della Scala. At some point in the 1360s Catherine also joined the group of Sienese laywomen associated with the Dominican Order and known as *mantellate*. In 1370, with severe famine in Siena, she further reduced her diet to water and raw vegetables and had a number of further intense mystical experiences, including a near-death experience usually described as 'her mystical death'. Although she was only in her early twenties, the circle of followers that

11 This biographical outline is based on the summaries of Catherine's life presented in the critical scholarly English language edition of Catherine's Letters, for which see Noffke (2000, pp. liii-lvi), supplemented by the biographical summaries in Dupré Theseider (1979); Falassi (1980); and Cavallini (2005). For the most recent critical analysis of her life and the sources for it see Luongo (2006).

had begun to form around her started to style themselves her 'spiritual family' or '*famiglia*' and to call her '*mamma*'. At this point the Dominican friar Bartolomeo Dominici joined her circle and became her second confessor, whilst her fame also began to spread beyond Siena and, in response to letters sent to her, she began her practice of sending letters to prominent figures, both political and ecclesiastical, dictating them to members of her circle because she still could not write. Continuing her habit of extreme fasting, by 1372 she could no longer tolerate any solid food and would vomit if she tried to eat.[12]

In early 1374 Catherine was summoned to Florence by the Dominican Order to be questioned before the General Chapter of the Order either – depending on how the incident is interpreted – to answer concerns as to her orthodoxy because of doubts prompted by the extravagant nature of her visions and mystical experiences, or as part of a process, within the Dominican Order, of assessing her suitability for a more public role in the life of the Order and its role in the contemporary church. Whatever the origins of her summons to Florence, during the General Chapter, Raymond of Capua was appointed as her confessor and sole Dominican authority and adviser, and from this point onwards her practice of sending letters to prominent political and ecclesiastical figures increased dramatically and her career took on an increasingly public and political character.[13] During the summer she assisted the sick in Siena during a severe outbreak of plague, and in the autumn she visited the Dominican community at Montepulciano, to the south of Siena, to venerate the body of its founder, Agnes of Montepulciano.

Catherine spent much of 1375 in Pisa and Lucca, working to prevent the outbreak of outright conflict between the papacy – still located in Avignon – and Florence, which sought to organize a league of Tuscan city states in opposition to the Pope. In particular, Catherine sought to dissuade Pisa and Lucca from joining the emerging Florentine league against the papacy, not least by advocating a crusade against the Turks as a means of uniting Christians against a common enemy. Her advocacy of such a crusade included a letter to the English condottiere John Hawkwood – also known as Giovanni Acuto – whose mercenary army had been released from service with the papacy, following the peace concluded between the papacy and Milan, and was now extracting payments from Florence, Siena and other Tuscan cities. On 1 April 1375 Catherine claimed to have received invisible stigmata during an ecstatic and mystical experience whilst praying in front of a painted wooden crucifix in the Pisan church of Santa Cristina. In June she also returned, briefly, to Siena to minister to a young Perugian, Niccolò di Toldo, who had been sentenced to death by the Sienese authorities for allegedly 'sowing discord' in the city.[14] By the end of the

12 For discussions of Catherine's extreme fasting and asceticism and their significance for her mystical experiences and spirituality see Bell (1985, pp. 22–53); Walker Bynum (1987, pp. 165–80); Slattery (1989); Scott (1999).

13 For a useful summary of the principal recipients of her letters, subdivided into popes, cardinals and bishops, kings and queens, condottieri, civic leaders, aristocratic women, lawyers, artists, disciples, family, members of religious orders and others, see Boccardi (2003, pp. 199–207).

14 The precise nature of Niccolò di Toldo's political offence in the eyes of the Sienese is not certain. However, as Luongo (2006, pp. 91–6), has recently suggested, given his letters to

year, Florence had indeed established a league of Tuscan cities – including Siena – in opposition to the papacy and had initiated severe taxation of clerical property in Florence, thus initiating the so-called 'War of Eight Saints'. Florence was therefore placed under a papal interdict, whilst Perugia and other cities in the Papal States were in revolt.

In 1376, with the papal interdict still in force, Catherine went first to Florence and then to Avignon to intercede with Pope Gregory XI on behalf of the Florentines and to urge Gregory to return the papal court to Rome. She also continued to call for the reform of the church and for a crusade to unite Christians in a common cause. In September, Gregory XI left Avignon for Rome and Catherine, leaving Avignon after him, re-encountered him at Genoa and renewed her insistence that he continue to Rome – which he did, arriving in January 1377. Catherine, meanwhile, returned to Siena in December 1376. In 1377 Catherine first founded a religious community at Belcaro, near Siena, in a castle given to her by a wealthy member of her circle of followers. She then spent the late summer and autumn in the Val d'Orcia, seeking to reconcile conflicting factions within prominent Sienese families and their followers – trying, in particular, to broker a peace between the Sienese civic authorities and the powerful but exiled Salimbeni family. During this period, she continued her increasingly prolific sequence of letters addressed to prominent figures, including the Pope, to whom she also sent her confessor Raymond of Capua with detailed proposals for the reform of the church.[15] Whilst in Rome, however, Raymond was elected Prior of Santa Maria sopra Minerva, the principal Dominican church in the city. Catherine, meanwhile, following further mystical experiences, had also begun to dictate what she called her 'book' – a work which came to be known as the *Dialogues*.

In 1378 Catherine again went to Florence, at the request of Pope Gregory, on a mission to mediate peace between the city and the papacy. In March, however, Pope Gregory XI died and Pope Urban VI was elected and rapidly prompted a threat of schism by his robust approach to the issue of reform of the church. In June, whilst in Florence, Catherine narrowly escaped death during the revolt of the Ciompi – and was apparently considerably disappointed not to have suffered martyrdom in the incident – whilst in July a peace was finally effected between Florence and the papacy. In September, however, the election by French cardinals of a rival Pope, Clement VII, initiated the previously threatened papal schism. Catherine was summoned to Rome by Pope Urban VI, together with 40 of her followers, to support his cause. Catherine duly went to Rome and sent numerous further letters in support of Urban VI. During this period Catherine also completed her *Dialogues*.

---

the Sienese civic authorities in relation to the matter and on Niccolò's behalf, it seems likely that Niccolò was in some way associated with Gerard de Puy, the vicar general of the papal states and de facto governor of Perugia – a major city within the papal states situated near to the borders of Sienese territory.

15 As Noffke acknowledges in the introduction to the first volume of her edition of Catherine's letters, it remains a matter of debate whether or not Catherine in fact learned to write – as traditionally claimed – during 1377 while she was staying at Rocca d'Orcia, or whether she remained unable to write and continued to dictate her letters to various scribes drawn from among her followers, for which see Noffke (2000, pp. xxi–xxii).

In April 1379, the forces of the schismatic Pope Clement VII – some of which had occupied Castel Sant'Angelo in Rome – were defeated by the *Compagnia di San Giorgio*, led by the condottiere Alberico da Barbiano, acting on behalf of Urban VI, and with the active encouragement of Catherine in letters she sent to him. The papal schism remained, however, and Catherine redoubled her efforts to secure the reform and unity of the church, not only sending numerous further letters to various figures but also performing a daily 'pilgrimage' from her community – housed near the church of Santa Maria sopra Minerva – to old Saint Peter's to pray for the unity of the church. It was in this final period of her life that she dictated her third literary legacy, her *Prayers*. At the end of January 1380 Catherine suffered two days and nights of seizures which left her unable to move or speak, thus causing her followers to think she was dead. She recovered, however, and resumed her daily pilgrimage to pray in Saint Peter's until, in late February, she experienced the 'mystical boat of the church' being placed on her shoulders and collapsed under its weight. By the end of February 1380, Catherine had become so weak that she lost the use of her legs and was confined to bed. She eventually died on 29 April 1380, worn out by her long-maintained regime of extreme fasting and prayer for the unity of the church – for which reason she was, and is, regarded as a martyr. Her remains were buried, initially, in the cemetery of Santa Maria sopra Minerva, but were then moved to a tomb located within the church itself. In 1384, however, the relic of her head was transported from Rome to Siena, where it was received with a solemn ceremony and procession – thus initiating the process by which, over the following six centuries, her cult came to be the vehicle for a succession of types of civil religion.

As already noted, in the present context, the central issue is not that of establishing a critically reliable account of Catherine's life but, rather, understanding the way in which Catherine's life has been perceived and interpreted by her followers in a process which merges biography with hagiography and then deploys this amalgam in the promotion of her cult, including the various civil religious meanings that have been associated with it. That said, however, it is nevertheless worth pausing to consider some aspects of recent discussion of Catherine's biography and the way in which it has been interpreted by her followers – not least because, as subsequent chapters will show, in the twentieth and early twenty-first centuries the civil religious associations and significances of Catherine have to some extent posed an at least implicit challenge to certain aspects of her conventional hagiography and historiography.

As recent scholars have pointed out, in the interests of successfully promoting her cult and seeking her canonization, even in the earliest hagiographical accounts of her life, Catherine was celebrated pre-eminently by appeal to the ascetic, mystical, 'supernatural' and 'miraculous' aspects of her life.[16] Thus, key hagiographical sources such as the *Legenda maior* written by Raymond of Capua, the *Legenda minor* and *Libellus de Supplemento* compiled by Tommaso Caffarini, and the first formal investigation of the case for her canonization, the *Processo Castellano*, all emphasized the supernatural and mystical dimensions of her biography, the

---

16 See for example Scott (1992, pp. 35–6; 1993, pp. 91–6; 1999, pp. 136–7, 166); Rattazzi Papka (1995, pp. 134, 140–42); Luongo (2006, pp. 7–8).

devotional intensity of her life, her self-sacrificial works of charity and compassion for the sick and the imprisoned, and her success in converting others.[17] Activities such as her ambassadorial roles on behalf of the papacy, her preaching before Popes Gregory and Urban, and her dictation of numerous letters to prominent figures notwithstanding, it was Catherine's mystical visions and experiences – such as her 'mystical marriage to Christ', her 'exchange of hearts' with Christ, her experience of receiving the host directly from Christ during the mass, her choosing a crown of thorns not a crown of gold from Christ, and above all her claim to have experienced the stigmata – that tended to be central to the promotion of her cult. The same emphasis on the ascetic, the ecstatic, the mystical and the visionary was also evident in the earliest cycles of images portraying Catherine's life. Thus, both the series of images of Catherine in the early manuscript of Tommaso Cafferini's *Libellus de Supplemento*, now held in the Biblioteca Comunale degli Intronati in Siena, and the mid-fifteenth-century cycle of painted panels portraying scenes from Catherine's life by the Sienese painter Giovanni di Paolo present Catherine, above all, as a visionary saint and emphasize the importance of her experience of the stigmata in establishing her claim to sanctity.[18]

The motive for such emphases on the part of Catherine's early hagiographers was, as Thomas Luongo has recently observed, the reconciliation of 'Catherine's exceptionally active and public career with the standard expectations of female sanctity'.[19] In order to conform to the highly gendered expectations regarding the appropriate modes of female behaviour – including the behaviour of female religious, mystics, and candidates for sainthood – Catherine's early hagiographers created a tradition which played down her high-profile public activities and portrayed her as a contemplative and mystic called into the world by God to shame and confound powerful and learned men by her divinely inspired authority – despite being a 'mere' woman.[20] Indeed, so pressing was the need to conform to recognized norms of female sanctity that, in the interests of the promotion of her cult and canonization, even Catherine's letters and preaching were presented in terms that explicitly emphasized the divine and supernatural origins of her 'literacy' and the direct inspiration of her speech by God, whether in dictating her letters or preaching.[21]

Not the least of the effects of the hagiographical tradition thus established in the period between Catherine's death in 1380 and her canonization in 1461 was the abstraction of Catherine from her social and political context. Indeed, so pervasive was the influence of such hagiography that, even in much modern writing on Catherine, she is still, unfortunately, effectively placed 'at a mystic remove from the politics of her day'.[22] Moreover, the tendency established by her early hagiographers was then reinforced in the sixteenth century as the *Legenda maior* 'established

---

17 For further discussion of these texts see Chapter 1, pp. xx–xx.

18 Moerer (2003, pp. 55–60, 165–6; 2005).

19 Luongo (2006, p. 8).

20 Luongo (2006, p. 8).

21 Scott (1993, pp. 91–6; 1999, pp. 136–7, 166); Rattazzi Papka, (1995, pp. 133–4, 140–42); Luongo (2006, pp. 7–8).

22 Luongo (2006, p. 7)

the mystical Catherine as a significant model for the lives of nuns in enclosed monasteries' and the Counter-Reformation insistence on monastic enclosure for all religious women 'meant that the only relevant aspects of Catherine's life for others could be the ascetic and mystical ones'.[23] Conversely, as the Counter-Reformation ideal thus came to dominate later interpretations of Catherine, the model of female sanctity implied by Catherine's letters – in which a young woman addressed popes and other influential political figures and reminded them forcefully of their duties and responsibilities – fell out of favour to such an extent that, for well over a century, between the 1580s and the second decade of the eighteenth century, no new editions of Catherine's letters were published.[24]

As Thomas Luongo has now demonstrated, however, far from being removed from her social and political world – and despite her own, itself highly political, plea that she was politically neutral – Catherine was in fact thoroughly immersed within the politics of Siena, Tuscany and the papacy during the mid 1370s. Basing his conclusions upon extensive archival research, Luongo argues that, even before 1374, there is substantial evidence that Catherine's family background suggested sympathy with the political aims and interests both of the powerful Sienese family of the Salimbeni and of the papacy. From 1374 onwards, however, it is clear that Catherine was even more directly under Dominican and papal protection and played a significant role in papal diplomacy in Tuscany. Her advocacy – not least in and through her letters and the network of contacts she thus established – of the pacification of Italy, the return of the papacy to Rome, the reform of the church and the unification of Christendom through a crusade were precisely the aims which Gregory XI wished to advance, and which the Dominican Order supported.[25] Luongo also persuasively argues, therefore, that Catherine's appearance before the Dominican General Chapter in Florence in 1374 had not been to face investigation for possible heresy, but rather to be vetted as a possible 'political visionary' through whom Dominican and papal interests might be advanced.[26] Similarly, whilst recognizing that a genuinely critical account of Catherine's early life is impossible given the existing sources, Luongo nevertheless challenges both the conventional assertion that Catherine came from a relatively poor background and the equally conventional tradition that her religious vocation faced opposition from her mother. He presents convincing evidence to show that, in fact, Catherine's family were probably 'close to the highest levels of social and political power' in Siena and that the 'opposition' of her mother was probably a hagiographical device rather than a historical reality. Catherine's mother, 'Monna Lapa', he suggests, may well deserve a positive role in Catherine's story, not the negative, nagging one assigned to her by

23 Scott (1992, p. 36). See also Matthews Grieco (1994, pp. 317–20, especially pp. 319–20) who nevertheless suggests that, until the full impact of the Counter-Reformation and '*il trionfo del modello estatico*', portrayals of Catherine, especially in xilografic prints, also emphasized her active life especially as an '*eroina domenicana*' and in relation to her writings and her role in the return of the papacy to Rome.

24 Zaggia (2006, pp. 154–5).

25 Luongo (2006, esp. Chapters 2, 4 and 5).

26 Luongo (2006, pp. 56–8).

tradition.[27] Similarly, he also demonstrates that the spiritual '*famiglia*' that gathered around Catherine in Siena included a number of young Sienese noblemen and other lay followers who held a variety of offices in Sienese civic life. Indeed, Luongo goes so far as to suggest that: 'Catherine's *famiglia* was simultaneously a spiritual association and a political movement.'[28]

Luongo's insistence, firstly, on the need to place Catherine firmly within her social and political context, and secondly, on the genuinely public and political nature of her words and actions, is both timely and appropriate. As he points out in his conclusion, moreover, his reinterpretation of her career calls for a similar re-evaluation of her writings, especially her letters which, he suggests, should be recognized as 'vehicles for her to interject her sanctity and prophetic authority into worldly affairs'.[29] Luongo's study of Catherine's public and political life specifically examines her role within Sienese and Tuscan politics and therefore focuses on the period between 1374 and 1378. After 1378, as Luongo rightly observes, Catherine's overwhelming concern became the papal schism and, indeed, in late November 1378 she moved to Rome where she spent the final years of her life. To this period Luongo gives only a brief postscript.[30] Clearly, however, given the concerns that dominated the final years of her life and the numerous letters that she continued to send, Catherine's immersion in the politics of her day did not diminish during this period. An equally close analysis of her actions and writings during this period would surely confirm and enhance the reinterpretation of Catherine as a figure deeply and directly involved in pressing political issues.

This reinterpretation of Catherine also, however, serves to highlight a certain irony in the modern development of Catherine's cult, especially in relation to the twentieth-century campaigns to secure her recognition as a patron saint of Italy and a co-patron saint of Europe. For it was precisely Catherine's public and political roles – as ambassador for the papacy, as alleged prompter of Gregory XI's return to Rome from Avignon, as opponent of the papal schism, as preacher of a particular message concerning peace and social justice, as author of letters to political leaders, monarchs, soldiers and popes, and as perceived proto-advocate of both Italian and European unity – that were central to her promotion as a focus first for Italian and then for European identity, values and civil religion. And it was more often than not to her letters that appeal was made to demonstrate and substantiate her claim to be a worthy patron saint – whether of Italy or of Europe.

The greater part of the present book will focus on the various stages in Catherine's promotion as a patron saint of Italy and Europe. In so doing it will show how, despite the persistence of many of the hagiographical traditions laid down in earlier centuries, a distinctly political Catherine – or, more correctly, a sequence of political Catherines – nevertheless re-emerged in the course of the twentieth and early twenty-first centuries and became the focus for a series of versions of Italian and then European civil religion. Before that, however, it is necessary, first, to examine the process by

27 Luongo (2006, pp. 28–32, 51–4).

28 Luongo (2006, p. 135; see also pp. 123, 126–8, 140, 156).

29 Luongo (2006, p. 207).

30 Luongo (2006, p. 202).

which – before becoming the focus of Italian and European civil religion – Catherine and her cult became a vehicle for a more particular and specific civil religion. It is, therefore, to the development of her cult as an expression of Sienese civil religion – and her emergence as the pre-eminent figure within the Sienese civic pantheon of saints and *beati* – that the first chapter now turns.

Chapter 1

'*La santa senese*': Catherine and the Civil Religion of Siena 1384–1857

Catherine of Siena, it has been observed, would never have been made a saint had it not been for the interest of the Dominican Order – and in particular the reformers within the order – in promoting a saint with her profile.[1] There is much evidence that may be cited in support of this claim. Thus, as already noted in the introduction to this book, Catherine's first confessor and spiritual instructor, Tommaso dalla Fonte, was a Dominican and by the end of the 1360s she had associated herself with the group of Sienese Dominican lay-women known as the *mantellate*.[2] As early as 1374, moreover, the Dominican Order had apparently already recognized Catherine's potential as a prophetic and mystical representative of their interests, especially in relation to the papacy and its future. Consequently, in the summer of 1374, Catherine appeared before the Dominican General Chapter in Florence, as a result of which Raymond of Capua became her official confessor and spiritual director and she effectively began to speak and act with the authority and under the protection of the Dominican Order and the papacy.[3] In the final two years of her life in Rome, Catherine and her community of followers lived in a house close to Santa Maria sopra Minerva, the principal Dominican church and community in the city.[4] When she died in 1380 her remains were taken to Santa Maria sopra Minerva where they were first placed in a tomb in the cemetery of the community and subsequently, on the initiative of Raymond of Capua, who was by then Master General of the Order, were transferred to a marble tomb in a chapel – customarily referred to as the Capranica chapel – located near to the high altar.[5] In 1384, Raymond secured permission from Pope Urban VI for the translation of the relic of Catherine's head to Siena, where it was received, with great ceremony, by the civic and religious authorities in May 1385 and placed in the sacristy of the church of San Domenico – thereby ensuring that both Santa Maria sopra Minerva in Rome and San Domenico in Siena became sites of pilgrimage and devotion to Catherine's cult.[6]

1 Kieckhefer (1997, p. xxi).

2 Luongo (2006, pp. 33–40).

3 Luongo (2006, pp. 54–8).

4 Cavallini and Giunta (2000, pp. 45–6).

5 Drane (1914, vol. 2, pp. 272–3, 276, 282); Bianchi (1988, pp. 21, 43, n. 38); Norman (2008).

6 Drane (1914, vol. 2, p. 284); Riedl and Seidel (1992b, p. 458); Norman (2008). This process is also discussed in more detail later in this chapter. The separation of Catherine's head and body – which may initially prompt some surprise – conformed to at least two prestigious precedents within Dominican history. In the case of both Dominic himself and of Peter Martyr,

Unsurprisingly, it was also a series of Dominican authors who produced the early accounts of Catherine's life and thus established her hagiographical tradition. Thus, the *Legenda maior*, the first '*vita*' of Catherine, probably compiled between 1385 and 1395, was the work of Raymond of Capua, her confessor and spiritual adviser from 1374 onwards, and subsequently Dominican Master General.[7] Similarly, in the first two decades of the fifteenth century, it was the influential Dominican Tommaso di Antonio de Senis – more commonly known as 'Caffarini'[8] – who created the *Legenda minor* – as its title suggests, an abbreviated version of the *Legenda maior* – and the much longer *Libellus de Supplemento*, which provided additional biographical-hagiographical details.[9] A native of Siena and a devoted follower of Catherine, Caffarini was a member of the community at San Domenico, Siena, rising to become its prior, and also, in 1380, the year of Catherine's death, the director of the Sienese *mantellate*. In 1394 he was called to Venice and assisted in the founding of Corpus Domini, a convent for Venetian *mantellate*, becoming its spiritual director two years later, and subsequently becoming responsible for the spiritual oversight of the *mantellate* throughout Italy. Together with Bartolomeo Dominici, another high-ranking Sienese Dominican then in Venice, Caffarini energetically promoted both the interests of the reform movement within the Dominican order and the cause of papal recognition of the *mantellate* – the promotion of the cult of Catherine of Siena being central to the latter project.[10]

It was, moreover, in Venice – and as a result of the enthusiastic celebration of her cult by local devotees – that the first formal investigation of the case for Catherine's canonization took place. Not only had Caffarini had woodcuts of Catherine made in order to further the popular diffusion and dissemination of her reputation,[11] but in 1398 Caffarini had returned briefly to Siena, primarily to collect additional evidence of her life, including some of her letters,[12] and to obtain various relics of

---

the order's second saint, their heads had been separated from the rest of their remains for the purposes of popular devotion. I am grateful to Dr Joanna Cannon for information on this and for access to her unpublished paper, 'Founders and Followers (II)', given at the Association of Art Historians Conference, Edinburgh, 2000. The ideas in the paper will be included in Dr Cannon's forthcoming book provisionally entitled *Religious Poverty, Visual Riches: Art in the Dominican Churches of Central Italy in the Thirteenth and Fourteenth Centuries*.

7 For the text of the *Legenda* see Raymond of Capua (1866; 1980). For discussions of the presentation and hagiographical construction of Catherine in this text see Boesch-Gajano and Redon (1982); Scott (1993, pp. 91–6; 1999, pp. 136–7); Rattazzi Papka (1995, pp. 133–4, 138); Luongo (2006, pp. 23–55). For Raymond of Capua see also Kearns (1980, pp. xiii–lii).

8 The family name 'Caffarini' was wrongly associated with Tommaso di Antonio, for which see the introduction, by G. Cavallini and I. Foralosso, to Tommaso di Antonio Caffarini (1974, pp. vi–viii).

9 Tommaso di Antonio Caffarini (1942; 1974).

10 Freuler (1987, pp. 571–3); Moerer (2003, pp. 49–51).

11 Drane (1914, vol. 2, p. 322); Tommaso di Antonio Caffarini (1974, pp. 407, 409); Laurent (1942, pp. 92–3); Freuler (1987, p. 573). It has been suggested that it was the still relatively new art of wood engraving that contributed most to the development of Catherine's cult between her death and her canonization, for which see Matthews Grieco (1994, p. 317).

12 Tommaso di Antonio Caffarini (1974, p. 394); Laurent, (1942, p. 73).

Catherine – including a finger, a tooth and her first habit. These he brought back to Venice, to the convent of Corpus Domini, which became a centre for devotion to Catherine, with a major procession and exposition of her relics on her annual feast day.[13] Indeed, so prominent were these and other celebrations of her cult in Venice[14] that they prompted complaints that the Dominicans were inappropriately honouring Catherine as if she were already canonized and therefore officially a saint – whereas in reality she was, as yet, no more than a *beata*, a holy individual, celebrated by her devotees, but not yet recognized as worthy of sainthood by the church.[15] As a result of the complaints, Francesco Bembo, the Bishop of Castello, initiated a diocesan investigation to review the charges. The investigation – which became known as the '*Processo Castellano*' – and was conducted between 1411 and 1416, first rejected the complaints against the Dominicans and then became an enquiry into Catherine's claim to sainthood. After hearing the evidence of 24 witnesses, the enquiry was favourably impressed by the evidence for Catherine's sanctity. Despite this, however, her devotees nevertheless remained unable to secure the initiation of a full papal review of the case for Catherine's sanctity through a formal examination of the case by a committee of cardinals.[16]

It was, therefore, not until a further four decades had elapsed that the cause of Catherine's canonization was again – and this time successfully – pursued. Moreover, whilst the early promotion of her cult and the production of the key texts for her hagiography had indeed been the result of the efforts of members of the Dominican Order, the eventual success of the subsequent campaign which led to her canonization in 1461 owed much to the efforts and influence of the Sienese, and especially the Sienese civic authorities. In accounts of Catherine's eventual canonization it is habitually remarked – and not without reason – that it was a Sienese pope, Pius II, who finally accorded her the status of sainthood.[17] Clearly, this was indeed no coincidence. Neither, however, was it merely a simple matter of Pius II favouring the city of his familial origins. Catherine's canonization was, in fact, also the culmination of a sustained effort on the part of the Sienese to secure such recognition for a figure who had already become an important member of the

13 Laurent (1942, pp. 363, 443); Tommaso di Antonio Caffarini (1974, pp. 406–7); Zaggia (2006, pp. 131–2).

14 Catherine's cult was also celebrated, for example, in the Dominican communities of SS. Giovanni e Paolo and S. Domenico di Castello, for which see Laurent (1942, pp. vi–vii); Heusinger (2000, p. 45).

15 For the distinction between saints and *beati*, see Vauchez (1997, esp. pp. 85–103).

16 Vauchez (1997, p. 97); Moerer (2003, pp. 89–90).

17 See for example Klaniczay (2002, p. 379); Wegner (2005, p. 174). Enea Silvio Piccolomini, a member of a branch of the powerful Sienese Piccolomini family, was elected Pope, taking the name Pius II, in August 1458, having previously been Bishop of Siena since 1450. In addition to his canonization of Catherine, he also raised the see of Siena to the status of an archdiocese, made various prestigious gifts to the cathedral and the city – including the relic of the right arm of John the Baptist – and added a prestigious loggia to the city's urban environment. He also appointed his nephew Francesco Todeschini-Piccolomini as Archbishop of Siena in 1460. For recent discussion of Pius II and his role in Siena see Nevola (2005; 2007a, pp. 59–89).

'civic pantheon' of Sienese saints and *beati* – and thus also a key figure in the civil religion of Siena.

It is well known that the principal focus of the civil religion and civic devotion of Siena and the Sienese is the Virgin. From 1260 and the famous victory of the Sienese over the Florentines at Montaperti onwards the Sienese have believed the Virgin to be the special and pre-eminent heavenly patron and protector of their city. Devotion to the Virgin has shaped Sienese civil religion throughout the centuries since Montaperti and continues to do so even to the present.[18] The city has been formally rededicated to the Virgin on various occasions, most recently in 1944 when the course of the Second World War brought renewed danger to the city.[19] Although it is thus the principal historical form of Sienese civil religion, devotion to the Virgin – and to the associated 'myth of Montaperti' – is not, however, the only expression of Sienese civic devotion. Alongside devotion to the Virgin, the Sienese and their civic authorities also developed a 'pantheon' of civic saints and *beati* whom they celebrated as subsidiary patrons and protectors of the city.

The origins of the Sienese 'civic pantheon' may be traced securely at least to the early fourteenth century. Thus, in both the famous double-sided altarpiece for the high altar of Siena cathedral – known as the *Maestà* – by Duccio di Buoninsegna, and also in the equally famous *Maestà* by Simone Martini in the Palazzo Pubblico of Siena, the Virgin is portrayed, surrounded by numerous saints but attended, most particularly, by saints Ansano, Crescenzio, Savino and Victor – the four early Christian patron saints and 'protectors' of Siena whose relics were possessed by the cathedral.[20] By the early fifteenth century Sienese government documents referred to these four saints as 'patrons and defenders of the community and people' and 'patrons and especial protectors and advocates of the magnificent city of Siena'.[21] During the mid fifteenth century, however, there is clear evidence that the Sienese embarked on a conscious and deliberate project to establish and celebrate a much more extensive 'pantheon' of civic saints and *beati*. Between the mid 1440s and the beginning of the 1460s, in a series of works of art – executed, significantly, for three of the most prestigious civic locations in Siena: the baptistery, the Spedale di Santa Maria della Scala and the Palazzo Pubblico – the painter Vecchietta portrayed Ansano, Crescenzio, Savino and Victor accompanied by a series of other local saints and *beati* including, most notably: the local thirteenth-century Dominican Ambrogio Sansedoni, a renowned preacher and papal diplomat; Andrea Gallerani who was believed to have founded the local charitable institution of the Spedale della Misericordia; Pier Pettinaio a late thirteenth-century layman and Franciscan tertiary renowned for his piety and

18 There is an extensive literature on this subject. For a recent study of the theme, which reviews much of the literature and interprets such devotion as an expression of Sienese civil religion, see Parsons (2004a).

19 Parsons (2001; 2004a, pp. 89–92).

20 For discussion of these saints and their role as heavenly patrons of Siena, see Consolino (1991); Norman (1999, pp. 35–6, 40–41, 49, 54, 67–85); Parsons (2004a, pp. 11, 15–16); Argenziano (2003); Steinhoff (2006, pp. 125–9, 138–49, 152–68).

21 Webb (1996, p. 290), citing, respectively, the Sienese *Liber Censuum* of 1400 which listed the tributes due at the annual celebration of the Feast of the Assumption, and the records of the Sienese *Consiglio Generale* for 14 May 1413.

charity; the blessed Sorore, mythical founder of the prestigious Sienese Spedale di Santa Maria della Scala; the renowned local Franciscan preacher Bernardino, who had died only as recently as 1444 – and Catherine of Siena.[22]

The promotion of this expanded pantheon of civic saints and *beati* has been described as 'visual propaganda for local saints', an expression of 'hagiographic chauvinism'[23] and also – in the felicitous turn of phrase of the late nineteenth and early twentieth century Sienese scholar Vittorio Lusini – as the cultivation of a community of '*santi cittadini*'.[24] It also seems probable, however, that the determined promotion of this expanded civic pantheon in the three works by Vecchietta was closely related to the efforts of the Sienese authorities to secure the canonization – and thus the transition from *beati* to full sainthood – of two of its most recent members.[25] In 1450, a mere six years after his death and after a brief but intense campaign on the part of the civic authorities of Siena – as well as those of Aquila (where Bernardino died, where his body remained and where his tomb rapidly became associated with miraculous cures), and the efforts of the Observant Franciscans – Bernardino of Siena was canonized by Pope Nicholas V.[26] The Sienese marked Bernardino's canonization with extended and elaborate civic celebrations, culminating in a festival in the Campo, in front of the Palazzo Pubblico, which included a celebration of mass and the ascent of an actor representing Bernardino into a wooden 'paradise'.[27] The Sienese civic authorities also resolved immediately that Bernardino should now be invoked as the 'fifth advocate and protector of the magnificent commune and people of the city of Siena'.[28]

With one member of their civic pantheon of '*santi cittadini*' thus raised to sainthood, the Sienese then sought to secure the canonization of Catherine as well. Thus, in May 1458, the Sienese government wrote to its ambassador in Rome, Leonardo Benvoglienti, asking him to raise the possibility of Catherine's canonization both

22 For discussion of the three works of art by Vecchietta, including identification of the various other *beati* also portrayed in one or other location see, van Os (1974, pp. 16–23); Norman (2003, pp. 197–210); Parsons (2004a, p. 18). Norman has also explored the development of the civic pantheon in these three works by Vecchietta in a paper, '"Santi cittadini": Vecchietta and the Civic Pantheon in mid Fifteenth Century Siena', given at the College Art Association of America Conference in Boston, 2006. For an expanded version of this paper see Norman (forthcoming). For discussion of the way in which the cults of other individual members of this expanding civic pantheon developed, see for example the cases of Ambrogio Sansedoni in Torriti (1993) and Redon (2004, pp. 20–41), and of Andrea Gallerani in Norman (2007).

23 van Os (1974, pp. 18, 23).

24 Lusini (1901, p. 77). I am indebted to Diana Norman for drawing my attention to this source. Mons. Vittorio Lusini was a member of the cathedral chapter in Siena, a prominent member of the religious, cultural and civic life of the city, and the author of one of the first modern scholarly studies of Siena cathedral. For his obituary see the *Bollettino Senese di Storia Patria*, 32, 1925, pp. 108–14.

25 Webb (1996, pp. 300–307); Norman (2006; forthcoming).

26 Moerer (2003, pp. 103–6); Norman (forthcoming).

27 Webb (1996, p. 302); Rossi (2002, p. 21).

28 Webb (1996, p. 302), citing the records of the Sienese *Consiglio Generale*.

with 'our most reverend Cardinal' (that is to say, Enia Silvio Piccolomini) and with Pope Calixtus III, emphasizing the high regard in which Catherine was held, not only in Siena but also in '*tutta Italia*'.[29] In so doing, however, the Sienese were not merely following – and opportunistically trying to capitalize upon – the successful precedent set by the recent canonization of Bernardino, but were also seeking to consolidate a civic commitment to Catherine and her cult that was already well established within Siena. Indeed, the strength of the civic enthusiasm for Catherine and her cult had been evident even in the early 1380s. Following Raymond of Capua's authorization of the transfer of the relic of Catherine's head to Siena in 1384, it was transported, in secrecy, to Siena in the care of two Sienese Dominicans, Tommaso della Fonte and Ambrogio di Luigi Sansedoni, and placed in the sacristy of the church of San Domenico. Whilst visiting Siena in 1385, and after consulting other local followers of Catherine, Raymond of Capua then informed the civic authorities of the fact that the relic was now in San Domenico. The Sienese authorities responded by organizing an elaborate series of festivities. Initiated by eight days of prayers and preaching, beginning on 23 April, in which eminent figures proclaimed Catherine's achievements, on Sunday 1 May, at San Domenico, the Sienese were informed that the head would be received into the city on 5 May in a solemn procession in which the civic authorities had invited all the bishops and abbots of the territory of the Sienese republic to participate. On the evening of 4 May the head was taken from San Domenico to the Hospital of Saint Lazarus, outside the Porta Romana, where it was placed in a richly decorated tabernacle. The following day the beginning of the procession was announced by the bell of the Palazzo Pubblico, which continued to toll, together with the bells of the city's churches, throughout the procession.

The procession was led by 200 boys and 200 girls dressed in white and carrying flowers, and included all the neighbourhoods and guilds of Siena, as well as all the religious confraternities of the city – each of the latter performing a *tableau vivant* portraying an incident from Catherine's life, the cost of which was paid for by the civic authorities. These were followed by representatives of religious communities, secular priests and canons, the Sienese civic authorities and the bishops from dioceses within the Sienese state. Finally came the tabernacle containing Catherine's head, carried by four Dominicans beneath a *baldachino* of gold brocade adorned with jewels, accompanied by Raymond of Capua and the Bishop of Siena, and followed by the Sienese *mantellate*. The procession carried the relic into the city and through the streets to San Domenico where, after a Te Deum, a sermon from Raymond of Capua and a blessing from the bishop, the head was again placed in the sacristy. There then followed a further fifteen days of preaching.[30]

The presence of the relic of Catherine's head further enhanced the status of San Domenico as an early location for Catherine's cult within Siena. The anniversary of

29 Laurent (1942, pp. 475–6), citing the records of the Sienese *Balìà*.

30 Lombardelli (1593); Angiolini (1683); Drane (1914, vol. 2, pp. 283–8); Falassi (1980, pp. 77–9); Giunta (1988, p. 71, nn. 2, 3); Riedl and Seidel (1992b, 2.1.2, p. 458); Moerer (2003, pp. 106–7). Sources differ as to whether these events occurred in 1384 or 1385, for which see the sources above (indeed Lombardelli even gives the date as 1388). What is not in doubt, however, is the strongly civic character of the procession and attendant ceremonies.

her death had already become the focus of an annual celebration, using ceremonies permitted for the memorialization of local *beati* who were not canonized, including the placing of floral tributes in front of her image and the recitation of verses in her honour.[31] Similarly, the chapel known as the Cappella delle Volte – where Catherine and her fellow *mantellate* had gathered to pray and where several of Catherine's most intense mystical experiences were believed to have occurred[32] – was also located beside San Domenico. In particular, on the outside wall of the chapel, a painted image of Catherine became a focal point for her Sienese devotees (Plate I). Attributed to the Sienese painter Andrea Vanni, who was himself one of her followers, the image was revered as a 'true portrait' of Catherine – and because of this was, in the seventeenth century, detached from its original location and moved inside the chapel, which in turn was itself incorporated within the walls of San Domenico.[33] The precise date of the painting continues to be a matter of debate, most traditional accounts suggesting that it may have been completed as early as 1380 or 1381, whilst one proposal suggests that it might plausibly be linked to the will of a wealthy Sienese woman, Giovanna Piccolomini, who died in August 1383 and left a bequest for a chapel to be erected in San Domenico in honour of Catherine. Since a chapel could not be erected – because Catherine was not canonized – the bequest was used, it is suggested, for the painting, the female devotee also included in the painting being a representation of the donor figure.[34] What is not in doubt, however, is that the image significantly contributed to the role of San Domenico as a site for Catherine's cult from the early 1380s.

By the beginning of the second decade of the fifteenth century, Catherine's cult within Siena had also achieved sufficient prominence within civic life and consciousness for her to be included by the Sienese Capitano del Popolo, Meo di Giovanni, in a list of local 'saints' – as he chose to describe them – whom he invoked as patrons of the city in the presence of Florentine ambassadors. Thus, Catherine followed Ambrogio Sansedoni, Andrea Gallerani, Pietro Pettinaio and Peter the Martyr – the latter a Sienese Franciscan martyred in the early fourteenth century – in Meo's litany on behalf of the Commune.[35] In 1446, a festival celebrated in Catherine's honour in the piazza in front of the church of San Domenico, was attended – according to the Sienese chronicler Tommaso Fecini – by some twenty thousand people, including the civic authorities. The festival involved great splendour and spectacle and was described by the early sixteenth century Sienese writer, Sigismondo

---

31 Chavin de Malan (1846, vol. 1, pp. 383–7; vol. 2, pp. 557–8); Pastor (1894, pp. 290–91); Laurent (1942, p. 37); Giunta (1988, p. 69); Moerer (2003, p. 78).

32 Including her vision of Christ as a beggar to whom she gave clothing and her 'exchange of hearts with Christ', Raymond of Capua (1980, pp. 130, 174–5); Moerer (2003, pp. 79–81).

33 Riedl and Seidel (1992b, pp. 505–6).

34 Torriti (1982, pp. 39–42); Bianchi and Giunta (1988, pp. 155–8); Bähr (1984); Moerer (2003, p. 81). For the proposal that the painting is linked to the will of Giovanna Piccolomini, see Bähr, above.

35 Lisini (1892); Laurent (1942, pp. 468–9); Giunta (1988, p. 71); Moerer (2003, p. 107).

Tizio, as being for the '*festa di Santa Caterina Vergine e Martire*'.[36] Nine years later, in 1455, on 28 April – the eve of the anniversary of Catherine's death – the Sienese *Consiglio Generale* resolved, by a majority of 291 to 51, to give an annual offering of six elaborate ceremonial candles, each of at least three pounds weight in wax, to the Dominicans of San Domenico, together with other acts of veneration, in celebration of the 'very blessed' (*beatissima*) Catherine of Siena '*mantellata*' at her festival. The record of the resolution also noted that Catherine was revered and her cult celebrated not only in Siena, but also in Venice, in other parts of Italy and beyond Italy, citing in particular the enthusiasm for her cult in Hungary.[37]

It was also from the mid 1440s onwards that Catherine appeared, with increasing prominence, within the three depictions of the Sienese civic pantheon by Vecchietta, each of which, as noted above, was for a prestigious civic location. In the first of the sequence – the series of civic saints and *beati* portrayed on the doors of a large reliquary cupboard for the sacristy of the church of the Spedale di Santa Maria della Scala which Vecchietta was paid for painting in 1445 – Catherine is shown kneeling in an attitude of intense devotion in front of a crucifix (Plate 1).[38] Significantly, however, her holy status is portrayed not with a full halo, but with the rays of a *beata* – as officially deemed appropriate for a figure not yet canonized.[39] Vecchietta also portrayed Catherine with the rays of a *beata* in the series of Sienese saints and *beati* which he painted – as part of a much larger decorative scheme – in the baptistery of Siena cathedral, dated to between 1450 and 1453.[40] In this instance, Catherine is shown with two of her attributes, a lily and a book,[41] and her continued depiction specifically as a *beata* is made the more significant because Bernardino – who had been canonized in 1450 – is now portrayed as a haloed saint whereas on the earlier reliquary doors he too had been shown with only the rays of a *beato*. A similar distinction also appears to have occurred in images of Bernadino and Catherine that

36 Fecini (1931, p. 857); Webb (1996, p. 301); Rossi (2002, p. 21); Moerer (2003, p. 107–8). See also the manuscript of Sigismondo Tizio, 'Historiarum Senensium, IV', 269, Biblioteca Comunale degli Intronati, Siena, BCI.Cod. B. III. 9.

37 Toncelli (1909, pp. 45, 60, n. 1); Laurent (1942, pp. 474–5); Moerer (2003, p. 108), all citing the records of the *Consiglio Generale*.

38 van Os (1974, pp. 16–23); Moerer (2003, pp. 116–19); Norman (2003, pp. 197–200; 2006; forthcoming); Parsons (2004a, p. 18). These sources also discuss the other saints and *beati* portrayed.

39 For the background to this convention see Vauchez (1997, pp. 86–7, 98).

40 Lusini (1901, pp. 48–9, 77–8, 80); Moerer (2003, pp. 114–15); Parsons (2004a, p. 18); Norman (2006; forthcoming). Again, these sources also discuss the other saints and *beati* portrayed in this work. Lusini, it should be noted, incorrectly identified Bernardino as Francis of Assisi.

41 It is true that this image bears the inscription 'STA KATRINA DE SENIS' and that the rays of a *beata* seem to emanate from a halo. It is likely, however, that the title was added after her canonization, replacing an earlier 'BEATA' which would have corresponded both to the rays around her head and to her location within a sequence of other Sienese *beati*. I am grateful to Diana Norman for this observation. Similarly, Strehlke (1988b, p. 222) observes that the original rays of this image were later 'clumsily altered into a saint's halo after her canonization'.

were added to the decoration of the Sala di Biccherna, located on the ground floor of the Palazzo Pubblico, in the early 1450s. This room contained a fourteenth-century painting, by Lippo Vanni, of the Coronation of the Virgin, accompanied by the four early patron saints of Siena. In 1445 this work was repainted by Sano di Pietro and in 1450–51 he also added, on either side of the Coronation, full-length images of Bernardino and Catherine. Bernardino is portrayed as a saint, complete with halo; Catherine as a *beata*, with the appropriate rays around her head, but without a halo.[42]

The third in Vecchietta's sequence of depictions of the Sienese civic pantheon is more complex, both in overall design and in the matter of its dating. Located within the Palazzo Pubblico, in the room known as the Sala del Biado, the painting is known as the *Madonna della Misericordia* because of its central figure of the Virgin, surrounded by saints, and with her cloak protectively extended above figures representing Siena's citizens. In this instance, however, whilst a large number of Sienese *beati* are portrayed in the inner arch above the main image of the Virgin, both Bernardino and Catherine are portrayed unambiguously as saints – complete with haloes – and are associated with the other saintly figures in the overall composition, including the four early patron saints of Siena who are also represented.[43] Despite the appearance of both Bernardino and Catherine as fully fledged saints – which might well be taken as an indication that this painting was completed after Catherine's canonization in 1461 – art historians generally date the work to between 1453 and 1457, a judgement based, in the absence of any documentary evidence, on stylistic considerations.[44] If this conventional dating is correct, however, it would represent a remarkably bold pre-emptive assertion on the part of the Sienese civic authorities of Catherine's status as a formally recognized saint. It would also, moreover, represent a considerable and somewhat puzzling contrast to the way in which the Sienese civic authorities approached the task of lobbying the papacy for Catherine's canonization. Thus, in the various documents which record the diplomatic efforts of the Sienese to secure Catherine's canonization, rather than anticipating the success of their cause, it is striking that the Sienese consistently and scrupulously refer to Catherine as '*beata Caterina*'.

---

42 The precise history of these images is complex and much debated and the documentation is inconclusive. A further complication is that the image of Catherine was subsequently much restored. Since the restored version still portrays her as a *beata*, we may however reasonably assume the original version also did so. For the history of the image see Carli (1963, p. 203); Southard (1978, pp. 171–3); Borghini (1983, pp. 162–3); Bianchi and Giunta (1988, pp. 246–7); Moerer (2003, pp. 122–3).

43 Carli (1963, pp. 209–10); Southard (1978, pp. 179–87); Borghini (1983, pp. 188–9, 191–3); Moerer (2003, pp. 120–21); Norman (2003, pp. 209–10; 2006; forthcoming); Parsons (2004a, p. 18). Once again, these sources also discuss the other saints and *beati* portrayed in this work. The extensive damage to this painting makes it difficult to identify SS. Crescenzio and Victor.

44 These dates were first proposed by Giorgio Vigni in 1937, for which see Vigni (1937, pp. 42–5) and have subsequently been followed by the majority of art historians writing on this painting.

As already noted above, in May 1458, the Sienese *Balia* asked the Sienese ambassador in Rome, Leonardo Benvoglienti, to raise the possibility of Catherine's canonization with Pope Calixtus III. Calixtus died on 6 August 1458, however, and on the 19 August the Sienese Enea Silvio Piccolomini was elected as his successor. The Sienese lost little time in renewing their request for Catherine's canonization. On 4 October 1458 eight ambassadors were sent to the Pius II and the College of Cardinals with letters of introduction. Although charged with much other business as well, they were instructed to seek to expedite the canonization of the '*beata Caterina*'. In November, the eight ambassadors reported on their endeavours in Rome, including the various diplomatic tasks and requests that they had been instructed to pursue. In respect of the *beata* Catherine, they suggested that her canonization would be difficult in respect of the collection of evidence, but also added that the Pope had said that he intended to do much good for Siena – although he needed reciprocal help from the Sienese. In March 1459, the Sienese authorities wrote to the prior of the Certosa at Pontignano, near Siena, and to the vicar of the Carthusian Order asking for various writings and works to assist in the canonization of *beata* Catherine. In April, Sienese government records again referred to ambassadorial contacts with the Pope and also noted that cardinals had been appointed to review the case for the canonization of *beata* Catherine. In May, the ambassadors reported their attempts to secure the support of Cardinals de Coëtivy and Bessarion regarding Catherine's canonization, whilst in July a letter instructs the Sienese ambassador in Mantua – where the Pope was then attending a council which was hotly debating a crusade against the Turks and in defence of the Catholic faith – to acquire the necessary papal bulls to be sent to the Archbishop of Siena and to determine the necessary payments for papal notaries and scribes involved in this task. On 1 August the ambassador replied to the priors and Capitano del Popolo of Siena and, at the end of a long account of other political and diplomatic matters, reported that, together with the procurator of the Dominican Order, he had visited the notaries and established the costs involved.

In mid September, Sienese ambassadors at Mantua were again required – amongst much other diplomatic business – to raise the related issues of Catherine's canonization and the need for the appointment of the necessary papal officials and cardinal deputies required for its progression. On 25 September the ambassadors replied to the priors and Capitano del Popolo, concluding their report with an account of progress on the process for the canonization of *beata* Catherine and in obtaining the necessary papal bulls. The same letter also reported Pius II's desire to return to Siena – which he described as his '*patria*'. On 28 September, however, the ambassadors had to report a delay in the canonization process, and on 1 October they wrote requesting more funds to pay for the papal bulls, whilst on 5 October they wrote again to confirm that progress was being made with the help of the additional funds that had been sent by the Sienese government and the intervention of the Dominican procurator. By 20 October the papal bulls for the commission for the canonization had been obtained, had been examined by the Dominican procurator and been sent to Venice, Florence, Siena and Rome. At the end of November the Sienese authorities sent a request to the Vicar General of the Roman Province of the Dominican Order asking permission for the Dominican doctor, master and professor,

Alessandro of Bologna, to be allowed to preach in Siena in honour of the *beata* Catherine.[45]

In February 1460 the Sienese Commune wrote to the governors of Rome and the Doge of Venice to obtain their support for the cause of Catherine's canonization, and in March they also asked the Doge to send them the original copy of the *Processo Castellano*.[46] In April members of the Sienese consistory noted that the painter Vecchietta had been paid 20 *lire* for work on a figure of *beata* Catherine[47] – arguably a significantly perplexing way of describing work by Vecchietta on a new image of Catherine if, indeed, he had already portrayed her as a saint in the Sala del Biado. Between November 1460 and May 1461 the Sienese authorities also took a series of decisions concerning the expenses and the practical arrangements for the canonization of Catherine – an event which was now clearly anticipated as imminent, although in March 1461 the Sienese again wrote to various cardinals in Rome to seek their continuing support for the cause.[48] At the end of May 1461, lengthy instructions were issued to two Sienese ambassadors to Pius II, specifically in regard to the issue of the canonization of the *beata* Catherine. The ambassadors were to commend Siena to the Pope and assure him of Sienese devotion towards him; to express the ardent desire of all the Sienese people for the amplification of the dignity and glory of the *beata* Catherine that her canonization would represent; and to press the need for rapid progress in the matter. In addition, the ambassadors were also to commend Siena to all the cardinals in Rome; to confirm that the necessary funds for the canonization were available; await approval of the process, and then return home. Further letters to the ambassadors were sent in June, again addressing aspects of the canonization process.[49] Catherine was eventually canonized by Pius II on 29 June 1461, the formal ceremony taking place in Saint Peter's in the morning, followed by a second ceremony in Santa Maria sopra Minerva in the afternoon.[50]

As the records of Sienese diplomatic initiatives and payments cited above indicate, however true it is that Catherine would never have been made a saint without the interest and support of the Dominican Order, it is also the case that her eventual canonization – and in particular its timing – owed a great deal to the efforts and commitment of the Sienese civic authorities. The extent of their desire to secure Catherine's elevation, above the level of a mere *beata*, to the full status of a *santa senese* – thus, indeed, making her the first Sienese '*santa*', the first female Sienese saint – alongside the also recently canonized Bernardino, is both clear and consistent. Indeed, the eventual canonization of Catherine is a striking demonstration of the effective combination of Dominican and Sienese civic interests and influences. Thus, when Pius II agreed to the initiation of the formal process for the consideration of Catherine's canonization, he also sanctioned the use of the records and testimonies

45 Laurent (1942, pp. 476–8, 481, 484–6), in each case citing *Concistoro* records in the Sienese Archivio di Stato; Norman (forthcoming).

46 Laurent (1942, pp. 486–8), again citing *Concistoro* records.

47 Laurent (1942, p. 488).

48 Laurent (1942, pp. 489–95, 502–7).

49 Laurent (1942, pp. 505–7, 511–12).

50 Laurent (1942, pp. 513–30).

originally gathered in Venice several decades earlier for the *Processo Castellano*, an initiative that, as we have seen, was thoroughly Dominican in origin and character.[51] In addition, as the Sienese diplomatic records show, at various points, the procurator of the Dominican Order had assisted in furthering the canonization process. But it was the diplomacy and the financial support of the Sienese civic authorities, combined with the opportune circumstance of a pope whose family origins were Sienese, that provided the crucial momentum for a successful campaign at the end of the 1450s and the beginning of the 1460s. It should not be overlooked, moreover, that Pius II – together with the papal court – was resident in Siena for two periods during 1459 and 1460. In the first instance he arrived in February 1459 – on his way to Mantua for the council – and stayed for two months. In the second, he arrived at the end of January 1460 and stayed for seven and a half months.[52] It is striking – and surely can hardly be coincidental – that the Sienese government records cited above focus particularly on diplomatic activity during 1459 involving Sienese ambassadors at Mantua. The presence of Pius II in Siena for over seven months in 1460, meanwhile, must have offered further opportunities to urge the cause of Catherine's canonization, whilst the Sienese had earlier established their enthusiasm over the election of a Sienese pope by virtue of their lavish celebration of Pius II's coronation in 1458.[53]

Given the care with which the Sienese authorities and their diplomats consistently referred to Catherine as a '*beata*' in their official correspondence and deliberations between 1458 and 1461, it is surely worth asking whether – stylistic issues notwithstanding – it is not more likely that Vecchietta's portrayal of Catherine as a saint among other saints in the Sala del Biado *Madonna della Misericordia* was, in fact, painted after Catherine's canonization.[54] If so, this image would then be one of a group of early post-canonization portrayals of Catherine which portray her new official status. For example, Vecchietta also painted a full-length image of Catherine, shown as a saint, on one of the piers in the Sala del Mappamondo in the Palazzo Pubblico, the figure being located, significantly, adjacent to another full-length figure of Bernardino (Plate ii). The document from 1460 referring to Vecchietta receiving payment for an image of the *beata* Catherine is usually associated with this painting and the painting is therefore dated to 1460–61. If the connection of the document with the painting is correct, it would seem entirely plausible that the

51 Of the 24 depositions supplied to the *Processo*, two were from laypersons and 22 from regular clergy, of whom 16 were Dominicans, the others comprising a Cistercian, two Carthusians, two Benedictines and a Franciscan, for which see Laurent (1942, p. xi); Heusinger (2000, p. 49).

52 Nevola (2006; 2007a, pp. 64–8).

53 Rossi (2002, p. 21); Nevola (2006, p. 67; 2007a, pp. 64–5). The Sienese celebrations included a simultaneous enactment, in the Piazza del Campo in Siena, of Pius's coronation in Rome on 3 September 1458. In the Sienese event, the figure representing Pius was crowned by another representing the Virgin, Siena's supreme patron and advocate.

54 See also the careful argument presented in Norman (forthcoming). Although not addressed to the matter of the dating of this particular painting, Strehlke (1988b, pp. 222–3) also emphasizes the care taken by the Sienese government to 'do everything correctly' in the matter of Catherine's canonization and concludes that 'precocious representations of Catherine as an aureoled saint' would therefore be unlikely.

Sienese authorities were at this point commissioning an image of Catherine in the now confident anticipation (given the extent and progress of their diplomatic efforts with Pius II by this time) of her shortly to be recognized new status, but nevertheless still chose to refer to her as the *beata* Catherine in the official documents.[55] The plausibility of this is supported by another document, dated 27 June 1461 – and thus just two days before Catherine's canonization – which reports the decision of the Sienese *Concistoro* to commission a further painting of the *beata* Catherine for a room in the Palazzo Pubblico. The document refers to an otherwise unknown painter – Francesco di Lorenzo di Bartolomeo Migliore – and there is continuing debate as to whether a full-length image of Catherine located in a room on the ground floor of the Palazzo Pubblico should be attributed to this painter or to Sano di Pietro.[56] Regardless of the issue of attribution, however, it is significant that the painting in question showed Catherine as a saint, complete with halo. Finally, the years immediately following Catherine's canonization also saw the production of a cycle of panels, attributed to the Sienese painter Giovanni di Paolo, which depict a series of scenes from her life. Although, once again, debate continues concerning their precise function – whether as predella panels for an altarpiece, or as a narrative sequence of scenes to accompany a large painted panel or wooden sculpture of Catherine herself – the fact that, in each case, Catherine is portrayed with a halo points to a date after her canonization in 1461. The sequence of scenes, it has plausibly been argued, represents a celebration of Catherine's historical importance and of the success of her cult at the moment of her canonization.[57]

It was not only by means of new paintings, however, that the Sienese celebrated the canonization of Catherine and also, thereby, their city's acquisition of a new '*santa cittadina*'. Collectively, the Sienese chronicle of Tommaso Fecini, the later history by Sigismondo Tizio and the records of the Sienese *Concistoro* together record that the canonization was celebrated on 16 August 1461 with an elaborate and splendid festival that included processions through the streets of Siena with numerous floats and the construction of a scene of paradise in the chapel in the Campo at the foot of the tower of the Palazzo Pubblico, whilst the house where Catherine had been born was turned into a 'beautiful chapel' with offerings from the civic authorities and the various guilds of Siena.[58] At its meeting of 19 March 1462 the Sienese *Consiglio Generale* resolved – by an almost unanimous vote of 163 to 1 – that Saint (*sancta*) Catherine was now to be numbered among the holy advocates of the city of Siena who would intercede with God for the well-being of the city and its liberty and government. As such she was also to be honoured by an annual

---

55 Carli (1963, p. 209); Southard (1978, pp. 250–52); Bianchi and Giunta (1988, pp. 252–3); Moerer (2003, pp. 124).

56 Carli (1963, p. 209); Southard (1978, pp. 197–9); Borghini (1983, p. 163); Bianchi and Giunta (1988, p. 249); Moerer (2003, pp. 125–6). The room is now known as the Ufficio del Personale.

57 Moerer (2003, pp. 127–72, especially pp. 166, 174). See also Strehlke (1988b, pp. 218–38).

58 Fecini (1931–39, p. 869); Laurent (1942, p. 538); Riedl and Seidel (1992a, 2.1.1, p. 59, n. 20); Webb (1996, pp. 307–8); Rossi (2002, p. 22); Moerer (2003, p. 110). See also Tizio, 'Historiarum Senensium, V', 30, BCI.Cod. B. III. 10.

festival at the church of San Domenico, on the first Sunday of May, at which the civic authorities would make the same kind of solemn procession and the same type of offering as they did each year at the church of San Francesco for the feast of Saint Bernardino.[59] Initially the various guilds of Siena were not explicitly required to render the same offerings to Catherine as to Bernardino. In May 1466, however, the community at San Domenico successfully petitioned the Sienese government for the imposition of the same penalties – for all the guilds – for failure to honour Catherine in the same way as Bernardino.[60] The annual procession in honour of Catherine each May also included the release of a prisoner in Catherine's honour. When the civic procession – which carried relics of Catherine through the city – reached the Campo and the chapel in front of the Palazzo Pubblico, a prisoner from the Commune's jail joined the procession and was subsequently released during the mass celebrated at the altar dedicated to Catherine in San Domenico.[61]

Following Catherine's canonization, her cult also continued to flourish and expand within Siena in other ways. In the very year of her canonization in 1461, the *Compagnia di Santa Caterina da Siena in Fontebranda* was founded. Also known as the *Confraternita di Santa Caterina da Siena in Fontebranda*, the new organization of lay devotees of Catherine initially met in San Domenico.[62] In 1479, meanwhile, a number of the *mantellate* who had continued to meet in San Domenico resolved to live as a religious community and took up residence in a palace, near to San Domenico, in the area of Siena known as the Poggio Malavolti, their community becoming known as the Convento di Santa Caterina del Paradiso.[63] In due course both of these institutions were also to receive the recognition and support of the Sienese civic authorities in virtue of their shared devotion to Catherine and her cult. Thus, in 1464, the Sienese civic authorities responded favourably to a petition from the inhabitants of the neighbourhood of Fontebranda when they sought funds to buy the house in which Catherine's family had lived in order to turn it into an oratory, complete with an altar dedicated to her. The people of the *contrada* of Fontebranda were also to furnish the new oratory, using funds provided by the Commune, which would then have patronage over it.[64] Subsequently the Commune made further grants in 1465 and 1470 for the furnishing of the oratory and the decoration of its façade,[65] whilst in 1474 there are references in civic accounts to payments to the

---

59 Webb (1996, p. 308); Moerer (2003, p. 110), citing the records of the *Consiglio Generale* which are also reproduced in Riedl and Seidel (1992a, 2.1.1, p. 59, n. 2).

60 Webb (1996, p. 308); Moerer (2003, pp. 111–12).

61 Toncelli (1909, p. 61, n. 5); Koenig (2001, p. 286).

62 For the early history of the *Compagnia di Santa Caterina da Siena in Fontebranda*, see Steinz-Kecks (1990, pp. 2–3); Turrini (1998, pp. 286–93); Ceppari Ridolfi and Turrini (2002, pp. 254, 259); Bacci (2003, pp. 8–11).

63 For the origins of the community of Santa Caterina del Paradiso see Riedl and Seidel (1992a, pp. 6–9); Calamati (1988, p. 25); Campanini and Rossi (1988, pp. 31–2).

64 Riedl and Seidel (1992a, 2.1.2, p. 59, n. 24); Steinz-Kecks (1990, p. 4); Moerer (2003, pp. 112–13); Sabelli (2002, p. 70). See also the exhibition catalogue entry by Simona Di Nepi in Syson et al. (2007, pp. 102, 104, n. 4).

65 Riedl and Seidel (1992a, 2.1.1, pp. 59, n. 25, 60, 61, n. 30); Steinz-Kecks (1990, pp. 4–5); Moerer (2003, p. 113); Sabelli (2002, p. 71).

sculptor Neroccio di Bartolomeo de' Landi for his work on a wooden statue of Saint Catherine for the Oratory.[66] The painted statue which resulted, which clearly displays her stigmata – and for which, it has been suggested, Vecchietta's image of Catherine in the Sala del Mappamondo of the Palazzo Pubblico may have been the model – quickly became and still remains one of the most revered images of Catherine in Siena.[67] Moreover, in addition to those who lived within the neighbourhood, the *Compagnia di Santa Caterina in Fontebranda* also began to meet in the Oratory, instead of, as originally, in San Domenico.[68]

Similarly, the Sienese civic authorities also contributed to the decoration of the chapel within San Domenico that was constructed, between 1466 and 1475, to house the relic of Catherine's head (Plate 3). The construction of the chapel was funded by Niccolò di Buonsignore Benzi, a Sienese citizen whose cousin Andrea had been a canon lawyer at the papal court of Pius II – and had been closely involved in the process of Catherine's canonization – and who himself later worked in Rome at the papal court.[69] As documents dating to the period 1466 to 1470 indicate, however, the new silver reliquary for the relic of Catherine's head and the marble tabernacle in which it was to be to housed (Plate 4) were funded jointly by Niccolò Benzi, the Dominicans of San Domenico and the Sienese government.[70] There also remained a strong link between the chapel and the *Compagnia di Santa Caterina in Fontebranda*. Members of the *Compagnia* could be buried in a communal vault located in front of the chapel in the body of the church – a practice that began in the last decade of the fifteenth century and continued regularly during the sixteenth century, a second vault for the *Compagnia* also being established.[71] By 1526, meanwhile, the community of *mantellate* at Santa Caterina del Paradiso had flourished to such an extent that they had not only been able to build a new church and convent but also received an offering of 20 *libre* of wax and 25 *staia* of salt from the Sienese government.[72]

The celebration of Catherine and her cult by the Sienese government in the decades following her canonization also continued in other ways. In addition to the embellishment of Catherine's main cult sites in Siena – at the expense of wealthy devotees and with an emphasis upon the portrayal of scenes from her life including,

---

66 Di Nepi in Syson et al. (2007, pp. 102–3, 104 nn. 5–6).

67 Torriti (1983, p. 14); Bianchi and Giunta (1988, pp. 260–61); Riedl and Seidel (1992a, 2.1.1, pp. 147–50). For the suggestion that Vecchietta's painting in the Sala del Mappamondo was the primary model for this statue, see Di Nepi in Syson et al. (2007, p. 103).

68 Turrini (1998, p. 286); Bacci (2003, p. 8).

69 Riedl and Seidel (1992b, 2.1.2, pp. 462, 562); Norman (2008).

70 Riedl and Seidel (1992b, 2.1.2, pp. 571–4); Norman (2008).

71 Riedl and Seidel (1992b, 2.1.2, pp. 777–9, including notes 117–23). As the documents cited in this source indicate, the proposal for a communal vault for the *Compagnia*, in front of the chapel in San Domenico, can be dated to July 1491, with the first burial occurring in 1493. A second vault is mentioned for the first time in 1531, and in 1622 the *Compagnia* was given papal permission to continue burials in San Domenico. A plan of San Domenico dated 1713 indicates the location of the vaults, for which see Riedl and Seidel (1992c, 2.2, plate 463).

72 Campanini and Rossi (1988, p. 34).

significantly, her experience of the stigmata[73] – the civic authorities of Siena also chose to celebrate Catherine in explicitly civic contexts. Between the last years of the fifteenth century and 1550, Catherine was portrayed on at least five occasions on the painted panels which formed the covers – known as *biccherne* – for the books containing Sienese government accounts. On a panel dated to 1498 Catherine is shown, on the left, at the moment of her stigmatic experience in 1375 in Pisa, whilst on the right Pius II is portrayed, enthroned and gesturing towards Catherine (Plate 2). In 1527 a panel depicted Catherine's mystical experience of exchanging her heart with Christ's; in 1539 another showed her mystical marriage with Christ; one in 1545 depicted her stigmatization; and in 1548 her mystical marriage was again represented.[74] It has been pointed out that the four appearances of Catherine on *biccherne* between 1527 and 1548 outnumber those of any other holy figure portrayed on surviving *biccherne* from this period, including even the Virgin.[75] Although true in itself, the statistic should not be over-interpreted because so many of the *biccherne* panels have not survived. It is thus possible that other now lost panels portrayed the Virgin and other holy figures equally frequently – or indeed that Catherine herself may in fact have been portrayed an even greater number of times. At the very least, however, it may reasonably be claimed that the five appearances of Catherine on *biccherne* between 1498 and 1548 clearly demonstrate her importance, and the importance of her cult, to the civic authorities of Siena during this period.

The decision to portray the subject of Catherine's stigmata twice within the profoundly civic context of *biccherna* covers was particularly significant. Nor, moreover, were these the only such examples of civic celebration of this theme. In the images of Catherine in the Palazzo Pubblico by Vecchietta (in the Sala del Mappamondo) and by either Sano di Pietro or Francesco di Lorenzo di Bartolomeo Migliore (in what is now the Sala degli uffici del Personale), and on the painted statue of Catherine by Neroccio di Bartolomeo de' Landi for the Oratory in Fontebranda, she was also portrayed with the signs of her stigmata prominently represented. This in turn reflected the prominence of the stigmata in the post-canonization fresco cycles of the Oratorio della Cucina, the Oratory of Saint Catherine in Fontebranda, the Chapel of Saint Catherine in San Domenico (Plate 3), and the cycle of panels by Giovanni di Paolo. Such representations of this theme in the Palazzo Pubblico and on the covers of *biccherne* clearly demonstrated the determination of the Sienese civic authorities to support the cause of the official recognition of the authenticity

73 In 1495, Bernardino Fungai was commissioned to paint an altarpiece – portraying the moment of Catherine's stigmata – for the chapel known as the Oratorio della Cucina in the sanctuary that was created out of the house in which Catherine and her family lived, for which see Torriti (1988, pp. 18–19); Riedl and Seidel (1992a, 2.1.1, pp. 203–6); Sabelli (2002, pp. 54–6). In the first four decades of the sixteenth century two major fresco cycles celebrating Catherine were also added to her Sienese cult sites, one in the Oratory of Saint Catherine in Fontebranda and the other in the chapel in San Domenico built to house the relic of Catherine's head. For the former see Riedl and Seidel (1992a, 2.1.1, pp. 134–40); Riedl (1990). For the latter see Torriti (1982, p. 44–6); Riedl and Seidel (1992b, 2.1.2, pp. 577–80); Norman (2008). In both cases Catherine's experience of the stigmata was again prominent.

74 Borgia et al. (1984, pp. 200–201, 230–31, 236–7, 240–41, 242–3).

75 Wegner (2005, p. 179).

of Catherine's experience of the stigmata – an issue that was a matter of serious and prolonged dispute between the Dominican and Franciscan orders. Anxious to protect the uniqueness of Francis of Assisi's stigmatic experience and status, Franciscan preachers and theologians argued that Catherine's experience of 'invisible stigmata' was not verifiable, should not be officially recognized by the church and also, therefore, should neither be celebrated nor portrayed as part of her cult. Such objections had even been voiced on the very day of Catherine's canonization by a Franciscan, Fra Roberto Caracciolo da Lecce, preaching at the celebration of the event in Santa Maria sopra Minerva. A highly polemical controversy ensued in which, initially, Franciscan objections secured papal support. In 1472 Pope Sixtus IV – himself a Franciscan – forbad, under threat excommunication, the portrayal of Catherine as a stigmatic either in images of her or in sermons on the subject. Although he subsequently lifted the threat of excommunication, he maintained the ban, which even the Dominican Order submitted to at their General Chapter in 1478. Confronted by the reality that depictions of Catherine as a stigmatic had continued, in 1490 Sixtus IV's successor, Innocent VIII, ruled that existing images of Catherine that portrayed her in this way could remain unchanged, but reiterated the ban on new portrayals of this kind. His successor, Pope Alexander VI – who was convinced that Catherine's experience was authentic – in practice allowed depictions of Catherine with the attributes of the stigmata, although he did not issue any formal pronouncement to reverse the previous ban or resolve the underlying issue. Thus, it was not until 1598 that Pope Clement VIII formally set aside the ban imposed by Sixtus IV whilst also referring the entire matter to the Sacred Congregation for Rites. It was then only three decades later, in 1630, that Pope Urban VIII officially recognized Catherine's stigmata as authentic and authorized their liturgical celebration.[76]

Such debate over her status as a stigmatic did not, however, impede the development of Catherine's status with the Sienese civic pantheon. In 1490 her status as one of the six officially recognized saintly advocates and protectors of the city was also celebrated by her inclusion in a group of huge gilded stucco statues of Siena's special patron saints that was added to the cathedral. Located at the crossing of the cathedral, the six statues – of Ansano, Savino, Crescenzio, Victor, Bernardino and Catherine – were placed high up in the angles immediately below the cupola at the top of the six piers that frame the crossing.[77] Her position as one of the six heavenly advocates of the city was also recognized in 1514 in the statutes of the newly formed *Compagnia di San Sebastiano*. Catherine was listed, together with Bernardino, after the Virgin and the four early Christian advocates and protectors of the city, and before the three saints to whom the *Compagnia* was especially dedicated.[78] Civic commitment to Catherine's cult, meanwhile, was also reaffirmed in November 1524 when the Commune resolved to give 25 *ducats* annually to the *Compagnia di Santa Caterina in Fontebranda*.[79] It is possible, moreover, that this new annual offering by

76 For more detailed discussion of the issue and references to the relevant papal documents see Giunta (1988, pp. 79–80; 1999, pp. 319–24).

77 Carli (1979, pp. 109–10); Torriti (1988, pp. 97–8).

78 Nevola (2007b, pp. 22, 28, n. 30).

79 Toncelli (1909, pp. 68–70); Turrini (1998, p. 290, n. 353); Bacci (2002, p. 10).

the civic authorities to one of the Sienese institutions that maintained and promoted Catherine's cult may have been prompted by the expulsion of Fabio Petrucci from Siena in September 1524. The Petrucci family had dominated Siena since 1487, ruling in a manner that resembled a hereditary dictatorship. The fall of the Petrucci regime and its allies – a process completed in April 1525 with the assassination of Alessandro Bichi who had dominated Siena since the fall of Fabio Petrucci – was therefore widely conceived within Siena not only as a reintroduction of a republican form of government but also as the regaining of liberty. Indeed, the members of the party that took over the government were known as the '*Libertini*'.[80]

The case is not conclusive, but at least three pieces of evidence may be cited in support of the proposal. First, the annual offering from the Commune to the *Compagnia*, initiated in November 1524, was given specifically in thanks to Catherine, the patron of the *Compagnia*, 'for her intercession for the regaining of liberty'.[81] Second, also in 1524, on 1 August, another Sienese lay company, the *Compagnia di San Salvatore*, invoked not only the four early patron saints and advocates of the city, but also Bernardino and the '*seraphica Catherina*', to intercede for the preservation and maintenance of peace and liberty, and for divine defence against anyone who wished to threaten this 'holy liberty'.[82] Third, on a painted cover for a group of documents requesting an annual offering of wax by the Commune to the *mantellate* of Santa Caterina del Paradiso and dated 1526, Catherine is shown above the Palazzo Pubblico of Siena, with arms and cloak spread protectively in the manner of the traditional Marian image known as the Madonna della Misericordia (Plate 5). In her right hand she holds a lily, and in her left hand she holds an open book upon the pages of which appear the words: 'LIBERTAS VIVAT'. The letters are painted in gold, as are Catherine's halo and the marks of the stigmata on each of her hands. The documents are principally notarial copies of petitions presented in April 1526 by the *mantellate* at Santa Caterina del Paradiso to the Sienese *Consiglio Generale* – requesting the same offerings of wax from the Commune that the civic authorities gave to other religious communities in the city – together with records of the votes taken in the *Consiglio Generale* in favour of the petition. Significantly, in the present context, in return for the annual offering of wax by the Commune on Catherine's annual feast day, the community undertook to pray continually for the preservation of the liberty of Siena – '*la dolce liberta nostra*' – asking God to maintain this state of affairs.[83]

Catherine's growing significance within the civic devotion and civil religion of Siena was also confirmed in 1545, in the final version of the Sienese government's

---

80 Jenkins (1972, p. 431); Ascheri (2000, p. 162); Norman (2003, p. 225); Mussolin (2006, p. 119); Jackson (2007a, p. 71; 2007b, p. 77).

81 Turrini (1998, p. 290, n. 353); Bacci (2002, p. 10).

82 Ascheri, Cornice, Ricceri and Santini (2004, p. 3).

83 The image and related documents are held by the Sienese Archivio di Stato, *Conventi*, 1150, *c*.77–84. The crucial phrase reads '... *volere obtone[n]do ci davere consa et con maggior obligo havemo ad pregare del continuo per la dolce liberta nostra che idio la mantenga alle quali humilmente ci raccoma[n]diamo et idio in soliati*', *Conventi*, 1150, *c*.78v. In a series of votes the *Consiglio Generali* agreed to the petition, each time by a large majority. See also Bisogni (1988, pp. 76–8); Barzanti, Cornice and Pellegrini (2006, p. 198).

statutes to be issued before the loss of Sienese independence in 1555. The statutes reaffirmed the obligation of the civic authorities to attend Catherine's annual feast days, visiting the altars dedicated to her and attending masses in San Domenico. They similarly noted the requirement for the authorities to attend the celebrations for the feast days of Bernardino, Ambrogio Sansedoni and Ansano as well.[84] In addition, however, the statutes also meticulously listed the specific offerings – in the form of varying weights in wax – that the Commune was to offer annually at Siena's various churches and religious institutions on the feast days of particular saints and on other religious festivals.[85] The level of the different offerings in wax clearly revealed a spiritual hierarchy within Siena's civic devotion and civil religion. At the pinnacle was the Virgin, the pre-eminent and historic heavenly patron and protector of Siena who, on the Feast of the Assumption, the most important day in the Sienese religious calendar, received no less than 160 pounds ('*librae*') of wax from the Commune. In addition, a number of other Marian festivals and religious institutions dedicated to the Virgin also received substantial amounts of wax annually (the Spedale di Santa Maria della Scala received 48 *librae*, for example, and the churches of Santa Maria dei Servi and Santa Maria a Fontegiusta received 24 *librae* each). What is most striking in the present context, however, is the fact that the second highest amount of wax to be offered annually by the Commune was the 80 *librae* which were to be presented at San Domenico on the first Sunday of May in honour of Catherine of Siena – an amount which, it has been observed, is not only half as much as that for the Virgin on the Feast of the Assumption, but also, therefore, confirmed Catherine as the first in status of the Sienese saints.[86] Catherine was, indeed, in these statutes, no longer simply one of the six advocates and defenders of Siena, but had already become the most prominent member of the Sienese civic pantheon. After her in rank within the civic pantheon of '*santi cittadini*' came Saints Bernardino and Ansano – both at 58 *librae* – with Ambrogio Sansedoni following at 18; Andrea Gallerani, Pier Pettinaio and Giovacchino Piccolomini all at 16; and Savino, Crescenzio and Victor at 12 each. In addition, moreover, Catherine was also honoured, above and beyond the 58 *librae* for her festival at San Domenico, by a further 24 *librae*, also on the first Sunday of May, to be presented to the community of *mantellate* at Santa Caterina del Paradiso.[87]

During the early sixteenth century Sienese devotion to Catherine and her cult also achieved new status in Rome. From the late fifteenth century members of the Sienese community in Rome had formed a confraternity called, variously, the *Compagnia della Nazione Senese* and the *Compagnia di Santa Caterina presso la tomba* – the latter title deriving from its custom of meeting in the Capranica chapel in Santa Maria sopra Minerva which housed Catherine's tomb. In 1519, however, the *Compagnia della Nazione Senese* received official recognition from Pope Leo X

84 Ascheri (1993, p. 7).

85 Ascheri (1993, pp. 366–70).

86 Ascheri (1990, p. 39).

87 Thus, arguably, making it all the more significant that, in 1526, the image of Catherine protecting the Palazzo Pubblico (Plate 5) was associated with petitions for, and agreements to make, offerings of wax from the Commune to the community.

and began to collect funds to build a church dedicated to Catherine of Siena for the use of the Sienese community in Rome. The building of the church, which in due course became Santa Caterina da Siena in Via Giulia, began in 1519 and attracted the generous financial support of both Cardinal Giovanni Piccolomini, the current Archbishop of Siena and great nephew of Pius II, and the wealthy Sienese banker and Roman resident, Agostino Chigi. The church was located not only on the new road – the Via Giulia – that linked the Vatican to the commercial centre of Rome, but also in the heart of the area that, in the late fourteenth century, had been known as the '*castrum senense*' because of the number of Sienese who had settled there.[88]

Catherine's growing importance and status during the first half of the sixteenth century as the new '*santa senese*' – both in Rome and in Siena itself – was, however, increasing just as the power of the Sienese republic decreased. In 1555 Siena ceased to be an independent city-state, having been forced to capitulate to the superior military strength of the emperor Charles V and his Florentine allies, after a long and bitter siege of the city during 1554–55. Siena became part of the Grand Duchy of Tuscany, ruled by the Florentine regime of the Medici. Despite the traumatic loss of their independence, however, the Sienese nevertheless managed to retain a significant degree of autonomy, albeit within the context of overall Florentine control. Such relative autonomy was expressed in a variety of ways: through the continuance of various Sienese government institutions and offices; through the continuing role of the Sienese nobility within the government of the city; and through the formal distinction, within the Grand Duchy, between the *Stato vecchio* or *Stato di Firenze* and the *Stato nuovo* or *Stato di Siena*.[89] Sienese identity was also maintained and reasserted through its religious life and, especially, its traditions of civil religion. Thus, between the final decade of the sixteenth century and mid-seventeenth century, the traditional Sienese devotion to the Virgin was reaffirmed in a variety of ways, most notably through the development of the cult of the Madonna of Provenzano and the construction of the Cappella del Voto in the cathedral as a shrine to the revered image of the Virgin known to the Sienese as the *Madonna del Voto*.[90]

Civic devotion in Siena was also reaffirmed, however, through an emphatic reassertion of the civic pantheon of Sienese saints and *beati*. In the era that followed the fall of the Sienese republic, the Sienese civic pantheon continued not merely to function but to flourish. In a variety of ways, from the late sixteenth century to the second half of the seventeenth century, the civic and religious authorities of Siena celebrated an expanded civic pantheon in which, whilst many of the saints and *beati* of the existing pantheon were re-acclaimed and re-portrayed, new members were also added to the community of Sienese '*santi* and *beati cittadini*'.[91] Within this newly expanded civic pantheon, the two most recent '*santi cittadini*' and the newest members of the select group of advocates and protectors of Siena – Catherine and

88 Nozzoli (1928; 1930); Borghini (1984); Spezzaferro (2005); Boccardi (2006); Norman (2008).

89 Parsons (2004a, pp. 32–3).

90 Parsons (2004a, pp. 34–8).

91 Argenziano (1996); Parsons (2004a, pp. 39–42).

Bernardino – figured particularly prominently.[92] It has been said of Catherine's and Bernardino's canonization and consequent celebration in the mid-fifteenth century that they 'became the city's new patron saints, effectively replacing the traditional ones, Ansano, Victor, Savino and Crescenzio'.[93] This is an overstatement, certainly in respect of the celebration of the civic pantheon in the mid-fifteenth century, but arguably also for its subsequent celebration in the late sixteenth and early seventeenth centuries. In the mid-fifteenth century Catherine and Bernardino were added to the four earlier advocates and protectors of the city, but did not simply replace them. The other four protectors and advocates continued to be portrayed together with Catherine and Bernardino.[94] It is correct, however, that Catherine and Bernardino began to assume a shared prominence within the group of six special saintly advocates and defenders of Siena. Thus, as we have seen, according to the statutes of 1545, Bernardino and Ansano were to be given a markedly higher than average annual tribute by the Commune of 58 *librae* of wax, whilst Catherine was to receive an even larger payment of 80 *librae*. This trend was subsequently accentuated in portrayals of the civic pantheon as the expanded community of Sienese *santi* and *beati cittadini* was emphasized and celebrated as part of the reassertion of Sienese identity that followed the fall of the republic and the loss of independence in 1555.

In a variety of contexts of civic devotion, Catherine and Bernardino increasingly came to the fore as the now pre-eminent members of the Sienese civic pantheon, with Catherine continuing to establish a prominence even in relation to Bernardino. In the new Marian cult of the Madonna of Provenzano, for example, Catherine and Bernardino were twice portrayed on early seventeenth-century *biccherne* covers in the act of venerating the Madonna.[95] Later in the century, Catherine and Bernardino were also given prominent places in the decoration of the church of Santa Maria di Provenzano, bronze statues of the two saints being placed above the high altar, in poses of adoration, on either side of the actual bust of the Madonna of Provenzano which provided the focus of this new Sienese civic cult.[96] In the cathedral, similarly, Catherine and Bernardino appeared in three prestigious locations, each of which reflected their prominence within Sienese civil religion. First, they were both portrayed in the large fresco on the right hand side of the chancel – one of a pair of paintings on either side of the chancel by Ventura Salimbeni, completed between 1608 and 1611 and depicting groups of Sienese saints and *beati*. Catherine, moreover, constituted the focal point of the painting, standing centrally placed within the group

92 It is also notable that the late sixteenth- and seventeenth-century expansion of the Sienese civic pantheon included a number of women – such as the *beate* Nera Tolomei, Aldobrandesca Ponzi and Caterina Colombini – whereas the only *beata* in the mid-fifteenth-century celebration of '*santi cittadini*' was Catherine.

93 Strehlke (1988a, p. 42).

94 Parsons (2004a, pp. 16–19).

95 Borgia et al. (1984, pp. 294–5, 300–301). The covers were for the periods July 1601 to June 1604 and January to June 1608 respectively.

96 Bianchi and Giunta (1988, p. 458); Parsons (2004a, p. 39). In the early eighteenth century, the four early advocates and protectors of the city were also portrayed in the pendentives of the cupola of the church, for which see Torriti (1988, p. 367).

of '*santi cittadini*' portrayed in this instance.[97] Both Catherine and Bernardino also featured – in the form of statues – in the prestigious Cappella del Voto – placed on either side of the revered image of the *Madonna del Voto*[98] – and again, in the form of gilded bronze statues, located in the two lateral pediments on the upper part of the façade of the cathedral, each portrayed in the act of genuflecting towards a third statue of the Virgin of the Assumption located in the central pediment.[99]

In addition, in 1616, Catherine was portrayed in a fresco that was added to the façade of the Oratory of Saint Ansano, located in the district of Siena known as Castelvecchio. One of the four early Christian martyrs who were recognized as Siena's special advocates and protectors – and honoured as such in Duccio and Simone Martini's paintings of the *Maestà* theme for both the cathedral and the Palazzo Pubblico – Ansano had long enjoyed a particular status as the saint who, it was believed, brought Christianity to Siena and baptized the first Sienese Christians. Traditionally believed to have been martyred in AD 303, during the Diocletian persecution, at Dofana, just outside Siena and close to the site of the battle of Montaperti – a location which itself came to occupy a central place in Siense civil religion – by the early fourteenth century Ansano had become the focus of a significantly enhanced civic cult which raised him above his fellow advocates and protectors Savino, Crescenzio and Victor. In 1325 the Sienese civic authorities decreed that Ansano's annual festival on 1 December should be a major holiday and that government officials would attend services in the cathedral bringing candles as offerings.[100] In the 1440s the Sienese civic authorities further demonstrated their commitment to Ansano's cult by commissioning the building of an oratory in Castelvecchio which incorporated the tower in which it was believed – according to Sienese tradition – that Ansano had been imprisoned before his martyrdom.[101] And, as the calendar of offerings of wax on saints' days in the statute of 1545 indicated, the annual festival of Ansano was marked by an offering of 58 *librae*, equal to that for Bernardino and second only to that for Catherine among the offerings to saints and *beati*. It is also significant, therefore, that when, in 1616, a new fresco by the painter Francesco Rustici was added to the lunette above the entrance to the oratory of Saint Ansano, the two saints chosen to accompany the portrayal of the Virgin and Child were Ansano and Catherine.[102]

Some of the late sixteenth and early seventeenth century paintings that were added to rooms on the second floor of the Palazzo Pubblico further exemplified this trend. The series of frescoes painted in the rooms known as the Sala and Saletta del Capitano celebrated Sienese civic identity by portraying a variety of scenes from Sienese secular and religious history including numerous depictions of Sienese saints and *beati* and incidents from their lives and legends. Among the saints and *beati* thus

97 Argenziano (1996, pp. 316–17, 319, 325); Parsons (2004a, pp. 40–41).

98 Parsons (2004a, pp. 39–40).

99 Parsons (2004a, p. 40); Barzanti, Cornice and Pellegrini (2006, pp. 296–7, 308, 316–18, 320–21).

100 D'Accone (1997, pp. 97–117); Parsons (2006, pp. 50–51).

101 Riedl and Seidel (1985, 1.1, pp. 325–8; 513); Nevola (2007a, pp. 151–5).

102 Bagnoli (1980, p. 186); Riedl and Seidel (1985, 1.1, p. 328).

portrayed, Catherine and Bernardino appeared most frequently, each being depicted four times. In the Sala del Capitano two scenes from Catherine's life – by the artist Rutilio Manetti – were added to the decoration in 1597. In the first scene Catherine was portrayed kneeling in front of Pope Gregory XI in Avignon and appealing to him to return to Rome. In the second scene Gregory's re-entry into Rome was depicted, with Catherine symbolically leading the papal procession into the city.[103] In the Saletta del Capitano, meanwhile, Catherine and Bernardino were twice portrayed together, once on either side of Bernardino's characteristic symbol, and once on either side of the Madonna of Provenzano.[104] Similarly, between the 1580s and the 1630s, the painted miniatures that, during this period, decorated the covers of the official government records known as the *Libri dei Leoni* also frequently portrayed Sienese saints and *beati*. Again, Catherine and Bernardino – or scenes and symbols directly associated with their cults – appeared more frequently than any other saints or *beati*, Catherine and her cult again appearing most frequently.[105] Whilst no other saint or *beato* featured more than four times (a level of representation achieved by Ansano), Bernardino and his cult were represented 11 times, and Catherine and her cult were depicted on no less than 14 occasions. In seven of these instances Catherine or aspects of her cult were the sole subject of the miniature.[106] Her experience of the stigmata was the subject of four images. Two of them portrayed her original experience of the stigmata in Pisa.[107] The other two showed the crucifix in front of which the experience of the stigmata occurred being carried in procession through Siena, depicting in particular the crucifix passing in front of the Palazzo Pubblico (Plate 10).[108] A further miniature portrayed the relic of Catherine's head – again being taken in procession through the Campo and in front of the Palazzo Pubblico (Plate 9)[109] – and another showed her in front of Pope Gregory XI appealing for his return to Rome.[110]

The calculated affirmation of the specifically civic significance and context of the processions with the crucifix of the stigmata – which is so clearly implied by their portrayal in the Campo and directly in front of the Palazzo Pubblico – is further emphasized by the particular year in which these images were painted. Both occurred in 1623, the year in which the construction of a church – located within the Sanctuary

---

103 Borghini (1983, pp. 298, 304).

104 Borghini (1983, p. 310).

105 Redon (1992); Pallavicino, (1996); Pallavicino, Ceppari Ridolfi and Turrini (1996).

106 See the miniatures for September–October 1587, September–October 1595, May–June 1608, May–June 1617, May–June and September–October 1623, July–August 1629, for which see Pallavicino, Ceppari Ridolfi and Turrini (1996, pp. 418, 432, 444, 457, 468–9, 476).

107 The images for September–October 1587, July–August 1629, for which see Pallavicino, Ceppari Ridolfi and Turrini (1996, pp. 418, 476).

108 The images for May–June and September–October 1623, for which see Pallavicino, Ceppari Ridolfi and Turrini (1996, pp. 468–9).

109 May–June 1617, for which see Pallavicino, Ceppari Ridolfi and Turrini (1996, p. 457).

110 September–October, 1595, for which see Pallavicino, Ceppari Ridolfi and Turrini (1996, p. 432).

of Saint Catherine, to house the crucifix before which Catherine experienced the stigmata (Plate 6) – was completed and in which the crucifix was transferred to the new church. In May 1565, the Sienese had acquired the painted crucifix from the church of Santa Cristina in Pisa (Plate 7).[111] Two years later, in 1567, the crucifix was chosen as the sacred image to be carried in the first penitential procession for the festival of Domenica in Albis, to mark the close of the celebration of Easter – a procession and festival which subsequently became an annual event in Sienese religious life.[112] Between 1614 and 1623 the new church – which became known as the Chiesa del SS. Crocifisso – was built on the site believed to have been the garden of Catherine's family house. The new church was consecrated on 23 April 1623 and on 21 May the crucifix was transferred to it after a long progress through the streets of Siena, according to a route defined by the Capitano del Popolo to insure the maximum public participation and in a procession that included the civic authorities – precisely the events depicted, at the moment of passing in front of the Palazzo Pubblico, on the *Libri dei Leoni* miniatures for May–June and September–October 1623 (Plate 10).[113] A similar civic procession also took place in 1630 to celebrate Pope Urban VIII's official recognition of the authenticity of Catherine's stigmata. On that occasion, however, not only the crucifix of the stigmata but also the relic of Catherine's head was carried through the streets of the city.[114]

The Sienese celebrations and processions in honour of the completion of the Chiesa del SS. Crocifisso also included a reaffirmation of the link between the cult of Saint Catherine in Siena itself and its continuing expression among the Sienese community in Rome. Thus, in 1625 the *Compagnia di Santa Caterina in Fontebranda* donated a copy of the crucifix of the stigmata – commissioned from the painter Rutilio Manetti – to the *Confraternita della Nazione Senese* in Rome. Manetti's copy sought to produce the style of the original painted crucifix, whilst on the reverse side he portrayed Catherine, kneeling with arms outstretched and displaying the stigmata, with the city of Siena shown below her, and with the church of San Domenico in the foreground and both the cathedral and the tower of the Palazzo Pubblico prominent in the background (Plates 7, 8).[115] The gift once again confirmed the link between Siena's civic devotion to Catherine and her cult among the Sienese in Rome – just as, some thirty years earlier, the confraternity in Rome had been quick to signal its allegiance to the new Sienese civic cult of the Madonna of Provenzano, making a pilgrimage to Siena to the new cult site as early as 1595.[116] Manetti also contributed paintings to the fresco cycle that was added to the Oratorio della Cucina during the

---

111 Gigli (1854, vol. 1, pp. 188–9); Toncelli (1909, p. 90); Gianni (2002, p. 326). The translation of the crucifix to Siena was facilitated by Angelo Niccolini who was both Archbishop of Pisa and first Governor of Siena on behalf of the Medici, for which see Fusai (1999, pp. 10, 78); Ascheri (2000, pp. 189–90).

112 Gianni (2002).

113 Toncelli (1909, pp. 94–6); Pallavicino, Ceppari Ridolfi and Turrini (1996, p. 380), citing records of the *Consistoro*; Sabelli (2002, p. 34).

114 Gigli (1854, p. 174); Toncelli (1909, pp. 96–7).

115 Turrini (1998, p. 288, n. 350); Colucci (2005); Barzanti, Cornice and Pellegrini (2006, pp. 72, 96–7).

116 Sbaragli (1943).

late sixteenth and early seventeenth centuries. Chiefly comprised of scenes from Catherine's life, the overtly civic nature of her cult was nevertheless also reaffirmed in this painted programme by the inclusion of portrayals of four other members of the Sienese civic pantheon, namely the *beati* Giovanni Colombini and Andrea Gallerani (both painted by Alessandro Casolani in 1585), and the *beata* Nera Tolomei and the *beato* Bernardo Tolomei (portrayed by Francesco Vanni in 1600 as heavenly 'witnesses' of Catherine's canonization).[117]

The portrayal of the city of Siena beneath the figure of Catherine on the Rutilio Manetti copy of the crucifix of the stigmata (Plate 8) also, moreover, echoed two earlier images in which Catherine and Bernardino – the two most recently recognized official saintly advocates and protectors of the city – were shown with the Virgin and invoking her protection and oversight of Siena, which was, in turn, itself depicted in great topographical detail. In 1580 Catherine and Bernardino were portrayed in this way in a fresco painted in the vault of the ceiling of the lower part of the Oratory of San Bernardino in Siena.[118] The inclusion of Catherine in this instance constituted a particularly striking example of her status within Sienese civic devotion, given the dedication of the Oratory itself to Bernardino. Both saints then also appeared in this manner in an image published in the three-volume edition of Orlando Malavolti's history of Siena published in 1599.[119] Similarly, the use of the crucifix of the stigmata for the first Sienese procession for the celebration of Domenica in Albis in 1567 proved to be a precedent for subsequent occasions. Thus, relics and images associated with Catherine's cult were chosen for the annual penitential procession and devotions for this festival twice more in the sixteenth century and a further six times during the seventeenth century. The crucifix itself was chosen again in 1571, and 1600, whilst the relic of Catherine's head was chosen in 1576 and 1683, the relic of her finger in 1606, 1625 and 1697, and the relic of her rib in 1638.[120] On the latter occasion it was claimed that Siena was saved from a series of earthquakes as a result.[121]

Catherine's status and cult continued to be celebrated in Siena during the eighteenth century and the first six decades of the nineteenth century. Her place within the community of '*santi cittadini*' was restated in two sets of statues that portrayed members of the Sienese civic pantheon. In 1772, Catherine was one of a sequence of eight members of the civic pantheon, statues of whom were added to the internal decoration of the church of San Pellegrino alla Sapienza.[122] In the early nineteenth century statues of Catherine and Bernardino were placed on the façade of the church of Santa Maria di Provenzano in the niches on either side of the main door (with statues of Ansano and Victor above them in the niches at the top of the

117 Sabelli (2002, pp. 54–5, 58–9, 63).

118 Barzanti, Cornice and Pellegrini (2006, pp. 78–9). The painting is attributed to either Arcangelo Salimbeni or Francesco Vanni.

119 Barzanti, Cornice and Pellegrini (2006, pp. 50–52).

120 Gianni (2002, pp. 328–42).

121 *Mostra Cateriniana* (1962, p. 289).

122 Torriti (1988, p. 250).

façade).[123] Later in the nineteenth century the continuing association of Catherine with the Sienese civic pantheon was also reaffirmed by the addition of two further paintings to the fresco scheme within the Oratorio della Cucina in the Sanctuary of Saint Catherine. Thus, portrayals of Ambrogio Sansedoni and Bernardino were added in 1872 immediately to the left and right of the altar wall.[124] Catherine and her cult were also the focus for the procession and festival of Domenica in Albis on four occasions during the eighteenth century. In 1739 and 1777 the relic of her head was chosen as the sacred object for veneration in the cathedral during the festival, and in 1712 and 1750 the crucifix of the stigmata was chosen. The choice of the relic of Catherine's head in 1777 prompted not only the composition and publication of an account of her life in verse form by members of the *Contrada dell'Oca*,[125] but also a detailed account of the procession through the city with the relic, together with other poems and sonnets in celebration of the occasion.[126] In the first half of the nineteenth century both the relic of Catherine's head and the crucifix of the stigmata were again chosen on two occasions for the celebration of Domenica in Albis – her head in 1806 and 1827, the crucifix in 1816 and 1843.[127]

In the eighteenth century Catherine's status was also reaffirmed, and her cult promoted, by the work of the Sienese scholar Girolamo Gigli. The author of the famous *Diario sanese* in which he listed the annual festivals and celebrations for more than 450 saints and *beati* celebrated in Siena, Gigli had a particular devotion to Catherine of Siena, having become a member of the *Compagnia di Santa Caterina* in 1674, at the age of 14, subsequently serving as its prior and securing the official verification, by Archbishop Leonardo Marsili, of various relics of Catherine in the possession of the *Compagnia*.[128] Gigli's most important contribution to the development of Catherine's cult and reputation lay, however, in his ambitious project of producing a four volume edition of her complete works – a project that, as has recently been observed, had never been attempted previously (nor indeed subsequently).[129] Between 1707 and 1721 Gigli published a translation of Catherine's life by Raymond of Capua, two volumes of her letters, and an edition of her *Dialogue*.[130] He has a claim, therefore, to be regarded as the forerunner – if not the initiator – of the process

123 Torriti (1988, p. 367).

124 Sabelli (2002, pp. 55, 61).

125 *Breve Compendio della Vita della Serafica Vergine S. Caterina da Siena esposta in rima da A.I.P.A. e dai Sigg. della Contrada dell'Oca dedicate alla Quattro Compagnie Deputate dalla Domenica in Albis dall'anno MDCCLXXVII.*

126 *Relazione della Solenne Processione fatta in Siena nella Domencica in Albis l'anno MDCCXXVII dedicata all'illustrissimo e reverendissimo monsignore Antonio Felice Zondadori dei Marchese Chigi eletto inquisitore di Malta.*

127 Gianni (2002, 348–50).

128 Gagliardi, (1996, pp. 143–4).

129 Zaggia (2006, p. 155).

130 Scott (1993, p. 89); Gagliardi (1996, p. 144); Cavallini (1998, p. 21); Trifone (2004, p. 20; 2006, p. 189); Zaggia (2006, pp. 155–6). The first and third volumes, comprising respectively the life of Catherine by Raymond of Capua and Catherine's *Dialogue*, were first published in 1707. The second and third volumes, containing Catherine's Letters, were first published in 1713 and 1721.

whereby modern enthusiasts for and devotees of Catherine have used the publication and dissemination of her works as one of the principal means of promoting her reputation and her cult. In 1717 Gigli also published his *Vocabolario cateriniano*, a polemical work in which he championed the fourteenth century Sienese version of Italian used by Catherine and challenged the linguistic supremacy promoted by Florence and by the Florentine scholarly institution of the *Accademia della Crusca*. The *Vocabolario cateriniano* caused great controversy within the Grand Duchy of Tuscany and was even burned in public in Florence, whilst Gigli was expelled from the *Accademia della Crusca* and forced into exile.[131]

In addition to his edition of Catherine's works and the *Vocabolario cateriniano*, in his *Diario sanese* Gigli also, moreover, provided a detailed account of the way in which the annual civic procession in honour of Catherine on the first Sunday in May had developed by the early eighteenth century. The procession, he noted, formed initially in San Domenico in the morning and included the Dominicans, the members of the two Sienese confraternities dedicated to Catherine, members of the two Sienese *contrade* (the Oca and the Drago) who have Catherine as their patron saint, and representatives of the various professions and the university. Relics of Catherine were carried in procession through the streets, first to the convent of Santa Caterina del Paradiso, and then to the church of Santa Maria di Provenzano. The procession then went to the Piazza del Campo and the Palazzo Pubblico where it was joined by the civic authorities and then continued to the Sanctuary of Saint Catherine, stopping in front of the crucifix of the stigmata, and then continued finally back to San Domenico for mass, the relic of Catherine's head being exposed to the veneration of the faithful for the rest of the day.[132] It is thus particularly notable that, by the early eighteenth century, the route of the procession had come to include not only all the major sites of Catherine's cult in Siena and the civic centre of the Campo and Palazzo Pubblico, but also the church which was the centre of the cult of the Madonna of Provenzano – a striking illustration of the way in which Catherine's principal festival interacted with Sienese civic devotion and civil religion as a whole.

Gigli died in Rome in January 1722. It was also in Rome, in the middle of the following century, that the cult of Catherine of Siena received further significant enhancement. Between 1848 and 1855 the church of Santa Maria sopra Minerva was the subject of a major restoration. After the restoration, the high altar was re-consecrated by Pope Pius IX on 4 August 1855. Five days later, after three days of prayer in honour of Catherine, her remains were transferred from their former location in the Capranica chapel to a new one below the high altar. The ceremonies for the translation included three days of festivities and culminated in a procession in which Catherine's remains were carried through the streets of Rome, with the participation of the civic as well as religious authorities.[133] Two years later, Pope Pius IX also visited Siena. He did so, accompanied by the Grand Duke of Tuscany,

131 Gagliardi (1996, p. 147–8); Trifone (2004, p. 20; 2006, pp. 189–90); Zaggia (2006, pp. 156–8).

132 Gigli (1854, vol. 1, pp. 169–70); see also Grassi (1939, pp. 3–5).

133 Bianchi (1988, p. 40); Palmerio and Villetti (1989, p. 229).

Leopold II, on his way back to Rome after making a visit to the Papal States in central Italy. Arriving in Siena by train in the early evening of 28 August, Pius IX was escorted to the cathedral, amidst the acclamation of crowds of Sienese, where he was greeted by the ecclesiastical authorities. The next day he was accompanied to various sites in Siena, culminating in a visit to the Sanctuary of Saint Catherine in Fontebranda. There he was received by the representatives of the *Compagnia di Santa Caterina in Fontebranda* and the *Contrada dell'Oca* and visited the oratories and churches within the Sanctuary where he signed the visitors' book and accepted a commemorative medal in honour of his visit. On 30 August, after celebrating mass at the cathedral, Pius IX visited the Palazzo Pubblico and spent time in veneration of the relic of Catherine's head which had been brought, in procession, from the church of San Domenico to the Campo and to the chapel within the Palazzo Pubblico. After a subsequent papal blessing of the crowds that had assembled in the Campo, the relic of Catherine's head was returned, again in procession, to San Domenico.[134]

The events of 28 to 30 August 1857 neatly encapsulated Catherine's status by the mid-nineteenth century. Catherine and her cult were central to Pius IX's visit and presence in Siena. He visited her Sanctuary in Fontebranda, whilst the relic of her head was brought to the chapel in the Palazzo Pubblico – the civic heart of the city – for Pius to venerate it before blessing the Sienese, assembled in their central piazza. Nine years later, in March 1866, Pius IX was to honour Catherine by officially proclaiming her a co-patron saint of the city of Rome, together with Saints Peter and Paul.[135] He thus began a process by which, in the twentieth century, subsequent popes would further enhance Catherine's official status, also proclaiming her, firstly, a co-patron saint of Italy and, secondly, a co-patron saint of Europe. Before the occurrence of the latter elevations, however, Catherine's cult had first to undergo a significant transition. Already an important focus of Sienese civil religion and civic devotion – and, indeed, the pre-eminent member of the Sienese civic pantheon of '*santi cittadini*' – Catherine was not yet a focus for Italian civil religion and national sentiment. The process by which Catherine and her cult assumed this further significance will be the subject of the next chapter.

134 Grassi (1991, pp. 94–8).

135 Vanni (1975, pp. 95–7).

Chapter 2

From '*santa senese*' to '*Patrona d'Italia*': The Cult of Catherine of Siena 1859–1939

For devotees of Catherine of Siena, it has been observed, the twentieth century may justly be regarded as the great era in the history of her cult.[1] Declared the official patron of the women's section of *Azione Cattolica* by Pope Pius X in 1909, proclaimed the co-patron saint of Italy in 1939 and the patron of Italian nurses in 1943, on both occasions by Pope Pius XII, made a Doctor of the Church by Pope Paul VI in 1970, and finally proclaimed a co-patron saint of Europe by Pope John Paul II in 1999, Catherine's status among the saints of the Catholic church assumed ever greater recognition. In respect of her new roles as an official patron saint first of Italy and then of Europe she also, moreover, became the focus for two further forms of civil religion. To her role as the pre-eminent member of the Sienese civic pantheon of saints and *beati*, were added, first, the further role of being a representative figure for one expression of Italian civil religious identity, and subsequently the role of a symbol of a form of European civil religion and its values. The present chapter explores the beginning of this process, culminating in her proclamation as *Patrona d'Italia* in June 1939.

Although the crucial decades in the process by which Catherine came to be proclaimed a co-patron saint of Italy were the 1920s and 1930s, it is nevertheless possible to trace the origins of Catherine's emergence as a potential symbol of Italian national sentiment – and hence also a potential national patron saint – back into the latter half of the nineteenth century and the first two decades of the twentieth century. In both 1859 and 1861 Sienese celebrations of Catherine linked her explicitly to the cause of Italian independence. In 1859 the prestigious relic of her head was once again chosen as the focus for the annual Sienese festival of Domenica in Albis. In announcing this choice the *Avviso Sacro* – the official public notice – for the festival drew attention to the fact that Catherine had lived during a period in which the Catholic church was reduced to a condition of mourning, the Pope being absent from Rome in Avignon and unable to perform his proper pastoral role. Italy and Europe, meanwhile, the notice continued, suffered from a lack of religion, justice and law, and also, consequently, from factional strife and conflict. Because of this, however, Catherine had sought to resolve dissension, reconcile factions and promote peace and

1 Giunta (1988, p. 145).

harmony – and above all had persuaded the Pope to return from Avignon to Rome.[2] In adopting this line, the *Avviso Sacro* provided an early example of an appeal that was to become one of the most prominent and consistent themes in the interpretation and celebration of Catherine as a national – and later a European – saint in the next century. Even more significantly, the official accounts of the expenditure for the festival concluded with an explanation of what was to be done with the surplus funds that had been collected. Of the total surplus of 2,305 *lire*, 1,652 *lire* were allocated to two particular projects. A silver lamp for the chapel in San Domenico that housed the relic of Catherine's head cost 767 *lire*. The largest single sum – 885 *lire* – was, however, to be passed to the Sienese civic authorities to be given 'to the Italian war of independence', specifically for the cost of spiritual assistance for the army, for chaplains, for the care of the wounded and for families in need as a result of the war.[3]

Also in 1859, immediately after the festival of Domenica in Albis, a group of devotees of Catherine, together with the religious community in San Domenico, organized a further *ottavario* of prayer dedicated to seeking Catherine's intercession with God for the protection, blessing and victory of the Italian forces fighting 'for the holy cause of the independence of her and our Italian homeland'.[4] Similarly, two years later, as part of the Sienese celebrations of the fourth centenary of Catherine's canonization, the committee responsible for the festivities wrote to the Sienese civic authorities in May 1861 – to the Gonfaloniere del Municipio on 13 May, and to the Prefetto on the 18th. The committee explained that they proposed to celebrate the centenary of Catherine's canonization and at the same time give thanks to God for the much desired independence of Italy, an independence that had now been obtained, although not without the intercession of '*nostra Santa Concittadina*' who had herself greatly loved her '*Patria*'. The committee also sought the support of the civic authorities for the relic of Catherine's head to be placed on the high altar of San Domenico for public veneration on 29 June – the day of her canonization in 1461.[5] The celebrations on 29 July 1861 included numerous masses in San Domenico – which was richly decorated for the occasion – and a spectacular procession through

2 'Sacro Avviso: Domenica in Albis', 1859, copy in a collection of documents relating to this festival in the Archivio della Nobile Contrada dell'Oca, Siena, inventory number XIII B. 4 95.

3 'Rendi-Conto dei Deputati alla Festa che si faceva in Siena nella Domenica in Albis l'anno 1859', copy in the Archivio della Nobile Contrada dell'Oca, Siena, inventory number XIII B. 4 95.

4 'Deliberazione della deputazione per la commemorazione anniversaria e centenaria della canonizzazione di S. Caterina da Siena', Archivio della Compagnia di S. Caterina (1792–1970), inventory number 97 [5], now held by the Associazione Internazionale dei Caterinati, Siena.

5 'Copialettere e Petizioni della Festa centenaria di S. Caterina del 1861, no. 1 al Gonfaloniere del Municipio di Siena, 13 maggio, 1861, no. 2 al Prefetto di Siena, 18 maggio 1861', Archivio della Compagnia di S. Caterina (1792–1970), inventory number 98 [71]. See also Bacci (2003, pp. 118–19).

the city in the evening, followed by an *ottavario* of prayer in San Domenico in Catherine's honour until 7 July.[6]

Almost two decades later, in 1880, the celebration in Siena of the fifth centenary of Catherine's death was marked by controversy arising from the considerable tensions in Siena during this period between Catholic and anti-clerical groups. Thus, for example, religious processions through the streets were routinely prohibited for fear of disturbance to public order and requests to the civic authorities in 1880 to allow a solemn procession through the streets of Siena with the relic of Catherine's head were similarly rejected. The civic authorities did allow the tolling of the bell of the tower of the Palazzo Pubblico to mark the occasion – but even this act prompted protest in the pages of the strongly anti-clerical local paper *Il Libero Cittadino*. The paper complained that the civic recognition implied by tolling the bell of the Torre del Mangia was inappropriate because the celebrations of Catherine's death had not been in honour of Catherine as an 'illustrious Sienese woman' but for 'the saint who had brought the Pope back to Rome'. The paper also protested that a prominent representative of the clerical party in Siena had claimed that the celebrations were a protest against the 'revolution' that had resulted in the Unification of Italy.[7] Despite the absence of public processions, the centenary was nevertheless celebrated in San Domenico in a festival lasting from 28 April to 6 May. San Domenico was richly decorated for the duration of the festival and Catherine's head was displayed on the high altar for the devotion of the many people who attended the services both there and at the Sanctuary of Saint Catherine. On Sunday 2 May a large congregation attended the pontifical mass celebrated by the Archbishop of Siena in San Domenico, with music composed especially for the service, which culminated in a papal blessing, delivered by the archbishop with the permission of Pope Leo XIII. There was also, moreover, a degree of civic recognition of the centenary through the participation of the civic authorities – accompanied by the town band – at the inauguration of the restored façade of the church of Santa Caterina in Fontebranda, and also by virtue of a series of lectures on Catherine held in the Sala del Mappamondo in the Palazzo Pubblico on 6 May.[8] The Sienese scholar and priest Alessandro Toti – who had previously published one of the first scholarly studies of the sources for the various dedications of Siena to the Virgin, thereby seeking to emphasize the role of religion in the civic life and history of the city – also now marked the fifth centenary of

6 These details are reported in a brief article published in 1962 in the Sienese Dominican periodical *La Patrona d'Italia*, for which see Paganucci (1962). The author cited a document – found by a fellow Dominican – then apparently in the Biblioteca Comunale in Siena, entitled, 'Rendiconto dei Deputati alla Festa che si faceva in Siena nella Chiesa abbaziale di S. Domenico dei MM. RR. Monaci Cassinesi nel 29 guigno 1861 – e successivo ottavario per solenizzare il Quarto centenario della Canonizzazione di Santa Caterina ecc.' I have been unable to trace the original document in the Biblioteca Comunale.

7 *Il Libero Cittadino*, 9/5/1880, p. 2; *Il Telegrafo*, 29/4/1939, p. 4; Luchini (1987, pp. 163–4). For the broader context of the tensions between clerical and anti-clerical groups in Siena in the period after Italian Unification see Parsons (2004a, pp. 65–9).

8 *Il Telegrafo*, 29/4/1939, p. 4. This account of the celebration in 1880, by the Sienese historian Virgilio Grassi, refers to contemporary newspaper reports, but without naming them specifically. I have been unable to track down the original reports.

Catherine's death by publishing a collection of the sources relating to the Sanctuary of Saint Catherine in Siena.[9]

In 1887, moreover, the Sanctuary proved to be the location for an event which, at the same time, transcended the conflict between clerical and anti-clerical factions in Siena and also reaffirmed the potentially national significance of Catherine within the new Italian state. Between Saturday 16 and Monday 18 July 1887 King Umberto and Queen Margherita visited Siena. The Sunday morning of the royal visit was devoted to the Sanctuary of Saint Catherine. Amidst great public enthusiasm, and with the same form of ceremony that had been used for the visit of Pope Pius IX in 1857, the king and queen were received in Fontebranda by the Governor and other officials of the *Contrada dell'Oca*. After a symbolic presentation to the king and queen of the fifteenth-century keys to the Sanctuary, they first visited the church of the *Contrada dell'Oca* – namely the Oratory of Santa Caterina in Fontabranda – and then continued to the rest of the Sanctuary, accompanied by the Italian prime minister Francesco Crispi, and escorted by the Prior of the *Confraternita di Santa Caterina in Fontebranda*. In the Sanctuary they attended a mass and were presented with a gold medal in commemoration of the event. The following morning Queen Margherita also visited the chapel of Saint Catherine in San Domenico to venerate the relic of Catherine's head.[10] The potential symbolism of the visit is all the greater if it is consciously placed within the context of the tensions between church and state, not only in Siena, but in Italy as a whole at this time. Despite the continuing conflict between church and state, in this instance, the king and queen, and the liberal prime minister, had all attended mass at the shrine of a saint much revered not only in Siena but also in Rome and by the papacy – and who, indeed, the previous Pope had made an official patron of Rome. Francesco Crispi, it was said, even remarked on the fact that it was a long time – prior to the visit to the Sanctuary – since he had attended mass.[11] Clearly, the figure of Catherine had the capacity, at least temporarily, to transcend the contemporary discord between the civil and religious spheres in Italy and to bring church, monarchy and liberal prime minister together.

Catherine's own capacity to combine the interests of church and state was also one of the themes of a lecture, presented in Siena in 1895 at the *Accademia dei Rozzi* under the auspices of the *Commissione Senese di Storia Patria*. The lecture was given by Carlo Calisse, Professor of History at the University of Siena from 1892 to 1895 and then subsequently at the University of Pisa. A specialist in the history of both Italian law and ecclesiastical law, Calisse was later appointed a Counsellor of State (in 1907) and a member of the Senate (from 1919 until his death in 1945), where he was to prove an early and a consistent supporter of the Fascist regime.[12] In his substantial lecture in 1895 – which ran, in its printed version, to some 32 printed pages – Calisse presented a detailed account of Catherine's life, structured around

9 Toti (1880). For his earlier study of the dedications of the city to the Virgin see Toti (1870), and for Toti himself and his support for the new kingdom of Italy see Nardi (2005, esp. pp. 347–8, 352, 358).

10 Grassi (1972, pp. 14–15).

11 Grassi (1972, p. 15).

12 *Dizionario biografico degli italiani*, 16, pp. 730–32.

detailed references to her letters. In so doing he made use of the first modern attempt at a critical edition and commentary on the letters, published in four volumes in 1860 by the Italian patriot, nationalist and republican Niccolò Tommaseo, who had himself prefaced his edition of Catherine's letters with a study of her life, thought and works, including her political as well as her religious aims and activities.[13] Towards the middle of his lecture, Calisse addressed the theme of Catherine's advocacy of – and her strategy for – peace both within Italy and among the Christian rulers and nations of Europe. At the end of a section of his lecture on her call for charity in the hearts of the powerful, and thereby the possibility of an end to injustice and war, Calisse observed that it was not war in itself that Catherine hated, but war born of worldly aims and interests, and which therefore oppressed the weak and innocent and divided Christians as enemies. Referring to a phrase from her letters that was to be quoted repeatedly in the next century by advocates of Catherine as either an Italian or European patron saint, Calisse noted that, in the face of conflict between Christians, Catherine urged, memorably, *'Pace, pace, pace'*. As part of her strategy to overcome such conflict between Christians, however, Catherine in fact advocated another kind of war, namely a crusade against the Turks – '*gli infedeli in oriente*' – which would unite Christian Europe in a common cause, and thus also bring peace to Europe itself. This strategy, Calisse argued, constituted an example of Catherine's political wisdom, united with her fervent love of both her country and the church. By the single means of carrying the war to the Levant, Catherine proposed to defend Europe against the threat of Turkish expansion, to bring peace to Italy, to provide a means of calming the schism between eastern and western Christianity, to renew the Christian faith in the lands of its birth and to aid the reform of the state of the Roman church.[14]

In 1904 the relic of Catherine's head was again chosen, for the first time since 1859, as the focus for the Sienese celebration of the festival of Domenica in Albis – although the crucifix of the stigmata had been so honoured in 1889, and the statue of Catherine by Nerrocio di Bartolomeo de' Landi, from the Oratory of the *Contrada dell'Oca*, in 1897.[15] In 1904, the festival was still in progress – and Catherine's head therefore still on display for public veneration on the high altar of the cathedral – when King Victor Emanuel III visited Siena on 17 April to open the epoch-making *Mostra dell'Antica Arte Senese* that was held that year in the Palazzo Pubblico. The cathedral was, moreover, included in the crowded itinerary for the king's time in Siena – thus once again associating the celebration of Catherine's cult not only with Sienese civic devotion, but also with the interaction between such civic devotion and the royal dynasty of the Italian state.[16]

---

13 Tommaseo (1860). The biographical introduction to the edition was re-published twice in the following century as a separate volume, for which see Tommaseo (1922, 1979). For Tommaseo himself, see Zaggia (2006, pp. 162–3).

14 Calisse (1895, pp. 18–22). For the phrase '*Pace, pace, pace*' see Catherine's letter to Pietro d'Estaing, Cardinal of Ostia, for the text of which see Meattini (2005, pp. 128–31).

15 Gianni (2002, pp. 353–4).

16 Grassi (1972, p. 25). For the significance of the Mostra dell'Antica Arte Senese see Parsons (2004a, p. 64–5); Cantelli, Pacchierotti and Pulcinelli (2005).

Interest in Catherine and her cult was also sustained, in the first two decades of the twentieth century, by a number of significant publications. In 1909 Domenico Toncelli published his study *La Casa di Santa Caterina a Siena* which not only examined the history of the Sanctuary dedicated to her in Siena but also presented a history of her cult, supported by references to Sienese archival sources, thus supplementing the work previously begun by Alessandro Toti in 1880.[17] In 1909 Catherine was also made the official patron of the women's section of the Italian Catholic social movement *Azione Cattolica*, an initiative of Pope Pius X which – following his predecessor's proclamation of Catherine as a co-patron of Rome in 1866 – now signalled, for the first time, papal recognition of Catherine's possible role in a national Italian context. The Sienese publishing house of Giuntini-Bentivoglio also played an important role in raising the profile of Catherine and her cult. In 1913 alone their imprint included the Sienese writer, Federigo Tozzi's *Antologia d'antichi scrittori senesi dalle origini fino a Santa Caterina*, which culminated in a celebration of the works of Saint Catherine; a new and substantially expanded edition of Piero Misciattelli's *Mistici Senesi* (first published in 1911) in which Catherine received particularly full treatment; the first part of a new six-volume edition of Catherine's *Letters*, and a collection of Catherine's thoughts for a popular audience, both also edited by Misciattelli.[18] In the present context, it is Misciattelli's interest in Catherine – and especially his account of her life in the expanded version of his *Mistici Senesi* – that is of greatest significance. An historian of Sienese art and religion, from a distinguished Catholic family, Misciattelli was subsequently to play a prominent role in the promotion of Catherine's cult – and especially her potential significance as an advocate and embodiment of both 'Italian' and 'Roman' values – in the 1920s and 1930s. Even in 1913, however, the shape of such an interpretation of Catherine was already clearly evident. Thus, in the preface to his anthology of Catherine's thoughts, Misciattelli not only described her as the greatest of Italy's female saints, but also expressed the hope that contemporary Italians would listen to her voice 'returning' to them from the fourteenth century, take her message to heart, take comfort from her in times of difficulty and be inspired by her example to cultivate similarly 'heroic virtues' in their own lives.[19]

The treatment of Catherine in the expanded version of Misciattelli's *Mistici Senesi* was, however, even more revealing and significant. In the 1911 version, Misciattelli had given Catherine a single chapter – as he had to each of the other five Sienese saints and *beati* addressed in the book. Indeed, in the original version Catherine had actually received less extensive treatment than the other figures, the chapter devoted to her being substantially shorter than the rest.[20] In the 1913 edition, however, the space devoted to Catherine was greatly expanded, to the point

17 Toncelli (1909).

18 Tozzi (1913); Misciattelli (1913a, 1913b, 1913–21). Tozzi subsequently published a selection of extracts from Catherine's writings under the title *Le cose più belle*, for which see Tozzi (1918). For the role of the Giuntini-Bentivoglio publishing house and the impact of their initiative beyond Siena, see Zaggia (2006, p. 171).

19 Misciattelli (1913a, 'Prefazione', unpaginated).

20 Misciattelli (1911, pp. 130–47).

of being subdivided into what amounted to two sub-chapters – albeit presented as parts I and II of a single chapter. Part I was titled '*L'attività politica*' and Part II, '*L'attività mistica*'.[21] In contrast to the earlier version, Catherine was now treated in greater detail than any other saint. It was not only the amount of space devoted to Catherine in the new version, however, that was significant: the content of the new material was also revealing. By far the greater part of the additional material was to be found in the section now entitled '*L'attività politica*'. Two passages in particular provided a foretaste of a style of interpretation of Catherine that was to become common in subsequent decades. In the first, Misciattelli located Catherine within the context of fourteenth-century Italy, a land, as he characterized it, beset by fratricidal conflict and at the mercy of mercenary bands, and in which the image of the Roman Catholic church, ['*la gran madre Roma*'], was darkened by the disgrace and cowardice of a prince, [the Pope], who was in exile in Avignon. In this context, Misciattelli argued, Dante and Catherine – one Florentine, the other Sienese, one of aristocratic background, the other of humble origin – were both models of 'a race created for victories', and representatives of the Tuscan people in an era when they could be regarded as the legitimate heirs of all the traditional Roman virtues. In the political thought and action of Catherine, moreover, he continued, it was clear that she continually sought to restore the dignity and power of the nation through Rome.[22] In the second passage, Misciattelli presented his analysis of Catherine's political action in relation to the papacy and Italy. Catherine, he affirmed, was indeed Sienese, but was also, and above all, Italian, and specifically appealed to fellow countrymen and women as '*italiani*'. She therefore sought to bring peace to Italy and to inspire a sense of unity which would liberate Italy from foreign domination, but at the same time understood that to achieve these aims it was also necessary to secure peace in Europe by reviving a religious unity among the divided nations of Catholic Europe. And this she sought to achieve by calling for Christian alliance in the form of a crusade to free the Christian holy places from occupation by the 'infidel' and at the same time establish a barrier to any future 'infidel' invasion of Europe. Thus she sought an Italian unity through a federation under the leadership of the papacy – as the heir of the Latin empire – and an alliance of European Christians against the common enemy of the Catholic world, namely the Turks. In seeking to achieve these ends, moreover, Catherine combined both her religious and her political aims and agendas, seeking internal reform of the church and the return of the papacy to Rome, and then the leadership of the papacy in a crusade against the Turks.[23]

In interpreting Catherine's political thought and actions in this way, Misciattelli not only placed himself in continuity with the portrayal of Catherine set out by Carlo Calisse in 1895 but also implicitly drew attention to the contemporary relevance and resonance of Catherine's political ideas at the beginning of the second decade of the twentieth century. It can, after all, hardly have escaped the attention of Misciattelli's original readers that, between the publication of the first edition of *Mistici Senesi* in 1911 and the second edition in 1913 – with its much expanded discussion of

21 Misciattelli (1913b, pp. 132–61 and 162–81).

22 Misciattelli (1913b, pp. 135–6).

23 Misciattelli (1913b, pp. 146–9).

Catherine's political activity, including her call for a Christian coalition against the Turks – Italy had been engaged in a war with Turkey both in Libya and the Dodecanese islands. The Bishop of Cremona, Geremia Bonomelli, had even described the attack on Libya as a 'crusade' in which the Italian flag and the Christian cross together triumphed over Islam.[24]

The Italian entry into the First World War in May 1915 prompted a more explicit connection between Catherine, the interests of the Italian nation and the Italian armed forces. At the end of June 1915, a month after the Italian entry into the war, three days of prayer to Saint Catherine were held in Santa Caterina in Fontebranda – the Oratory of the *Contrada dell'Oca* – to ask for peace and the victory of the Italian armies.[25] In September a further '*triduo*' of prayer to Catherine was held in the Chiesa del SS. Crocifisso, at the instigation of Don Leopolodo Tuci, the priest responsible for the Sanctuary of Saint Catherine (Plate 6). The local Catholic paper reported that the response of the Sienese could not have been more favourable and that a 'river' of people attended the highly Christian and patriotic addresses.[26] In September 1917 a further day of prayer was held, again in the Chiesa del SS. Crocifisso – and in front of the crucifix itself. Held this time in response to Pope Benedict XV's call to the belligerents to end the war, the theme of the day of intercession was the request for a swift peace with justice.[27] In 1918, however, the specific association between Catherine, Italy in time of war and conflict with Turkey was once again in evidence. That year the committee responsible for the festival of Domenica in Albis in Siena again chose the highly revered fifteenth-century statue of Catherine owned by the *Contrada dell'Oca* as the sacred image to be honoured.

In February 1918 Archbishop Prospero Scaccia wrote, on behalf of the committee, to the *Contrada dell'Oca* explaining the choice of this image for the festival. He began by noting that the choice could hardly be more appropriate, since only a brief time had elapsed since the 'liberation of the Holy Places' – a reference to the fact that allied forces had entered Jerusalem in December 1917 as part of their campaign against Turkish forces in Palestine and Mesopotamia – a cause for which, he observed, Catherine had also worked in her own lifetime. In addition, Scaccia continued, it was also appropriate that, in the same days in which this great and historic event had occurred, Catherine should intercede with God on behalf of thousands of Italians now exiled from their homes (in north-eastern Italy, after the disastrous Italian defeat at Caporetto the previous October) and for Italy itself, that the nation might obtain a true peace, that was just, enduring and victorious.[28] The

---

24 The Italian government had declared war on Turkey – after a dispute over Italian interests in Libya – in September 1911. Italy invaded the two Turkish provinces of Tripolitania and Cyrenaica and, in November 1911, declared Libya annexed to the Italian crown. The following year Italy also bombarded the Dardenelles and occupied the Dodecanese islands. By the Treaty of Lausanne in October 1912 Turkey withdrew its forces from Libya. For Bishop Bonomelli's remarks, see Bosworth (2005, p. 48).

25 *Il Popolo di Siena*, 19/6/1915, p. 3.

26 *Il Popolo di Siena*, 18/9/1915, p. 3.

27 *Il Popolo di Siena*, 1/9/1917, p. 3

28 The letter may be found in the Archivio della Nobile Contrada dell'Oca, Siena, inventory number XIII B. 9 168, 'Comitato per il 2nd Ottavario della Domenica in Albis in

public notices for the festival of Domenica in Albis adopted a similar tone. One, published in February 1918, announcing a novena of prayer in the Oratory of the *Contrada dell'Oca* in preparation for the festival, proclaimed that the statue had been chosen because the committee, believing itself to be reflecting the wishes of the Sienese, wished to invoke the protection of Catherine for Italy in a moment of such gravity both for the nation and for civilization. A second, published in March for the festival itself, asserted that, in a moment of great trepidation for Italy and the whole world, nothing could be more appropriate than to recall the message of Catherine, 'the great heroine of justice, charity and peace', and to pray to her for the beginning of the hoped-for reign of God, of justice, truth, liberty and love.[29] The local Catholic newspaper, meanwhile, reported that the festival of Domenica in Albis in 1918 had been celebrated with greater solemnity than for many years, with numerous people visiting the cathedral, especially in the evenings, to honour Catherine and seek her intercession on behalf of the nation in which she had herself been an apostle of justice, truth and peace.[30]

The distinctly patriotic tone of the references to Catherine during the festival of Domenica in Albis in 1918 gave a foretaste of a phenomenon that was to become increasingly common during the next two decades as Catherine was systematically promoted as a '*santa nazionale*' and a potential official '*Patrona d'Italia*'. In the immediate aftermath of the First World War, however, progress towards the promotion of Catherine and her cult was initially slow, not least, as one source put it, because of the 'difficulties of the time' – a reference, clearly, to the severe social, economic and political crises that Italy experienced in the post-war period, and especially between 1919 and 1922.[31] Such difficulties notwithstanding, however, in December 1920 the increasing interest in Catherine of Siena and her cult was given institutional form by the foundation of the *Società Internazionale di Studi Cateriniani*, under the guidance of a provisional organizing committee. Significantly, when, in 1941, one of the founding members wrote a brief summary of the history of the *Società*,

---

onore della imagine di S. Caterina della Contrada dell'Oca l'anno 1918'. Scaccia's reference to the 'holy places', although couched in terms that were specifically relevant to Catherine, reflected a broader strand in Catholic and Italian reaction to the allied capture of Jerusalem. Thus, in 1918, Italian propaganda directed at Austro-Hungarian troops contrasted the allied 'liberation of the holy tomb from its centuries old desecration' with the fact that Germany and Austria–Hungary were allied with Turkey, for which see Cornwall (2000, pp. 151–2, 215). In December 1917 the diocesan authorities in Siena had published a notice enthusiastically celebrating the capture of Jerusalem and organized a Te Deum of thanks in the cathedral, for which see *Il Popolo di Siena*, 22/12/1917, p. 4.

29 Copies of both public notices may, again, be found in the Archivio della Nobile Contrada dell'Oca, Siena, inventory number XIII B. 9 168, 'Comitato per il 2nd Ottavario della Domenica in Albis in onore della imagine di S. Caterina della Contrada dell'Oca l'anno 1918'.

30 *Il Popolo di Siena*, 13/4/1918, p. 3.

31 The source in question was the 'Programma' and 'Notizie' published in 1923 to introduce the first edition of *Studi Cateriniani*, the *Bullettino della Società Internazionale di Studi Cateriniani*. These texts appear as a preface to the first edition. The reference to the grave difficulties of the time is on page 7.

he began by referring to the lecture on Catherine given by Carlo Calisse in 1895 as the earliest origin of the idea for such a society.[32] The first formal event under the auspices of the new society – and also the official inauguration of the society itself – was a public lecture, in January 1922, in the Sala del Mappamondo of the Palazzo Pubblico, given by Count Giuseppe dalla Torre, the director of the Vatican newspaper, *L'Osservatore Romano*.[33] A year later, the *Società* began publication of its periodical, *Studi Cateriniani*, devoted to the study of Catherine's life and teaching and to the promotion of her cult. Other branches of the society were founded elsewhere in Italy, including, most notably, in Rome, where the local branch met in the premises of the *Arciconfraternita di Santa Caterina da Siena in Roma*.[34]

The opening article in the first edition of *Studi Cateriniani* in September 1923 was by Piero Misciattelli,[35] who had also, in 1922, edited a re-publication of Niccolò Tommaseo's introduction to his 1860 edition of Catherine's *Letters*. In the preface of the re-publication, Misciattelli not only celebrated Tommaseo as an Italian patriot and as one of the best interpreters of Catherine's thought, but also asserted that, after the great victory in the recent war, contemporary Italy was now intoxicated with sterile and useless political passions, and divided and afflicted by factional hatred. The sectarian spirit that now dominated Italy, he argued, unfortunately took the nation back to the tragic conditions of the time in which Catherine had lived. Italians therefore needed to return to the example of Catherine herself in order to learn how to heal their wounds and recover true freedom and social peace within the nation.[36] Misciattelli's preface was dated August 1922. Two months later, the Fascist March on Rome brought Mussolini to power and initiated a regime which would last for another 21 years. Misciattelli himself rapidly indicated his own strong support for Fascism, thus confirming the political stance that was already implicit in his preface to Tommaseo's work. Thus, in 1924, under the imprint of the 'Casa Editrice Imperia' – a publishing house run by the Fascist Party – he published a short book entitled *Fascisti e Cattolici*. The volume – which appeared in the series of *Quaderni Imperia*, directed by the future Fascist foreign minister Dino Grandi – presented a passionately argued case both for Fascism and for the need for Catholics to support Mussolini and his party.[37] Fascism, Misciattelli asserted, in a chapter also entitled 'Fascists and Catholics', would confront and combat all the modern ideologies that threatened to cause the disintegration of the nation's spiritual – and therefore Catholic – unity. It would resist the attempts of northern European and Anglo-Saxon nations to undermine Italy's Catholic culture and heritage. To this end, it was essential to retain a sense of discipline and of respect for both religious and civil authorities.[38] Similarly, in a chapter devoted to 'The Latin Tradition', Misciattelli insisted that

32 Nencini (1941, p. 45). See also Matteucci-Serpieri (1940, pp. 15–18).

33 Nencini (1941, p. 46).

34 See the 'Programma' and 'Notizie' referred to in note 29, pp. 7–8 for the origins of branches of the *Società* in Rome, Pisa, Florence and Bergamo.

35 Misciattelli (1923).

36 Misciattelli (1922, pp. vii, x).

37 Misciattelli (1924).

38 Misciatelli (1924, pp. 89–92, esp. pp. 90, 92).

there was now a fundamental choice between a Fascism which he characterized as 'Italian and Catholic' and a Bolshevism which he described as 'Asiatic'. In the coming confrontation between the forces of order and disorder, between the principles of Fascism and a resurgent Rome on the one hand and the barbarism of Bolshevism on the other, it would be – Misciattelli insisted – the imperial eagle of the former that won.[39] The book concluded with the appeal, published by socially prominent Catholics in Rome, for Italian Catholics to give their unreserved support to the Fascist government.[40]

Such texts as Misciattelli's book notwithstanding, as numerous studies over several decades have consistently demonstrated, the relationship between Italian Fascism and Roman Catholicism was, in fact, never simple, always ambiguous, and frequently subject to profound tensions.[41] On the one hand, Italian Fascism always included a strongly anti-Catholic element and there was ongoing tension between Fascist and Catholic organizations, especially in relation to youth movements. Mussolini consistently tried to bring the church under Fascist influence, whilst Fascism presented itself as an alternative 'religion' with its own rites, rituals, festivals, sacred symbols, myths and beliefs.[42] On the other hand, Mussolini – ever the pragmatist and opportunist in his pursuit of political advantage – presented the appearance of a positive relationship with the Catholic church whenever this might prove beneficial to his regime. In particular, the Catholic church in Italy offered Mussolini and Fascism a potential point of access to a mass audience and constituency. By calculatedly cultivating a rapport with the church – even if only amidst continuing ambiguity – Mussolini played skilfully to the 'cultural Catholicism' of Italian society. Conversely, by avoiding prolonged confrontation of an overt kind between Fascism and Catholicism, Mussolini avoided the threat of alienating the majority of Italian Catholics. The 1920s thus witnessed various gestures of goodwill towards the Church – as well as outbursts of anti-Catholic rhetoric and violence and sharp conflicts over Catholic youth movements – whilst, for Catholicism, Fascism appeared to offer an alternative to the threat posed by socialism and communism. Behind the scenes, meanwhile, from as early as 1926 both Mussolini and Pope Pius XI had begun to explore the possibility of finding a way to formally end the dispute between church and state that had endured since 1870.

It was against this background, therefore, that the promotion of the cult of Catherine of Siena – and the movement to secure her recognition as a '*santa nazionale*' and '*Patrona d'Italia*' – developed from the mid 1920s onwards. It is not difficult, moreover, to find evidence of the Fascist context within the history of the various projects that were initiated by Catherine's followers during these years.

---

39 Misciatelli (1924, pp. 109–17, esp. pp. 115, 117).

40 Misciatelli (1924, pp. 139–41).

41 See for example Binchy (1977, but originally published in 1941); Jemolo (1960, pp. 166–277); Webster (1960, pp. 57–161); O'Brien (1971); Pollard (1985); Koon (1985, pp. 116–42); Malgeri (1994, pp. 53–63); Gentile (1996, pp. 53–6, 62–4, 69–75; 2001, pp. 134–54); Bosworth (2005, pp. 231–2, 257–68); Zagheni (2006); Parsons (2008a, pp. 77–80).

42 Koon (1985, pp. 11, 26–8, 71); Gentile (1990; 1996; 2006); Bosworth (2005, pp. 3, 11, 78, 138–43, 196–202); Parsons (2007, pp. 471–2).

In 1926, for example, Rome was the location for the foundation of another society dedicated to the promotion of Catherine of Siena and her cult. The *Corporazione dei Caterinati* was founded in June 1926 in the church dedicated to the saint at Magnanapoli, near to the Quirinale. The second article of its statutes specifically committed the new society to making Italians more aware of Catherine in order to secure her recognition as a '*santa nazionale*'. The *Corporazione* attracted the support of influential members of Rome's civil and ecclesiastical elites – including ministers of the Fascist government such as Pietro Fedele and Emilio Bodrero.[43] Like the Sienese *Società Internazionale di Studi Cateriniani*, the *Corporazione* also founded branches in other Italian cities. It continued to meet in the church of Santa Caterina da Siena a Magnanapoli until 1932, by which time the church had become the seat of the *Ordinariato Militare*, the organization responsible for providing chaplains to the various branches of the Italian armed forces. Subsequently the *Corporazione* held its meetings in the church of Santa Maria sopra Minerva.[44]

Two further projects to celebrate and promote Catherine and her cult were also initiated in 1926. In both cases, moreover, the impact of the political context of the now firmly established Fascist regime was evident. In January, the *Corso Universitario di Studi Cateriniani* was inaugurated at the University of Siena, establishing annual lectures on Catherine of Siena that rapidly became known as the *Cattedra Cateriniana*.[45] Then, in May, the Governatore of the *Arciconfraternita di Santa Caterina da Siena in Roma*, Arturo Bruchi, wrote to the Governor of Rome, proposing to honour the figure of Catherine of Siena in Rome by placing a bust of the saint in the Pincio Gardens, among those of other famous Italians commemorated there. Bruchi also indicated that the Sienese wished to donate the bust to Rome, thereby commemorating both the relationship between the two cities where, respectively, Catherine was born and had died, and also her status as an official patron saint of Rome – an initiative that had also received the support of the Archbishop of Siena, Prospero Scaccia.[46] The proposal was accepted and a bust of Catherine, by the Sienese sculptor Arturo Viligiardi – who was also a founder member of the *Società Internazionale di Studi Cateriniani* – was duly inaugurated in the Pincio Gardens

43 Fedele was minister of education from 1925 to 1928, subsequently becoming a member of the senate and minister of state. Bodrero was undersecretary for education from 1926 to 1929 and subsequently vice-president of the Chamber of Deputies and appointed to the senate in 1934. For both of which see Cannistraro (1982).

44 Bianchi (1990, pp. 64–7); Carrara (1929). The church and convent of Santa Caterina da Siena a Magnanapoli had previously been the location of the female religious community in Rome dedicated to Catherine.

45 Nencini (1941, pp. 46–7).

46 Rossi (1928). The text of Bruchi's letter is reproduced in this article. Letters between Bruchi, Archbishop Scaccia and the Mayor of Siena, Vittorio Martini, show that Bruchi skilfully initiated the idea that the Sienese would donate the bust, writing first to Scaccia in February 1926, and then to Martini, on Scaccia's advice. Martini and Scaccia then exchanged letters confirming their mutual support for the proposal. The letters are preserved in the Archivio Arcivescovile di Siena, in a file entitled 'Arciconfraternita di S. Caterina da Siena in Roma', inventory number 3962.

in April 1928 during the celebration of Catherine's annual festival (Plate 11).[47] The broader ideological context of both these initiatives was clear. At the inauguration of the *Cattedra Cateriniana*, in the letter proposing the addition of a bust of Catherine to the Pincio Gardens, and at the inauguration of the bust in 1928, the celebration of Catherine was explicitly placed within the context of the rhetoric of national renewal associated with the Fascist regime and its promotion of a cult of both '*romanità*' and '*italianità*'.

The speeches and the lecture to mark the inauguration of the *Cattedra Cateriniana* in January 1926 set the pattern. On behalf of the government, the minister for public instruction, Pietro Fedele, asserted that the *Cattedra Cateriniana* would not only be a centre of scholarly research into the works of Saint Catherine, but also a spiritual flame that would inspire new generations with the same faith in '*romanità*' and '*italianità*' that had also been, he claimed, a central feature of Catherine's own thought. The rector of Siena University, Achille Sclavo, and the Mayor of Siena, Vittorio Martini, then both concluded their speeches with extravagant compliments to Benito Mussolini, including the claims that in Mussolini more than one of Catherine's own virtues had been revived, and that Catherine's vision of a restoration of Italy's and Rome's greatness in her day was now echoed in Mussolini's contemporary vision of a renewed Italy. Both speakers also emphasized the intensity of Catherine's sense of being Italian and her status as the 'most Italian of the Italian saints'.[48] The first lecture given under the auspices of the new *Cattedra Cateriniana*, was then delivered – very appropriately, given his numerous publications on Catherine in the previous two decades – by Piero Misciattelli. He took as his subject '*La romanità di Santa Caterina da Siena*', and argued that Catherine displayed her '*romanità*' above all in her efforts to secure the peace and unity of Italy – a project that he described as embodying a modern sense of nationalism, precisely because it extended to all of Italy, not merely to the Papal States.[49]

In his letter proposing the bust of Catherine for the Pincio Gardens, Arturo Bruchi recalled both Misciattelli's and Fedele's remarks at the inauguration of the *Cattedra Cateriniana* and concluded by reaffirming Fedele's insistence that Catherine's spirit would become the inspiration of new generations, placing this process firmly within the context of the contemporary – Fascist-inspired – revival of national sentiment, in which Rome and Italy, he said, 'vibrated' with new life and greatness.[50] Subsequently, on 29 April 1928, the official unveiling of the bust was accompanied by a ceremony which, once again, emphasized the themes of Catherine's devotion to Italy and Rome and related this devotion to the contemporary example of Mussolini and Fascism. Presenting the bust on behalf of Siena, the Podestà, Fabio Bargagli Petrucci, claimed

47 At the end of March 1928, before being taken to Rome, the bust was displayed to the public in Siena, near to the entrance to San Domenico, for which see Luchini (1994, p. 293).

48 Rossi (1928, p. 18); see also 'Inaugurazione della Cattedra Cateriniana', *Studi Cateriniani*, 3, 1926, pp. 1–14; 'Discorso dell Comm. Prof. V. Martini, Sindaco di Siena', *Studi Cateriniani*, 3,1926, pp. 119–21; and 'La Cattedra di Studi Cateriniani', *La Diana*, 1, 1926, p. 70; all of which are unsigned articles.

49 Misciattelli (1926a). A longer version of the lecture was also published, for which see Misciattelli (1926b).

50 Rossi (1928, pp. 18–19).

that the ceremony stood in continuity with the long association between Siena and Rome – a continuity that was symbolized, he claimed, not least by Catherine's sense, over five centuries earlier, that it was only in Rome that the papacy could properly be located, because Rome should be eternally the ruler of the world. Therefore, he affirmed, the Sienese now asked God that Saint Catherine would extend her protection over Rome, over Italy, and the world, in a springtime of spiritual re-birth which shone with the actions of Italy's eminent 'Condottiero', Benito Mussolini.[51] Emilio Bodrero, speaking as undersecretary for education, then spoke of Catherine's civic virtues and also recalled her role in securing the return of the papacy to Rome.[52] The ceremony at the Pincio in the afternoon had been preceded, in the morning, by a mass in Santa Maria sopra Minerva attended by the girls of the Roman branches of the *Piccole e Giovani Italiane* – the two Fascist organizations for girls. In their black and white uniforms, accompanied by their leaders, and with their flags, after the mass they had filed past Catherine's tomb beneath the high altar leaving flowers to honour '*la grande Santa e la grande italiana*'.[53]

The Fascist context and rhetoric of the inauguration of the bust of Saint Catherine in the Pincio were subsequently reiterated in an article first published in the 3 May edition of the Florentine Catholic newspaper, *L'Unità Cattolica*, and then re-published in both the Sienese Catholic paper, *Il Popolo di Siena* and the Dominican journal *Memorie Domenicane*. Written by the director of *L'Unita Cattolica* – who was a Dominican tertiary – and entitled '*Per la Nostra Santa*', it opened by reporting the inauguration of the bust the previous Sunday. Fascist intellectuals, it asserted, had indicated their admiration for the Saint – as the ceremony in the Pincio demonstrated – not least because of her role in persuading Pope Gregory XI to return to Rome, thus helping to restore Rome's spiritual and material life. The authentic glory of Saint Catherine, it continued, consisted in the triumph of the Church, the liberation of the papacy, the rebirth of Catholic Rome and the affirmation of the honour of Italy in being home to the Vicar of Christ. Historians and writers had therefore honoured Catherine and likened her patriotism to that of Joan of Arc, the 'liberator' of France. In the context of the fourteenth century, the article continued, Catherine had been the voice of peace, the angel of the unity of the church, and the apostle of both Roman-ness and of the re-establishment of the papacy in Italy, thus recalling and reaffirming the destiny that linked Catholicism to both Rome and Italy. And for this reason Catherine is still remembered and celebrated, the article concluded, whereas the kings of France and England and the cardinals in Avignon are now forgotten.[54]

---

51 *Il Popolo di Siena*, 5/5/1928, p. 3; Vegni (1928); 'Resoconto delle feste per l'inaugurazione del busto di S. Caterina al Pincio', *Studi Cateriniani*, 6, 1929, pp. 35–6; 'Un monumento a S. Caterina da Siena in Roma', *S. Caterina da Siena, Bollettino Mensile della Chiesa di San Domenico*, 7, 1928, pp. 186–7; both of the latter being unsigned.

52 *Memorie Domenicane*, 45, 1928, p. 221–2.

53 'L'omaggio delle Piccole Italiane a Santa Caterina', *S. Caterina da Siena, Bollettino Mensile della Chiesa di San Domenico*, 7, 1928, p. 184; *Memorie Domenicane*, 45, 1928, pp. 220–21. The *Piccole Italiane* were girls aged between eight and 13. Subsequently they graduated to the *Giovani Italiane* for girls from 14 to 18.

54 *Il Popolo di Siena*, 5/5/1928, p. 2; *Memorie Domenicane*, 45, 1928, pp. 222–4.

Such speeches, articles and ceremonies foreshadowed both the style and the content of the rhetoric that later became a standard feature of the campaign for Catherine to be officially proclaimed patron saint of Italy. At one level, this is unsurprising, because – as both Stefano Cavazza and Diana Medina Lasansky have pointed out – the promotion of the cult of Saint Catherine during the 1920s and 1930s was an initiative of which Fascists could easily approve. By virtue of her attempts to restore the papacy to Rome, Catherine could indeed be interpreted as a forerunner of the idea of Italian unity and of the moral renewal of the nation, whilst her sense of discipline and self-sacrifice and her recognition of the importance of hierarchy and unity within the church were highly compatible with Fascist values and ideology. Moreover, along with a 'patriotic' reading of her life, Catherine could also be presented as embodying attributes deemed appropriate to the ideal of the Fascist woman, whilst an emphasis upon her humble origins and the fact that, even after achieving fame, she remained approachable suggested parallels with the image which Mussolini liked to promote of himself.[55] At another level, however, the extent to which devotees of Catherine were willing to associate her explicitly, and even enthusiastically, with Fascist achievements remains, nevertheless, striking. As Paul Corner has recently observed in a critical analysis of the concept of 'consensus' in Fascist Italy, after its seizure of power the Fascist regime created a situation in which, for most Italians, a genuine choice of being Fascist or anti-Fascist just did not exist: 'there was simply no feasible alternative to toeing the line if you wished to continue to lead a normal life'.[56] Corner's observation is certainly sufficient to account for the absence of dissent from the regime and its values in celebrations of Catherine and her national significance in the 1920s and 1930s. It does not, however, account for the positive enthusiasm and alacrity with which her followers often associated Catherine and her legacy with Mussolini and his regime.

Part – although certainly not all – of the explanation for that enthusiasm may also lie in the particular circumstances and ethos of the Catholic church in Siena during the 1920s and 1930s. As recent historians of the Sienese church during the Fascist period have pointed out, by the late 1920s a clear affinity had already developed between the church in Siena and the local Fascist authorities. During the 1920s Prospero Scaccia – who was Archbishop of Siena from 1909 to 1932 – had quickly developed a sympathetic rapport with the local Fascist authorities. Thus, in 1928 the celebrations for the 25th anniversary of Scaccia's elevation to the episcopacy included a civic reception for Scaccia in the Palazzo Pubblico during which speeches – both by Scaccia himself and by the Podestà of Siena, Fabio Bargagli Petrucci – emphasized Scaccia's patriotism and support for the new and stable Italy that

55 Cavazza, (1997, pp. 189–90); Lasansky, (2007, pp. 123–4). The aptness of Lasansky's evocation of ways in which Catherine could be portrayed as a model for Fascist women and a symbol of Fascist virtues notwithstanding, considerable care should be exercised with regard to other aspects of her interpretation of Catherine during the 1920s and 1930s. Thus, for example, she suggests that the Sienese campaign for Catherine to be proclaimed *Patrona d'Italia* only began in 1932 and that the bust of Catherine (Plate 11) was placed in the Pincio gardens only in 1939 after her proclamation as co-patron saint of Italy.

56 Corner (2002, p. 349).

had emerged from the violent years following the First World War.[57] Nor was such reference to the violence of the post-war period of merely rhetorical significance. Siena had been described in contemporary police reports as 'the reddest province in Tuscany', whilst Tuscan Fascism has in turn been characterized as 'second to none in its violence', particularly during 1921 and 1922.[58] Moreover, of the ten local Fascists who were subsequently commemorated in Siena as 'martyrs' of this period of violence, two – a layman, Nazzareno Ciarrochi, and a local priest, Padre Angelico Galassi – had been killed at Abbadia San Salvatore in August 1920 as a result of left-wing attacks on religious observances during the annual celebration of the Feast of the Assumption. Galassi in particular was subsequently described by the local Fascist newspaper as 'a martyr for the church and the nation'.[59] In marked contrast to such left-wing violence against the church, however, in Siena in the 1920s the civic authorities were quick to add local expressions of a new rapport with the church to the general efforts of Italian Fascism to court Catholic opinion and support. Thus, in 1924 the church and civic authorities cooperated to restore the annual *Corteo dei Ceri* – a traditional Sienese religious procession at the Feast of the Assumption – and in 1928 they similarly cooperated to restore the annual celebration of mass in honour of the Virgin on 22 September in the chapel in the Palazzo Pubblico. Both ceremonies had been in a state of suspension since the 1860s as a result of the tensions between the local church and the civic authorities in the decades following Italian Unification.[60]

Indeed, so marked did the rapport between the local civic and religious authorities become during the 1920s and 1930s, firstly under Scaccia and then, even more emphatically, under Archbishop Mario Toccabelli – who became Archbishop of Siena in 1935 – that one recent historian of the Sienese church, Achille Mirizio, has argued that Sienese Catholicism combined with Fascism in a way that was self-conscious, radical and profound, to the extent that the city, province and diocese of Siena appeared to be a textbook example of such interaction. After the difficulties and conflicts of the decades following Italian Unification, Mirizio argues, the advent of the Fascist regime appeared to the leaders of the Sienese church to offer an excellent opportunity to re-model the relationship between church and state in a much more positive way – especially given the theological and pastoral outlook of both Scaccia and Toccabelli which he characterizes as a kind of nostalgia for a 'medieval' social vision in which respect for religion guaranteed the status of the church and its role in society.[61]

The use of pro-Fascist rhetoric in the particular context of the promotion of Catherine as a national saint was nowhere more evident – and not only among the Sienese – than in reactions to the *conciliazione* between church and state embodied in the Concordat and Lateran Treaties of February 1929. Even before the announcement

---

57 Bocchini Camaiani (1994, p. 77); Mirizio (2002, pp. 474–6; 2003, pp. 48–50).

58 Snowden (1989, pp. 1, 55–6).

59 *La Rivoluzione Fascista*, 27/11/1938, p. 2. See also *La Nazione*, 27/11/1938, p. 4; For the commemoration of these 'martyrs' in Siena see Parsons (2007).

60 Parsons (2004a, pp. 83–4, 101–2 n. 12).

61 Mirizio (2002, pp. 470–71).

of the *conciliazione*, however, the theme of Catherine of Siena as a national saint had already begun to assume a new prominence. In a process which it is reasonable to interpret as a deliberate and calculated prelude to the *conciliazione*, a series of articles and lectures on Catherine were published in December 1928. On 9 December an article entitled '*Caterina da Siena, Santa degli Italiani*' appeared in the *Corriere della Sera* and was subsequently reprinted in many other Italian papers – or, as the report of the article in the journal *Rassegna Cateriniana* put it, after first appearing in the *Corriere della Sera* the item had made a triumphal round of all the Italian papers.[62] Echoing an association that had already been established in the report of the inauguration of the bust of Catherine in the Pincio gardens published in *L'Unita Cattolica*, the article in the *Corriere della Sera* began by asking whether Italy should and would have a '*santa nazionale*' in the way that France already had Joan of Arc. The Fascist government, it continued, had already, a few years ago, recognized Francis of Assisi as the '*santo degli italiani*',[63] and now many of Catherine's most committed devotees proposed that Italy had need of both a female patron saint as well as a male one. The article then reported the foundation of the societies dedicated to Catherine and her cult in both Siena and Rome and noted that the *Corporazione* in Rome included in its membership members of the Fascist government such as

62 'Caterina da Siena, Santa degli Italiani', *Rassegna Cateriniana*, 8, 1929, p. 36. The publishing history of this periodical is complex. In 1922 the Dominican community at San Domenico in Siena began publication of a periodical entitled *S. Caterina da Siena, Bollettino Mensile della Chiesa di San Domenico*. In 1926, responsibility for publication of the periodical was transferred from San Domenico, Siena, to the Dominican community at Fiesole. In 1928 the title was changed to *Rassegna Cateriniana* and the periodical was described as an official publication of the 'movimento nazionale cateriniano'. In 1931, however, it reverted to its previous title and association with San Domenico, before adopting the title *S. Caterina da Siena, Bollettino Domenicano* in 1933, and finally, *S. Caterina da Siena, Patrona d'Italia* from 1940. It continued under this title until 1943 when it ceased publication during the crisis of the Second World War, resuming again in 1946. In 1948 it was replaced by a new periodical published from San Domenico, Siena, entitled *La Patrona d'Italia*.

63 In 1926, the Fascist government had participated with enthusiasm in the celebrations held at Assisi on 4 October to mark the seventh centenary of the death of Saint Francis. For example, in a message to Italians abroad to mark the occasion, Mussolini described Francis as 'the most saintly of [male] Italians and the most Italian of [male] saints'. The government was officially represented at Assisi by Pietro Fedele; the train carrying the Pope's representatives, led by Cardinal Raffaele Merry del Val, was greeted with military honours along the route and at Assisi; and at a reception held in the Palazzo del Comune and hosted by the Podestà of Assisi the representatives of church and state exchanged fulsome compliments. On the evening of the celebrations, Mussolini authorized the beginning of the negotiations that culminated in the *conciliazione*, dating the letter 'Rome, October 4th, 1926, Feast of Saint Francis of Assisi'; for all of which see Fortini (1937, pp. 259–66); Binchy (1977, pp. 140–41). Local publications and memorabilia produced in celebration of 1926 as an '*anno francescano*' also celebrated Francis as a forerunner of Mussolini and interpreted him in Fascist terms, for which see Franzinelli (2003a, pp. 28–9). In Assisi, local historians continue to emphasize the meeting between Pietro Fedele and Cardinal Merry del Val as the beginning of the process that culminated, in 1929, in the 'Conciliazione', Concordat and Lateran Treaties, for which see Ronci (2005).

Amedeo Giannini, Carlo Calisse, Corrado Ricci and Emilio Bodrero. After noting that a branch of the *Corporazione dei Caterinati* had now also been established in Milan, the article closed with the customary summary of Catherine's political role in the fourteenth century: her call to the Pope to return to Rome; her work for the unity of the church, and thus the pacification of Italy and Europe; and her 'great ideal' of a crusade against the Turks who threatened Constantinople.[64] On 29 December 1928 Emilio Bodrero then gave a lecture to the newly formed branch of the *Corporazione dei Caterinati* in Milan. Entitled '*Caterina da Siena, Santa Nazionale*', Bodrero affirmed that Catherine's political and moral ideas possessed a universal validity that transcended the contingencies and circumstances of her own time. He concluded by claiming that Catherine's authentically Italian character had never been more evident than in the present moment, when the governing regime wished to establish a new era of good government. The full text of the lecture was also printed in *Il Popolo d'Italia*, the newspaper run by Mussolini's brother, Arnoldo.[65]

With the announcement of the *conciliazione* on 11 February 1929, however, the expression of such sentiments reached new heights.[66] Thus, the first edition of *Studi Cateriniani* for 1929 opened with an article applauding the Concordat and Lateran Treaty. For all Sienese, it asserted, it was natural to see the parallel between the return of the papacy to Rome – which had been the great dream and aspiration of Catherine's life and work – and the reconciliation now brought about by the 'holy work' of Pope Pius XI and the 'genius' of Benito Mussolini who, like Catherine, desired 'the unity of the nation in the unity of faith'. Thus, the author affirmed, 'Italy was returned to God, and Rome to Italy' – thereby playing on Pius XI's comment that the Lateran Treaties and Concordat had 'given God back to Italy and Italy to God'.[67] This brief item was followed by an article celebrating Catherine as the 'herald of peace' whose efforts had restored the papacy to Italy in the fourteenth century, just as the relationship between Italy and the papacy had now been restored by the efforts of Mussolini – a parallel which the author, Bianca Flury-Nencini, professed herself surprised not to have found in other discussions of the *conciliazione*.[68] The article than proceeded, once again, to compare the achievements of Catherine of Siena and Benito Mussolini. Mussolini, it argued, had shown that he possessed a conscience characterized by Catherine's values, thus demonstrating an affinity linking the thought of the fourteenth century Dominican tertiary and the 'great man' of the twentieth century. In their desire for unity and peace between the church and Italy, the names of Catherine of Siena and Benito Mussolini were linked as heroes with

---

64 'Caterina da Siena, Santa degli Italiani', *Rassegna Cateriniana*, 8, 1929, pp. 36–9.

65 'Comunita da Milan: Conferenza di S.E. Emilio Bodrero', *Rassegna Cateriniana*, 8, 1929, pp. 52–4. The full version of the lecture appeared in the 30 December edition of *Il Popolo d'Italia*.

66 For the Lateran Treaties and Concordat, see Binchy (1941, pp. 167–253); Jemolo (1960, pp. 226–37); Webster (1960, pp. 109–11); Pollard (1985, pp. 15–74); Malgeri (1994, pp. 55–6); Margiotta Broglio (2000, pp. 1153–7); Riciotti (2004); Zagheni (2006, pp. 163–6).

67 'Il Patto Lateranense solennizzato nella Casa di S. Caterina da Siena', *Studi Cateriniani*, 6, 1929, pp. 1–3.

68 Flury-Nencini (1929, esp. pp. 6–7,). See also Vanni (1930).

the same mission of peace. Thus, a great contemporary Italian – Benito Mussolini – had now restored peace to an Italy torn by post-war disorder and had reconciled Italy and the church, just as Catherine had restored the Pope to Rome and peace to Italy in her day.[69]

Flury-Nencini also quoted from the predictably enthusiastic and extravagant response to the *conciliazione* issued by Archbishop Scaccia in the pages of the local Catholic paper, including his evocation of Pope Pius XI's description of Mussolini as a man sent by providence.[70] Scaccia's response in the pages of *Il Popolo di Siena* also described the coming of the *conciliazione* as 'the hour of God', announced a service of thanksgiving – which took place in the cathedral the next day – and concluded by describing Catherine as 'the herald sent by God for the glorification of both the church and the nation'.[71] The same page of the paper also carried photographs of Pius XI and Mussolini, as well as the texts of the notices published by the Podestà, Fabio Bargagli Petrucci, by the local head of the Fascist party, Giorgio Alberto Chiurco, and by the local representatives of *Azione Cattolica*. The notice issued by Bargagli Petrucci again referred to Catherine, linking her to Dante and all the other great Italians who had dreamed of peace between the authorities of church and state – or, as he put it, the '*concordia delle due supreme Gerarchia della Chiesa Romana e dello Stato Fascista*' – which had now come about, as a result of the efforts of the Pope, the king and the Duce.[72]

In similar manner, the February 1929 edition of *Rassegna Cateriniana* welcomed the *conciliazione* with an opening section that included photographs of Pius XI and King Victor Emanuel III and asserted that Catherine's intercession had contributed to the present reconciliation of church and state.[73] This was followed immediately by a brief article that presented the *conciliazione* as the fulfilment of Catherine's own hopes for Italy, centuries earlier: although her work to bring peace to Italy and end conflict between Italians by uniting in a crusade did not succeed in her lifetime, she had desired unity among Italians because they were the children of a single nation.[74] The April edition then included an article on the Lateran Accord and the thought of Catherine of Siena in which the anonymous author again compared the circumstances of Catherine's day – and especially her role as an ambassador and peacemaker – with the contemporary reconciliation of church and state. The author also reminded readers of Pius XI's statement that God had been restored to Italy and Italy to God, and concluded by simply asserting that the 'new Italy of the Concordat' had therefore proclaimed Catherine '*Santa Nazionale, Santa degli*

69 Flury-Nencini (1929, pp. 10–11, 14).

70 Flury-Nencini (1929, pp. 6–7). Both remarks by Pius XI – regarding Italy being restored to God and God to Italy, and describing Mussolini as a man sent by providence – may be found in Pollard (1985, pp. 49–50) and in Riciotti (2004, p. 26). For Archbishop Scaccia's response, see *Il Popolo di Siena*, 16/2/1929, p. 2.

71 *Il Popolo di Siena*, 16/2/1929, p. 2. He also entitled his pastoral letter, issued in February 1929, '*L'ora di Dio*', for which see also Bocchini Camaiani (1994, pp. 76–7); Mirizio (2003, pp. 52–3).

72 *Il Popolo di Siena*, 16/2/1929, p. 2. See also Mirizio (2003, p. 52).

73 'Conciliazione, 11 Febbraio 1929', *Rassegna Cateriniana*, 8, 1929, pp. 25–7.

74 Coiro (1929).

Italiani'.[75] The May–June 1929 number of the *Rassegna Cateriniana* continued this theme. An article by Giuseppe Fatini, first published in *La Sera*, again presented the case for Catherine to be recognized as the '*Santa degli Italiani*' – alongside Francis who, Fatini asserted, had already been recognized as the '*Santo degli Italiani*'. Catherine's attempt to 'regenerate' the Italian people and the Christianity of her day justified the popular desire for her to be proclaimed the representative female saint of the Italians, especially now that the new reconciliation between the papacy and Italy had restored the spiritual unity of the Italian people.[76] The same edition also carried a report of a lecture by a Dominican priest, Marco Righi, to the branch of the *Corporazione dei Caterinati* in Bergamo in which he expressed the hope that the appropriate authorities would officially proclaim Catherine the protectress of Italy, and that Italy, under the influence and government of Fascism and its Duce, would also become increasingly 'caterinian'.[77]

The first celebration of Catherine's annual festival after the announcement of the *conciliazione* was also marked by renewed and enthusiastic expressions of devotion to her cult on the part of the *Piccole e Giovani Italiane*. In Rome, at Santa Maria sopra Minerva, on the Sunday after Catherine's festival and at the initiative of the local *Fascio Femminile*, over 8,000 girls from every part of the city gathered for mass, during which they also presented a silver chalice – embellished with a Fascist emblem in gold and the inscription '*Le Piccole e Giovani Italiane a S. Caterina da Siena. 5 maggio 1929. A.VII.*' – in honour of Catherine. The presentation of the chalice, it was noted, was a revival – in a new form – of an older tradition whereby the civic authorities of Rome presented such a chalice in honour of Catherine as patron of Rome. This tradition had, however, remained unobserved since 1870 because of the conflict between the papacy and the new Italian state – a conflict now resolved by the *conciliazione*.[78] In similar fashion, as the *Rassegna Cateriniana* reported, at Massa in the morning of 30 April, the *Piccole Italiane* attended a mass in the church of San Giovanni in honour of the '*grande Santa italiana*', whose statue was left encircled by fresh flowers, whilst in the afternoon the *Giovani Italiane* in their turn attended a service in the same church.[79] In Siena, meanwhile, Catherine's annual festival was celebrated with renewed solemnity, and the local Catholic paper claimed that the whole of Italy took pride in Catherine as a '*Santa Nazionale*'.[80]

The cause of Catherine's proposed proclamation as '*Patrona d'Italia*' was given even greater prominence in early February 1930 – shortly before the first anniversary of the *conciliazione* – in a lecture, delivered on 3 February under the auspices of

75 'L'Accordo Lateranense nel pensiero di S. Caterina da Siena', *Rassegna Cateriniana*, 8, 1929, pp. 93–102.

76 Fatini (1929).

77 'P. Marco Righi O.P. ai Caterinati – Santa Caterina da Siena suprema bellezza Domenicana e Italiana', *Rassegna Cateriniana*, 8, 1929, pp. 145–9.

78 'La mistica offerta all'altare di S.Caterina da Siena nella Basilica di S.Maria sopra Minerva', *Studi Cateriniani*, 6, 1929, pp. 33–4; 'Omaggio delle Giovani e Piccole Italiane a S. Caterina', *Memorie Domenicane*, 46, 1929, pp. 148–50.

79 'Massa. Le Giovani e le Piccole Italiane per Santa Caterina da Siena', *Rassegna Cateriniana*, 8, 1929, pp. 161–2.

80 *Il Popolo di Siena*, 27/4/1929, p. 3.

the *Cattedra Cateriniana*, by Father Martin Gillet, the French Master General of the Dominican Order. Gillet spoke on '*Santa Caterina da Siena e Santa Giovanna d'Arco – Le Due Sante della Patria*'. Asserting that, despite their many differences, Catherine of Siena and Joan of Arc nevertheless displayed great similarities in their 'patriotic and religious mission', Gillet argued that what united the two saints was their common experience that love of country and love of the church were complimentary, not contradictory. Whilst in Catherine of Siena, Gillet argued, it was love of the church that inspired her love of country, in Joan of Arc it was love of country that led to love of the church. The histories of the two saints therefore demonstrated that there was no contradiction between Catholicism and patriotism. Indeed, according to Gillet, the two saints shared the aim of reconciliation between the church and their respective countries: in Catherine's case, in saving the church she also saved her country; in Joan's case, in saving her country she saved the church. Catherine had saved the church by securing the return of the Pope to Rome and thereby brought the possibility of peace and stability for Italy – although she subsequently suffered a form of martyrdom in seeing her briefly realized dream dashed by the schism following the election of Clement VII as rival to Urban VI. Joan, by contrast, sought to save her country, had suffered martyrdom in the process, but in so doing saved the church by preventing English domination of France and, therefore, in the long run of history, also prevented the potential triumph of Protestantism in Latin countries and the extension of this 'heresy' into the Mediterranean world. Joan of Arc had now been recognized as a national saint in France, but Catherine, although a co-patron of Rome, had not yet been proclaimed the '*Santa della Patria*' in Italy.[81]

Gillet's lecture was the catalyst for a determined campaign, during the 1930s, to secure Catherine's official recognition and proclamation as patron saint of Italy. Indeed, to this end, Gillet repeated his lecture several times for different branches of the *Corporazione dei Caterinati*: in Rome on 16 February and in Florence on 19 February; and in both Milan and Bergamo in May.[82] Similarly, Emilio Bodrero repeated his lecture on '*Caterina da Siena. Santa Nazionale*' – first given in December 1928 at Milan – in Bergamo in February 1930.[83] In both 1930 and 1931 the celebration of Catherine's annual festival in Siena was again marked by the participation of the *Piccole e Giovani Italiane*. On 30 April 1930 the local branches of the *Piccole e Giovani Italiane* marked the festival by attending a mass in San Domenico. As the local Catholic paper reported, the mass was celebrated by Father Luigi Sbaragli – a military chaplain during the First World War who was now the chaplain to the Sienese *Avanguardisti*, the Fascist youth movement for boys aged between 14 and 17 – and also included the blessing of the pennant of a newly formed group of the *Piccole Italiane* named after Elena Riccomani, a Sienese woman who

81 Gillet (1930, pp. 1–2, 8, 14–17, 19–20, 23). See also the report in the local Catholic newspaper, *Il Popolo di Siena*, 22//2/30, pp. 2–3.

82 *Rassegna Cateriniana*, 8, 1929, p. 278; 9, 1930, pp. 29, 33–42, 48, 60–61. The first of these references is an announcement of the lecture in Milan as forthcoming. See also *Memorie Domenicane*, 47, 1930, pp. 149–60.

83 *Rassegna Cateriniana*, 9, 1930, pp. 29, 124–5; *Memorie Domenicane*, 47, 1930, p. 159–60.

had died in the First World War whilst serving in a field hospital. The report also noted that that many Fascist youth groups elsewhere in Italy had indicated their celebration of Catherine's festival by sending telegrams to the ceremonies organized by the Sienese *Opera Nazionale Balilla*.[84] The following year it was observed that one of the most appealing aspects of the annual festival was the presence of more than a thousand members of the *Piccole Italiane* at a mass – again celebrated by Luigi Sbaragli – in San Domenico at which they presented not only floral tributes to Catherine but also a silver chalice paid for by their own contributions.[85] It was also reported that, at the national congress of the *Uffici di Cultura e Propaganda dell'Opera Balilla*, held in Florence in 1931, it had been proposed by the Sienese delegation that Catherine be formally elected as patron saint of the *Piccole e Giovani Italiane*. The proposal – it was noted – was well received and the head of the *Opera Nazionale Balilla*, Renato Ricci, confirmed that he would intervene to ensure that Catherine would be officially declared the heavenly patron of the *Organizzazioni Giovanile Femminile del Fascismo*.[86]

Catherine's annual festival was not, however, the only occasion for celebration of her cult in Siena in 1931: it was also the focus of the festival of Domenica in Albis that year. As an announcement published in February 1931 by the Dominican community at San Domenico explained, in 1930, two memorable anniversaries in the history of Catherine and her cult had coincided: the eleventh '*cinquantenario*' [half-century] of her death, and the third centenary of the official recognition, by Pope Urban VIII, of the authenticity of her experience of the stigmata. Because, in Siena, 1930 had also been the second centenary of the miracle of the '*Sacre Particole*' – which had been the focus of the Eucharistic Congress held in the church of San Francesco in Siena[87] – the Dominican community had agreed to postpone celebration of the two anniversaries relating to Catherine until 1931, also thereby making the celebrations a

84 *Il Popolo di Siena*, 3/5/1930, p. 3. For Sbaragli see a review of his war memoirs in the local Fascist paper *Il Popolo Senese*, 11/2/1929, p. 4, and his obituary in *Bollettino Senese di Storia Patria*, 57, 1950, pp. 228–9.

85 'I Grandi Festeggiamenti nella Basilica di S. Domenico in onore di S. Caterina da Siena', *S. Caterina da Siena, Bollettino Mensile della Basilica di San Domenico*, 10, 1931, pp. 1–3.

86 *La Rivoluzione Fascista*, 9/5/1931, p. 4; *S. Caterina da Siena, Bollettino Mensile della Basilica di San Domenico*, 10, 1931, p. 3. The chaplains appointed to the male and female sections of the *Balilla* – itself a highly militarized project – came under the oversight of the organization responsible for Italian military chaplains, the *Ordinariato Militare*. They duly sought to promote the cults of Saint Tarcisio and Saint Catherine, the 'protectors', respectively, of the youth groups for boys and girls, for which see Franzinelli (1995, p. 165). In 1930 the annual celebration in Santa Maria sopra Minerva attended by the *Piccole e Giovani Italiane* was addressed by both Bishop Angelo Bartolomasi – the head of the *Ordinariato Militare* – and Bishop Antonio Giordani who was responsible, within the *Ordinariato Militare*, for the spiritual oversight of the *Balilla*. Giordani also addressed the gathering in 1932. See *Memorie Domenicane*, 47, 1930, p. 277; 49, 1932, p. 244.

87 According to the miracle of the '*Sacre Particole*', in 1730 a number of consecrated hosts were stolen from the church of San Francesco in Siena, but were subsequently not only miraculously recovered but remained incorruptible.

fitting conclusion to the year-long recollection of the double anniversary.[88] Both the relic of Catherine's head and the crucifix of the stigmata were therefore chosen to be the joint focus of the festival of Domenica in Albis in 1931, '*in onore di S. Caterina da Siena*' and to commemorate the 'happy coincidence' of the two anniversaries.[89]

A careful reading of the descriptions of the detail of the organization of the exposition of Catherine's head and of the crucifix in the cathedral, and of the various texts that promoted and reported the event, reveals a striking combination of traditional Sienese devotion to Catherine as a Sienese saint and symbol of Sienese civic devotion and the more recent commitment to the energetic promotion of her claim to be both a '*santa nazionale*' and '*Patrona d'Italia*'. The continuity with traditional Sienese civic devotion was evident above all in the fact that the relic of Catherine's head and the crucifix of the stigmata were not presented alone for veneration in the cathedral. They were accompanied by relics from eleven other churches in Siena or its archdiocese, the majority of which were also relics of members of the Sienese civic pantheon of '*santi cittadini*'.[90] The publicity for the festival and the reports of it, however, equally strongly emphasized the contemporary concern that Catherine should be recognized as an Italian national saint. Thus, at the end of their announcement of the celebration of the 'double anniversary', the Dominicans of San Domenico called on the Sienese to prepare to give a solemn testimony of their love for the woman whom Pius IX had proclaimed '*Patrona di Roma*' and who, soon, they hoped would now be proclaimed '*Patrona d'Italia*'.[91] The public notice announcing the choice of objects for veneration during Domenica in Albis similarly called upon the Sienese to recall their pride in Catherine who would soon, 'without doubt', be the '*Patrona d'Italia*',[92] while the supplement to *Il Popolo di Siena* published for the occasion referred to the cult and memory of 'this Joan of Arc of the Papacy' who was also the greatest force for moral unity in the history of Italian politics.[93]

In 1932 the annual festival in honour of Catherine in Siena was the occasion for a further initiative to promote the cause of her proclamation as '*Patrona d'Italia*'.

---

88 'Feste Solenni in onore di S. Caterina', *S. Caterina da Siena, Bollettino Mensile della Basilica di San Domenico*, 10, 2, 1931, p. 1.

89 The statement that the festival was in honour of Catherine was made in the 'Programma' for the celebration of Domenica in Albis published in a supplement to *Il Popolo di Siena*, 4/4/1931, p. 8. The reference to the happy double anniversary appears on the title page of a *Relazione dei Festeggiamenti e Rendiconto Finanziario* published by those responsible for the organization of the festival, a copy of which is in the Archivio della Nobile Contrada dell'Oca in a collection of documents entitled 'Esposizione solenne in Duomo della Sacra Testa di Santa Caterina da Siena, Domenica in Albis dell'anno 1931–XI in Siena', [XII B. 11 92].

90 The '*santi cittadini*' whose relics featured included Ansano, Bernardino, Bernardo Tolomei, Francesco Patrizi and Antonio Patrizi. For the full list see *Supplemento al Il Popolo di Siena*, 4/4/1931, p. 9; *Relazione dei Festeggiamenti e Rendiconto Finanziario*, p. 9.

91 Feste Solenni in onore di S. Caterina', *S. Caterina da Siena, Bollettino Mensile della Basilica di S. Domenico*, 10, 2, 1931, p. 1.

92 *Relazione dei Festeggiamenti e Rendiconto Finanziario*, p. 4.

93 *Supplemento al Il Popolo di Siena*, 4/4/1931, p. 7.

The Sienese branch of the *Società Internazionale di Studi Cateriniani* called upon the Sienese to sign a petition requesting that Catherine should soon be officially proclaimed '*Patrona dell'intera Nazione*'. To this end, lists for signatures would be made available during Catherine's annual festival, on 29 April in the Sanctuary in Fontebranda, and on 30 April in San Domenico. The appeal to the Sienese from the local *Società Internazionale di Studi Cateriniani* included the affirmation that none of Italy's female saints was more Italian than Catherine, who had restored the papacy to Rome after its exile in France, and who also sought the liberty and greatness of both the church and of Italy. And today, the appeal continued, when the conflict between church and state has been resolved, and when both the *Piccole e Giovani Italiane* and the *Unione Femminile Cattolica Italiana* had recognized Catherine as their heavenly patron, the Sienese therefore hoped that Catherine would also be made patron saint of the whole nation.[94]

The festival itself, it was reported, was celebrated by an extraordinary number of people and was especially notable for the participation of all the educational and religious institutions of the city, and also of the *Balilla* and the *Piccole e Giovani Italiane*, accompanied again by their chaplain, Luigi Sbaragli. At the end of the festival, on 30 April telegrams were sent to Pope Pius XI, to the king, and to Mussolini, announcing the petition and urging that Catherine be proclaimed '*Patrona d'Italia*'. The lists of signatures – which totalled 25,976 – were bound in an elaborately decorated book, entitled *Voto Senese per Santa Caterina Patrona d'Italia*. The book was displayed for the Sienese public on the 29 May – in San Domenico in the morning and in the Sanctuary of Saint Catherine in the afternoon – and was then sent to Rome on 1 June 1932 for presentation to the Pope.[95] It is notable that, amidst general Sienese enthusiasm for the initiative, the petition was particularly warmly welcomed in the Sienese Fascist newspaper, *La Rivoluzione Fascista*, where it was observed that the celebration of Catherine's annual festival was more significant than usual in 1932 precisely because the petition demonstrated the desire of both Fascists and the Sienese in general that Catherine should be recognized as '*Santa Nazionale, protettrice della Patria nostra*', thereby following the example of the '*Giovani e Piccole Italiane*'.[96]

The campaign for Catherine's proclamation as '*Patrona d'Italia*' was maintained during 1933 and 1934. In 1933 Prospero Scaccia's successor as Archbishop of Siena, Gustavo Matteoni, wrote to all the Italian bishops, archbishops and other senior clergy seeking their support for the project and secured the positive responses of three cardinals, 29 archbishops, and 103 bishops. These too were bound into a single volume and presented to the Pope.[97] Also in 1933, both Piero Misciattelli and Emilio

94 A copy of the original appeal may be found among correspondence of Terenzio Nencini (who was both vice-president of the Società and Prior of the Confraternity of Saint Catherine in Fontebranda), now kept in the Archivio Arcivescovile, Siena, in a file entitled 'Statuti per varie Congregazione e Confraternite 1895–1956', inventory number 4033. The text is also reproduced in Nencini (1932, pp. 41–2).

95 Nencini (1932, pp. 43–7). See also Bianchi (1990, pp. 71–2).

96 *La Rivoluzione Fascista*, 8/5/1932, p. 4.

97 Bianchi (1990, p. 72).

Bodrero again drew attention to Catherine's political and national significance. In an article which discussed Catherine's civil idealism and political ideals – and related them to the international situation in which Italy found itself in the early 1930s – Misciattelli joined the ranks of those who emphasized the parallel between Catherine and Joan of Arc.[98] Emilio Bodrero, meanwhile, opened the 1933 lectures for the *Cattedra Cateriniana* in Siena with a restatement of the comparison between Catherine's era and contemporary Italy, concluding that Catherine should be recognized as '*Santa Nazionale*' because she, more than any other historical figure, reflected the ideals that Mussolini had restored to Italy and Italians.[99]

In 1934 Archbishop Matteoni called for Catherine's annual festival to be celebrated with greater fervour, whilst the report of the festival in the local Catholic paper repeated the description of Catherine as the 'Joan of Arc of the Papacy' and the greatest force for moral unity in the history of Italian politics which it had previously used in its celebration of the choice of Catherine's head and of the crucifix of the stigmata for the celebration of Domenica in Albis in 1931.[100] Six hundred Sienese members of the *Balilla* and the *Piccole Italiane* celebrated the festival of 'their patron' in San Domenico on 29 April, whilst a group of *Giovani e Piccole Italiane* from Pisa did so on 6 May, including giving a silver chalice.[101] In July, the Catholic paper then reported progress in the appeal organized by the *Società Internazionale di Studi Cateriniani* to fund the cost of a bust of Catherine, together with a chapel, altar and candlesticks for the church at Littoria, the new city founded south of Rome on land 'reclaimed by Fascism' from the Pontine marshes.[102] The same page of the paper also carried a report of a visit to Siena – and to the Sanctuary of Saint Catherine – by 250 young Fascists from Cadriglia, near Arezzo. Beyond Siena, the *Corporazione dei Caterinati* published and promoted a study by the Dominican priest, Marco Righi, entitled *Santa Caterina da Siena e la Conciliazione* in which he sought to demonstrate the influence of Catherine of Siena's writings on Pius XI in his preparation for the Lateran Treaties and Concordat. Righi's work was prefaced by a letter from the Archbishop of Bologna, Cardinal Giovanni Battista Nasalli-Rocca, asserting that Catherine would soon be proclaimed *Patrona d'Italia*.[103] The review of the book in *La Nazione* appeared under the headline, '*Santa Caterina da Siena e la sua italianità*'. It prefaced a highly appreciative assessment of Righi's work with an assertion of Catherine's own sense of the unity of Italy and the Italian people. Now, the review continued, after the victory of Vittorio Veneto in 1918, Italy was indeed finally unified – 'from the Alps to the Sea' – and was free of discord,

98 Misciattelli (1933, esp. p. 44). Misciattelli's article also included sharply polemical remarks about the nature of modern culture and its neglect of religion, and also concerning the 'pacifism' and 'hypocrisy' of the League of Nations, for which see pp. 35–6.

99 'La Cattedra Cateriniana all'Università di Siena', *S. Caterina da Siena, Bollettino Domenicano*, 1, 1933, pp. 59–60.

100 *Il Popolo di Siena*, 15/4/1934, p. 3; 22/4/1934, p. 2.

101 'All'altare della Santa', *S. Caterina da Siena, Bollettino Domenicano*, 2, 1934, p. 108.

102 *Il Popolo di Siena*, 22/7/1934, p. 3.

103 Righi (1934).

factional strife and servitude to foreign powers. It also recalled the language used in 1929 in celebration of Pope Pius XI and Mussolini.[104]

The national and patriotic significance of Catherine and her cult were given even greater prominence in 1935 and 1936 in the context of the Italian invasion and conquest of Ethiopia. It is generally acknowledged that the war in Ethiopia represented the high point in support for Mussolini and his regime, both among the Italian population as a whole and from within the Italian Catholic church.[105] The reaction to the war in Siena conformed to this pattern. Mario Toccabelli – who had become Archbishop of Siena in April 1935 following the death of Gustavo Matteoni – proved to be an enthusiastic supporter of the war, endorsing the invasion both in the pages of the local Catholic paper and at the *Solenne funzione propiziatrice in cattedrale per la vittoria delle armi italiane* held in Siena cathedral on 11 November 1935.[106] More significantly, in the present context, the Italian war in Ethiopia also prompted appeals to Catherine seeking her heavenly intercession on behalf of Italy and her protection of Italian soldiers. On 13, 14 and 15 October 1935, and again on 21, 22 and 23 February 1936, a 'triduo' of prayer was held in the church of Santa Caterina in Fontebranda, the Oratory of the *Contrada dell'Oca*. Arranged by the women of the *contrada*, the handwritten notices for these events defined their purpose as seeking the protection of Catherine over '*nostri Cari Soldati e sulla Patria armata*' and over '*nostri militari e sulla Patria*', whilst a prayer prepared for the occasions described those praying as devoted children of the Pope, to Italy, to the king, and to the Duce.[107] The local press reported the *triduo* of February 1936, describing it as an invocation of Catherine's protection for Italy's soldiers and a request for the nation's complete victory. The papers also noted that, as well as the *triduo* in Santa Caterina in Fontebranda, on 20 February there had also been a service of prayer in the Sanctuary of Saint Catherine, in front of the crucifix of the stigmata,

104 *La Nazione*, *Cronaca di Siena*, 18/12/1934, p. 4.

105 Jemolo (1960, p. 260); Binchy (1977, pp. 677–9); Bosworth (2005, p. 367); Zagheni (2006, pp. 203–4, 242–6).

106 *Il Popolo di Siena*, 22/9/1935, p. 1; Bocchini Camaiani (1994, pp. 81–2); Mirizio (2002, pp. 481–3; 2003, pp. 72–6); Parsons (2004a, pp. 84–5; 2007, p. 473). In December 1935 Toccabelli also gave his highly public support to the 'Giornata della Fede' when gold wedding rings were donated to the nation as part of the effort to offset the economic damage caused by the sanctions imposed on Italy by the League of Nations because of the war in Ethiopia. Toccabelli publicly donated his gold pectoral cross, for which see Luchini (1994, p. 517); Mirizio (2002, p. 482). A file of documents among Toccabelli's papers includes a letter, dated 19/12/1935, from Aldo Sampoli, the local Fascist party Federal Secretary, to Toccabelli, thanking him for this gesture. The file also includes a receipt, dated January 1936, for the precise weight of the gold from the cross. The two documents are in the Archivio Arcivescovile in Siena, inventory number 2995.

107 Copies of the notices and of the prayer may be found in the file of documents, 'Triduo a Caterina per la protezione dei nostri militari e volontari in Guerra in A.O. contro l'Etiopia, per la sicurrezza delle proprie Colonie e per la diffusione della civiltà Italiana in quell popolo barbaro e schiavista' in the Archivio della Nobile Contrada dell'Oca, inventory number XIII B. 12 52.

again seeking Catherine's protection of the Italian forces, peace with justice for the nation, and the safe return home of Italian soldiers.[108]

The Italian campaign in Ethiopia also prompted three projects to send copies of famous images of Catherine of Siena to both Ethiopia and Somalia, to be placed in churches used by the Italian military – initiatives that reflected the widespread practice in Italy during 1935–36 of sending copies of sacred images and statues, both of the Virgin and of particular saints, to the Italian forces serving in the Italian colonies in East Africa.[109] In March 1936, a committee representing the mothers and wives of Sienese soldiers serving in East Africa was formed to raise funds for a copy of the late fourteenth-century painting of Catherine by Andrea Vanni in San Domenico, Siena (Plate I), and send it to Somalia. The committee – which met for the first time in the Sanctuary of Saint Catherine on 1 March 1936[110] – commissioned the copy from the Sienese painter Vittorio Giunti. The initiative, it was noted, enjoyed the support of the archbishop, the Dominicans and the Sienese civic authorities, as well as the Sienese people, who thereby wished to show their support for those who, by their heroism, held Italy's name high and carried 'the light of Roman civilization' into the 'wildness' of Ethiopia.[111] Giunti had completed the reproduction of the Andrea Vanni image of Catherine by the end of April when it was placed on display in the Sanctuary of Saint Catherine during her annual festival for the public to again invoke her continuing protection of Italy's forces and of the king and Mussolini – the '*gloriosi condottieri*' who led the nation – and where it was also blessed by Archbishop Toccabelli.[112] The image was then transferred to San Domenico where it became the focus for a further *triduo* of prayer, culminating in a consecration of the image – which had been placed at the high altar – accompanied by a silver heart donated by the members of the *Contrada dell'Oca*. The image was then taken in procession to the station, carried by members of the *Confraternita di Santa Caterina in Fontebranda* and escorted by representatives of the Dominican Order, the military, the Sienese *contrade* and the public, to be sent to Naples, from where it was then sent on to the cathedral in Mogadishu, together with the silver heart and an album containing the signatures of the Sienese authorities and others who had signed the book during the *triduo* in San Domenico. The report of the ceremonies in *Il Telegrafo* also placed them firmly within a political rhetoric that extolled the Italian forces in East Africa as the bearers of '*la civiltà di Roma cesarea, cristiana e mussoliniana*' and also evoked the historical precedent of the era when the navies of Venice, Genoa and Pisa dominated the seas and carried Italian power

---

108 *Il Popolo di Siena*, 16/2/1936, p. 3; 23/2/1936, p. 4; *La Nazione*, 19/2/1936, p. 4; *Il Telegrafo*, 19/2/1936, p. 4.

109 Franzinelli (1995, pp. 217–22).

110 See the handwritten note accompanying press cuttings reporting the initiative in the collection of material relating to the Sanctuary compiled by Leopoldo Tuci, the priest responsible for the Sanctuary of Saint Catherine from 1915 to 1947: 'Notiziario riguardante il Santuario di S. Caterina Compilato dal Sac. Leopoldo Tuci', now in the Archivio Arcivescovile di Siena, inventory number 6546.

111 *Il Popolo di Siena*, 7/3/1936, p. 3; *La Nazione*, 14/3/1936, p. 4; *Il Telegrafo*, 14/3/1936, p. 4.

112 *Il Popolo di Siena*, 2/5/1936, p. 3; *Il Telegrafo*, 23/4/1936, p. 4.

to the east.[113] A brief item in the press in July reported that the committee of mothers and wives had received a letter from a military chaplain confirming its arrival in Mogadishu and assuring them that it would be sent on Addis Ababa to be placed in the capital of the new Italian empire.[114]

A second reproduction of a famous image of Catherine destined for East Africa was also blessed by Archbishop Toccabelli during the saint's annual festival in 1936. In this case the reproduction was of the image painted by Vecchietta in the Sala del Mappamondo of the Palazzo Pubblico in the mid-fifteenth century (Plate II). The painting was given by a number of the earliest supporters of Fascism in Siena and by the wife of Professor Giorgio Alberto Chiurco, one of the founding figures of Sienese Fascism. In 1936, Chiurco was serving as a military doctor with Italian forces in Somalia and the image was to be placed in the church, dedicated to Catherine, that Chiurco had had built at the field hospital of which he was the director. On this occasion, the blessing of the image took place in private – and at Chiurco's personal request to Toccabelli – in the chapel in the archbishop's palace, but the event was reported at some length in the local press.[115]

A third image of Catherine for the Italian forces in East Africa was produced as the result of a national collection organized by the *Piccole e Giovani Italiane*. Initiated by their branch in Milan, the project raised funds through appeals in the organization's magazine '*La Piccola Italiana*' in order to send a further copy of the Andrea Vanni image (Plate I), in this instance to be placed in a church built on the initiative of the intensely patriotic and pro-Fascist Dominican priest Reginaldo Giuliano who had been killed in Ethiopia whilst serving as a chaplain to one of the legions of the *Milizia Volontaria per la Sicurezza Nazionale*.[116] The image was eventually blessed in San Domenico, Siena, in December – having previously received a blessing in Milan – before being sent on to Ethiopia.[117] The *Piccole e Giovani Italiane* had also, again, been prominent in the celebrations for Catherine's annual festival in 1936. In the afternoon of 30 April, 400 of the *Giovane Italiane* had paraded in San Domenico to pray in front of the relic of Catherine's head, before then visiting the Sanctuary of the saint for an address from Luigi Sbaragli. The report of the event also noted that members of the *Piccole e Giovani Italiane* in Turin, Milan and Bologna took place in similar celebrations of their patron and protectress.[118]

---

113 *Il Popolo di Siena*, 23/5/1936, p. 3; *La Nazione*, 19/5/1936, p. 4; *Il Telegrafo*, 19/5/1936, p. 4; *Foglio d'ordine della federazione senese dei Fasci di Comabattimento*, 3/5/1936, p. 2; *S. Caterina da Siena, Bollettino Domenicano*, 4, n. 5, 1936, p. 76.

114 *Il Popolo di Siena*, 18/7/1936, p. 3; *Foglio d'ordine della federazione senese dei Fasci di Comabattimento*, 19/7/1936, p. 2.

115 *Il Popolo di Siena*, 2/5/1936, p. 3; *Il Telegrafo*, 30/4/1936, p. 4.

116 The MVSN was the fully military wing of the Fascist movement, organized in 'Legions' to evoke Roman military precedent. Existing alongside the Italian army, the units were also described as 'Camicie Nere' – Blackshirts – and included many of those most committed to the Fascist cause.

117 *Il Popolo di Siena*, 9/5/1936, p. 3; *La Nazione*, 14/7/1936, p. 4; 3/12/1936, p. 4; *Foglio d'ordine della federazione senese dei Fasci di Combattimento*, 6/12/36, p. 2. For Reginaldo Giuliano see Franzinelli (1995, pp. 249–57; 2003a, pp. 33–4, 108).

118 *La Nazione*, 3/5/1936, p. 4.

The announcement of Italian victory in Ethiopia in May 1936 was marked by enthusiastic celebration in Siena, including religious acts of thanksgiving. In the cathedral, after a civic procession from the Campo and the Palazzo Pubblico, a Te Deum was offered in thanks for victory and in celebration of the proclamation of the Italian empire, whilst the local Catholic paper reported the announcement of the Italian victory under the headlines '*Vittoria e Pace Romana*', '*Vittoria Romana*' and '*Impero di pace romana*'. The articles – which included sharply polemical remarks about British and northern European Protestant opposition to Italian policy – celebrated a victory that was interpreted as a triumph of both the sword and the faith; that initiated an empire of peace; and that represented a renewal of the destiny of an Italy that was at once '*Romana, Fascista e Cattolica*'.[119] In the Sanctuary of Saint Catherine, meanwhile, a service of thanksgiving was held with a Te Deum, a solemn blessing with the sacraments, hymns and the opportunity to kiss the reliquary of the saint. The report of this event also noted that there had been regular services for victory in the Sanctuary since the beginning of the war the previous October.[120]

As well as the particular circumstances of the invasion of Ethiopia and the declaration of the new Italian empire, the references to – and the entire rhetoric of – empire and '*romanità*' which accompanied many of the celebrations and invocations of Catherine during 1935 and 1936 recalled the much earlier evocations of her '*romanità*' by Piero Misciattelli in the first lecture for the *Cattedra Cateriniana* in 1926 (and again in his essay on the civic ideals of Catherine published in 1933), [121] at the inauguration of the bust of Catherine in the Pincio gardens in 1928, and in the various parallels suggested between Catherine and Mussolini a year later at the time of the *conciliazione*. In early 1937, moreover, in Santa Caterina da Siena a Magnanapoli – the Roman church that was the religious and administrative seat of the *Ordinariato Militare*, the organization for Italian military chaplains – volumes containing the names of the Italian casualties in the First World War were placed in the crypt, which had been dedicated as a 'living monument' to Italy's dead in that conflict. A section of the crypt was also dedicated to those killed in the Ethiopian campaign – an expedition which, it has been noted, was frequently presented as an example of the inter-relatedness of '*romanità*', Christianity and civilization.[122]

During the next three years, overtly patriotic references to Catherine continued in other ways, albeit with less intensity. In 1937 it was again noted that over a thousand members of the *Piccole e Giovani Italiane* participated in Catherine's annual festival in Siena to celebrate their patron and reflect on their role in the contemporary rebirth of the Italian nation.[123] In 1938 the theme of the intensely Italian quality of Catherine's character and personality was again emphasized in the biography of

119 *Il Popolo di Siena*, 9/5/1936, pp. 1, 3; 16/5/1936, pp. 1, 3; *Il Telegrafo*, 10/5/1936, p. 4; Grassi (1972, pp. 56–7).

120 *Il Telegrafo*, 12/5/1936, p. 4.

121 Misciattelli (1933, pp. 36–7).

122 Franzinelli (1995, pp. 104–8, 211–12, 237). For further discussion of the significance of ideas of '*romanità*' in relation to the campaign for Catherine to be proclaimed '*Patrona d'Italia*', see Parsons (2008a, pp. 79–80).

123 *S. Caterina da Siena, Bollettino Domenicano*, 5, n. 2, 1937, p. 9.

Catherine, entitled *La Santa degli Italiani*, published in 1938 by Giovanni Bitelli – who the previous year had published a biography of Mussolini. In its review of the book, *La Nazione* affirmed that Catherine was, indeed, one of the chosen symbols of her race – not simply in broadly Latin terms, but specifically and 'rigorously' in respect of her distinctively Italian character.[124] The same year, in August, the local press reported the inauguration of a new church in Addis Ababa dedicated to Catherine of Siena. The report asserted that Catherine looked benignly upon the re-conquest of an Italian empire in which her own ideals of faith and nation were expressed.[125] And in October, in an article published in the periodical of the various branches of the charitable organization of the Misericordia of the province of Siena, the author, writing of '*Siena e la sua Santa*', repeated the by now traditional line that Catherine was the most saintly of Italian women and the most Italian of the nation's female saints – but also concluded that, whereas her own era had been one of faction and conflict, now the Italian people could rejoice because Rome had recovered its imperial crown under the sign of the eagle and the cross.[126]

Archbishop Toccabelli, meanwhile, continued to press the cause of Catherine's proclamation as an official patron saint of Italy, first with Pope Pius XI and then, after his death in February 1939, with his successor Pius XII. In Siena, efforts were also redoubled in the late 1930s to re-order and improve access to the Sanctuary of Saint Catherine in Siena in anticipation of her now expected elevation to the official status of *Patrona d'Italia* and of the events and pilgrimages that would therefore ensue. Such projects had been proposed from the early 1930s onwards but had been subject to controversy over alternative schemes and had also lacked adequate funds. During 1938, however, the pages of *Il Popolo di Siena* carried regular reports of the work of the committee that was now responsible for the project and of the contributions that had been made to the fund for the work.[127] In April 1939, with Catherine's proclamation as *Patrona d'Italia* now known to be imminent, Toccabelli used the pages of *Il Popolo di Siena* to orchestrate a much more elaborate celebration of her festival than had recently been customary. Toccabelli appealed to the precedent set by the Sienese in past centuries in their devotion to Catherine, citing the processions by the civic authorities and people to the Sanctuary and to San Domenico, the veneration of the relic of her head, the freeing of prisoners, and the giving of alms to the poor. In more recent times, Toccabelli observed, although interest in Catherine and her cult had grown, her annual festival had not been observed with similar devotion. He therefore invited the Sienese to participate in a renewed and enhanced version of Catherine's annual festival, on 29 April in the Sanctuary in Fontebranda, and on 30 April in San Domenico. At the centre of the festival, Toccabelli announced, would be a new procession, to mark the closure of the festival in Fontebranda and the opening of the celebrations in San Domenico. The procession, which would

124 Bitelli (1938); *La Nazione*, *Cronaca di Siena*, 25/1/1939, 4.

125 *Il Telegrafo*, 12/8/1938, p. 4.

126 *Charitas: foglio di informazioni della Aggregazione delle Misericordie della Provincia di Siena*, 2/10/1938, p. 2.

127 *Il Popolo di Siena*, 13/2/1938, p. 3 and regular reports thereafter; Luchini (1994, pp. 295, 298–9, 301–2).

include the civic authorities, would move from the cathedral to the Sanctuary where it would receive a blessing with the relic of the saint. The procession would then continue to San Domenico for the uncovering of the relic of Catherine's head for veneration by the faithful during the rest of the festival. At both venues votive candles were also to be presented by the civic authorities.[128] After the festival at the end of April, the local Catholic paper asserted that, with the introduction of the procession from the cathedral to the Sanctuary and San Domenico, the Sienese had renewed their traditional homage and devotion to their saint. It was also noted that, after uncovering the relic of Catherine's head, Archbishop Toccabelli had repeated that Catherine – together with Francis of Assisi – would soon be proclaimed a patron saint of Italy.[129]

Just under two months later, on Sunday 18 June 1939, Catherine of Siena and Francis of Assisi were formally proclaimed co-patron saints of Italy by Pope Pius XII. The fact that the proclamation would be made the next day had been announced on the radio the previous afternoon, prompting a series of predictably ecstatic celebrations in Siena. The bell of the Torre del Mangia of the Palazzo Pubblico was rung, as was the bell of San Domenico and the other churches of the city. In San Domenico, at the chapel of Saint Catherine and in the Oratory of the *Contrada dell'Oca*, spontaneous services of thanksgiving were held, followed the next day by a solemn Te Deum of thanksgiving in the Sanctuary of Saint Catherine in front of the crucifix of the stigmata. Telegrams were also sent to Cardinal Maglione, the Vatican Secretary of State, by the Podestà of Siena, Luigi Socini Guelfi, and by the Governor of the *Contrada dell'Oca*, Alessandro Raselli.[130] On 27 June, in the main lecture room of the University of Siena, Cardinal Carlo Salotti, Prefect of the Congregation of Rites at the Vatican, then delivered the closing address for that year's sequence of lectures under the auspices of the *Cattedra Cateriniana*. After presenting a review of Catherine's life and character, culminating in a celebration of her support for the papacy and her desire that Italy should be saved through the Pope and his presence in Rome, he concluded his address with an assertion of the strength of Catherine's love of Italy. Eulogizing Italy as a land of saints, martyrs, heroes and soldiers – from the soldiers who fought at Lepanto to those who now carried the tricolour of Christ in Africa – he affirmed that Catherine was one of the great glories of Siena, and now more than ever a glory of Italy.[131]

Catherine's new status was also celebrated beyond Siena. At the end of July it was reported in *Il Popolo di Siena* that altars were being dedicated to Catherine in various parts of Italy,[132] whilst articles celebrating her proclamation as *Patrona*

---

128 *Il Popolo di Siena*, 16/4/1939, p. 1.

129 *Il Popolo di Siena*, 30/4/1939, p. 1; 7/5/1939, p. 3; *Il Telegrafo*, 30/4/1939, p. 4.

130 *Il Popolo di Siena*, 25/6/1939, pp. 1, 3; Luchini (1994, p. 301); 'Proclamazione di S. Caterina da Siena a Patrona d'Italia' – a collection of documents recalling the events of 17–18 June 1940, in the Archivio della Nobile Contrada dell'Oca, inventory number XIII B. 14 98. See also Toccabelli (1940).

131 Il Popolo di Siena, 25/6/1939, p. 1; 2/7/1939, pp. 1–2. The text of Salotti's address is also reproduced in 'Cinquantenario dei Patroni d'Italia San Francesco d'Assisi e Sanat Caterina da Siena', *Quaderni Cateriniani*, 54–5, 1989, pp. 8–11.

132 *Il Popolo di Siena*, 30/7/1939, p. 1.

d'Italia appeared in the journals *Memorie Domenicane, Vita e Pensiero* and *Vita cristiana* – in the latter cases focusing jointly upon Catherine and Francis as joint patrons of Italy, in the former, concentrating simply on Catherine.[133] Appropriately, however, it was in Siena that the single most compelling recognition of Catherine's elevation to the role of *Patrona d'Italia* occurred. The painted banner for the *Palio* of August 1939 – by the Sienese artist Bruno Marzi – was dedicated to Catherine and dominated by her image (Plate III). In common with the imagery required for every August *Palio*, the Virgin of the Assumption – whose festival the August *Palio* celebrates each year in Siena – was portrayed at the top of the banner. The focus of the banner, however, was a portrayal of Catherine of Siena shown standing above, and looking down upon, a walled city, with her arms spread so as to hold her cloak protectively over and around the city below her. To the left of her head appear the words 'S. CATERINA DA SIENA' and to the right the words 'PATRONA D'ITALIA'. The walls of the city bear Roman imperial eagles, whilst, upon close examination, the buildings inside the walls are seen to be depictions of famous monuments from various Italian cities, including Turin, Milan, Bologna, Rome, Siena, Florence, Perugia, Venice and Naples, thus encompassing the principal cities of the north and the south.[134] The imagery of the banner for the *Palio* of August 1939 was to be used again, in April 1940, for the celebration of the first annual festival of Catherine as *Patrona d'Italia*. That festival was take place less than two months before Italy's entry into the Second World War. It thus not only initiated a new era in the celebration of Catherine – focusing on her new identity as an official, national, patron saint – but also, as the next chapter will demonstrate, marked the beginning of the most dramatic and turbulent period in the modern history of her cult.

133 Cordovani (1939); Dalla Torre (1939); La Pira (1939).

134 Betti (1992a, pp. 113, 129); Caciorgna and Pierini (1995, pp. 42–3); Zetti (1999, pp. 97–8). The banner may now be seen in the Museum of the Contrada della Torre.

Plate 1 Vecchietta, Reliquary Doors, detail of *Catherine of Siena receiving the stigmata*, 1445, Pinacoteca Nazionale, Siena

Plate 2 *Pope Pius II indicating Catherine of Siena receiving the stigmata*, Archivio di Stato, Siena, Gabella n. 47

Plate 3 Chapel of Saint Catherine of Siena, San Domenico, Siena

Plate 4 Chapel of Saint Catherine of Siena, San Domenico, Siena, detail of the altar and tabernacle containing the relic of Catherine's head

Plate 5 Catherine of Siena protecting the Palazzo Pubblico, 1526, Archivio di Stato, Siena

Plate 6 Interior of the Church of the Crucifix, Sanctuary of Saint Catherine, Siena

Plate 7 *The Crucifix of the Stigmata*, Church of the Crucifix, Sanctuary of Saint Catherine, Siena

Plate 8 Rutilio Manetti, 1625, *Catherine of Siena above the city of Siena*, reverse side of a copy of the Crucifix of the Stigmata, Arciconfraternita di Santa Caterina da Siena, Rome

Plate 9 Antonio Gregori, 1617, *Procession in the Campo with the head of Saint Catherine*, Archivio di Stato, Siena

Plate 10 Attributed to Antonio Gregori, 1623, *Procession with Crucifix of the Stigmata in front of the Palazzo Pubblico*, Archivio di Stato, Siena

Chapter 3

Catherine of Siena and the Second World War: 1940–1945

Unsurprisingly, in 1940 the first *Festa Nazionale* held in honour of Catherine as patron saint of Italy was heavily coloured by overtly Fascist references and associations. In early December 1939 it had been announced in the pages of *Il Popolo di Siena* that, in his annual meeting with the Fascist Prefect of Siena, Mussolini had signalled his personal support for the renewal and improvement of the Sanctuary of Saint Catherine in Siena, as appropriate to her new status as a national patron saint, and to this end had contributed 50,000 *lire* to the cost of the project.[1] At the service in Siena cathedral at the end of December to mark the turn of the year, Archbishop Toccabelli then announced that 1940 was officially to be designated an '*Anno Cateriniano*' and that in Siena, from 4 to 14 April, there would be two weeks of missions and spiritual preparation before the celebration of the first *Festa Nazionale* in honour of Catherine as *Patrona d'Italia* during the final two weeks of April, culminating in processions through the city and ceremonies in the Sanctuary of Saint Catherine and in San Domenico on 28, 29 and 30 April.[2]

In March 1940, Toccabelli and the Podestà of Siena, Luigi Socini Guelfi, presented the plans for the restoration of the Sanctuary at an audience in Rome with Mussolini who gave a further substantial financial donation to support the work. Mussolini also gave permission for Toccabelli and Socini Guelfi to state publicly that he approved of the new *Festa Nazionale* and gave it his official patronage. He also agreed to the request that he send a personal representative to the first *Festa Nazionale* in honour of the new patron of Italy and formally authorized other Italian cities to participate in the festival. The Podestà then presented Mussolini with a four-volume edition of Catherine's letters, in a wooden box decorated with intarsio images of San Domenico and the Sanctuary. The meeting with Mussolini and his support for the forthcoming festival was reported with unrestrained enthusiasm not only in the local Fascist newspaper in Siena and the secular press, but also in the local Catholic paper, *Il Popolo di Siena*.[3] In the centre of the page of *Il Popolo di Siena* which carried the report of the meeting there also appeared a reproduction of the poster for the forthcoming festival. Designed by Bruno Marzi, it repeated the principal theme of the imagery of the *Palio* banner that he had painted the previous year, showing Catherine extending her arms and her cloak in protection over a

1 *Il Popolo di Siena*, 3/12/1939, p. 1.

2 *Il Popolo di Siena*, 7/1/1940, p. 1.

3 *Il Popolo di Siena*, 7/4/1940, p. 1; *La Nazione*, 31/3/1940, p. 4; *Il Telegrafo*, 30/3/1940, p. 4; 31/3/1940, p. 4; *La Rivoluzione Fascista*, 31/3/1940, p. 1.

walled city. The wall was again adorned with an imperial eagle, whilst within the city there appeared monuments representing the major cities of Italy.[4] A further variation on this imagery was used by the publishers of *Il Popolo di Siena* for the front pages of the series of special supplements that they published in March and April 1940 in preparation for the first *Festa Nazionale* of Saint Catherine. In each case, a half-length figure of Catherine was shown against a background of famous monuments representing particular Italian cities, beneath which appeared the title of the series of supplements: '*La Patrona d'Italia*'.[5]

In April 1940 the first *Festa Nazionale* in honour of Saint Catherine duly took place. The celebrations began on 14 April when the relic of Catherine's head was solemnly transferred from San Domenico to the cathedral and placed on the high altar. The procession – which included the civic and military authorities and the *contrade* of Siena, as well as various religious groups – was led by representatives of Fascist youth organizations. For the next week various groups – including clergy, religious orders and the Sienese *contrade* – visited the cathedral. Beginning on 21 April, for a week, the various dioceses of Tuscany and parishes of the archdiocese of Siena then visited the cathedral. The climax of the celebrations came on 28, 29 and 30 April. On the first day – in a ceremony described as the '*Omaggio dei Comuni d'Italia*' – the relic of Catherine's head was carried in procession, on a horse-drawn carriage, from the cathedral, through the streets of Siena, to the Campo (Plate 12). Cardinal Carlo Salotti then delivered an address in which he affirmed that all of Italy – from the Alps in the north to the islands of the south – was symbolically present in the Campo, especially through the presence of representatives of the royal family, of the government and of the various cities and *comuni* of Italy. Salotti then contrasted the Siena and Italy of Catherine's day, divided and prey to factions, with the Italy of the present: an Italy that was renewed; an Italy that was reconciled with the papacy; an Italy that now combined both political and spiritual unity; an Italy that was free, strong, independent and respected by all; and that was made powerful by the unanimity of its people and by its armed forces. Salotti concluded the address with a blessing that invoked Catherine's protection upon Siena and upon Italy. The procession then resumed, continuing to Fontebranda and the Sanctuary of Saint Catherine. At the Sanctuary the first symbolic stone for the Portico dei Comuni d'Italia – a new loggia to adorn the entrance to the Sanctuary – was presented by Prince Giangiacomo Borghese, the Governor of Rome. After being blessed by Cardinal Salotti, the stone was ceremonially laid by the Duke of Bergamo, who was present on behalf of the king (Plate 13). After an address by Prince Borghese, the representatives of other Italian cities then presented symbolic offerings towards the cost of the construction of the new Portico, and the ceremony concluded with the singing of the Fascist hymn, '*La Giovinezza*'. The following day the traditional celebration of Catherine's festival took place in the Sanctuary,

4 Caciorgna and Pierini (1995, pp. 42–3); 'Cinquantenario dei Patroni d'Italia San Francesco d'Assisi e Santa Caterina da Siena', *Quaderni Cateriniani*, 54–5, 1989, p. 17.

5 *La Patrona d'Italia: Solenni Festeggiamenti Nazionali in onore di S. Caterina da Siena Patrona d'Italia – Foglio di Informazione*, supplements to *Il Popolo di Siena*, published 3/3, 10/3, 31/3, 7/4 and 14/4/1940.

culminating in a further procession to take the relic of her head from the Sanctuary back to its customary place in San Domenico where the final acts of the first *Festa Nazionale* were observed on the 30th.[6]

The overtly Fascist dimension to the festival was not only revealed by the singing of '*La Giovinezza*' but is also amply confirmed by photographs which show the prominence of uniformed Fascists at the various ceremonies and processions. Particularly striking examples include the images of the laying of the first stone of the Portico dei Comuni and the moment in the Campo when, as the relic of Catherine's head passed in front of the Palazzo Pubblico, a group of officials in uniform gave the Fascist salute (Plates 12, 13).[7] The reports of the events and speeches in the local Catholic paper also strongly emphasized the contrast between the Italy of Catherine's day (in which the Pope was absent from Rome, and Italy itself was divided, the victim of factions and disorder, and held in contempt by foreign powers), and the Italy of 1940 (united with the papacy, renewed, spiritually and politically unified, free, strong and independent, and in which Rome was newly assertive).[8] Similarly, in his speech at the Sanctuary, Prince Borghese asserted that only now was it possible to understand fully the anguish felt by Catherine over the condition of Italy in her day, by means of comparison with contemporary Italy now under the influence of Fascism which, he affirmed, had brought strength and justice and had destroyed discord and division by appeal to a single faith and passion. It had also, thereby, made Italy not only truly united, in thought and in heart, but also secure in its power in following a leader who would not fail.[9] No less explicit in its

6 *Il Popolo di Siena*, 10/3/1940, p. 1; 14/4/1940, p. 1; 21/4/1940, p. 1; 28/4/1940, p. 1; 5/5/1940, pp. 1–2; *Quaderni Cateriniani*, 54–5, 1989, pp. 15–17; Luchini (1994, p. 302). The project for the 'Portico dei Comuni' in Siena provided a parallel to the earlier initiative, in Assisi, for a Votive Lamp, in honour of Saint Francis, given in the name of Italy's cities to symbolize their shared devotion to Francis as a '*santo nazionale*'. An idea first suggested in 1924 in connection with preparations for the celebration of the seventh centenary of Francis's death, the bronze lamp was eventually made and inaugurated only in 1939. On the 15 October 1939, on the final day of the celebrations of Francis's first annual festival after his proclamation as '*Patrono d'Italia*', the bronze '*lampada votiva dei Comuni d'Italia*' was lit for the first time by the vice-governor of Rome, on behalf of the cities of Italy. Placed at the entrance to the crypt which contains the tomb of Saint Francis beneath the lower church of the Basilica di San Francesco at Assisi, together with doves bearing olive twigs and appropriate inscriptions, the lamp includes four shields bearing, respectively, the symbols of the royal house of Savoy, Assisi, Rome and the axe and *fasces* of the governing regime. The lamp was – and remains – the focus of an annual rite in which representatives of one of the regions of Italy present oil for the lamp, on behalf of all Italian cities, at the annual festival in honour of Francis. For the origins of the lamp, its design, and its inauguration in 1939, see Gatti (1983, pp. 420–26).

7 See *Il Popolo di Siena*, 5/5/1940, p. 1; Luchini (1994, pp. 297, 300). A volume of photographs now in the possession of the *Associazione Internazionale dei Caterinati*, Siena, provides numerous further examples. I am indebted to the archivist of the *Associazione*, Dottoressa Franca Piccini for showing me this volume and for permission from the *Associazione* to publish a number of the images in this book.

8 See especially *Il Popolo di Siena*, 14/4/1940, p. 1; 21/4/1940, p. 1; 5/5/1940, p. 2.

9 *Il Popolo di Siena*, 5/5/1940, p. 2. The role of Prince Borghese in the ceremonies was recorded in the inscription that accompanied a bronze she-wolf suckling twins – the

association of the festival with Mussolini and his regime was the front page of the last of the special supplements produced for the first *Festa Nazionale* by the editors of *Il Popolo di Siena*. Below the image of Catherine portrayed against a background of representations of monuments from various Italian cities, there appeared a photograph of Mussolini, in military uniform and helmet, together with a brief text confirming his support of the festival (Plate 14).[10] The opening page of the book of tributes compiled to commemorate the festival similarly emphasized that the festival enjoyed Mussolini's patronage, whilst a pamphlet celebrating Catherine, published the month following the festival by the Sienese historian Virgilio Grassi, concluded by asserting that Catherine was no longer the heavenly protector of Siena alone, but also of all of Italy, 'returned, in our times, to Imperial greatness'.[11]

An account of the celebrations in Rome in April and early May 1940 to mark the first *Festa Nazionale* in honour of Saint Catherine, meanwhile, noted that the 'highly Italian' celebrations in Santa Maria sopra Minerva had opened with a mass conducted by Antonio Giordani, the bishop responsible for co-ordinating the spiritual oversight of the *Gioventù Italiano del Littorio*.[12] The mass, it was reported, was attended by 2,000 girls of the *Gioventù Femminile del Littorio*, each of whom presented a white rose at the high altar.[13] The edition of the Dominican journal in which this report appeared also carried a series of articles celebrating Catherine as '*Patrona d'Italia*'. One of the articles celebrated her specifically as the embodiment of the heroic virtues of her race,[14] whilst another concluded with a highly patriotic evocation of Catherine looking down protectively upon Italy: upon its cities, empire and colonies; upon its armed forces who guard the safety and prosperity of the nation; and upon the cemeteries of Italian soldiers killed in the campaigns in Africa and Spain. Finally the latter article sought Catherine's blessing upon Italy's victories – under the signs of the cross and the empire – and upon both the king-emperor and the 'far-sighted' Duce.[15]

Within two months of the first *Festa Nazionale* in honour of Saint Catherine, Italy entered the Second World War, declaring war on France and Britain on 10 June 1940. As in 1935, so also in 1940, the declaration of war prompted a *triduo* of prayer on 21, 22 and 23 June in the Oratory of the *Contrada dell'Oca*, to ask that Catherine

---

symbol of both Siena and Rome – that was given to the city of Siena by the city of Rome in commemoration of the first *Festa Nazionale* for Saint Catherine as *Patrona d'Italia*. Both the bronze wolf and the inscription may still be seen in the Cortile of the Palazzo Pubblico in Siena.

10 *La Patrona d'Italia: Foglio di Informazion, N.5, Supplemento al N.15 del Popolo di Siena*, 14/4/1940, p. 1.

11 Barbieri (1940, p. 1); Grassi (1940, p. 38).

12 The *Gioventù Italiano del Littorio* had been formed in 1937, combining the hitherto separate youth groups for boys and girls under one organization – whilst still retaining highly gendered roles for members, for which see De Grazia (1992, pp. 158–61).

13 'I Festeggiamenti Cateriniani', *Memorie Domenicane* 57, 1940, pp. 236–48, esp. p. 239.

14 Fiume (1940).

15 Villani (1940).

Plate I Andrea Vanni, *Saint Catherine of Siena*, c.1381, San Domenico, Siena

Plate II Vecchietta, *Saint Catherine of Siena*, c.1461, Sala del Mappamondo, Palazzo Pubblico, Siena

Plate III Bruno Marzi, banner for the *Palio* of 16 August 1939: *Catherine of Siena as Patrona d'Italia*. Museun of the Contrada della Torre.

Plate IV Alberto Positano, banner for the *Palio* of 16 August 2000: Catherine of Siena as *Patrona d'Europa. Museum of the Contrada del Leocorno*

Plate V Cover of the Album of signatures of military personnel 1942-1945, Archive of the Associazione Internazionale dei Caterinati, Siena

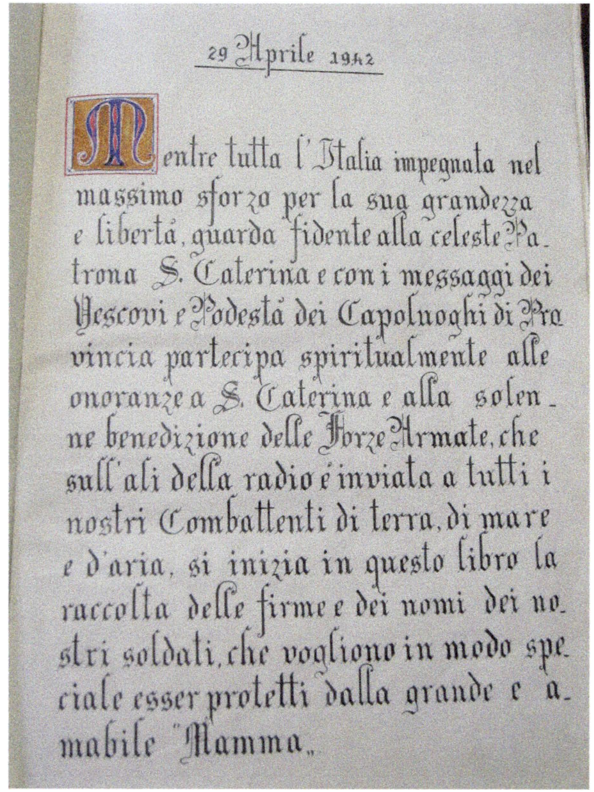

29 Aprile 1942

Mentre tutta l'Italia impegnata nel massimo sforzo per la sua grandezza e libertà, guarda fidente alla celeste Pa-trona S. Caterina e con i messaggi dei Vescovi e Podestà dei Capoluoghi di Pro-vincia partecipa spiritualmente alle onoranze a S. Caterina e alla solen-ne benedizione delle Forze Armate, che sull'ali della radio è inviata a tutti i nostri Combattenti di terra, di mare e d'aria, si inizia in questo libro la raccolta delle firme e dei nomi dei no-stri soldati, che vogliono in modo spe-ciale esser protetti dalla grande e a-mabile "Mamma"

Plate VI Frontispiece of the Album of signatures of military personnel 1942–1945, Archive of the Associazione Internazionale dei Caterinati, Siena

Plate VII Giovanni Cappelletti, Votive Lamp in honour of Catherine of Siena, 1943, Church of the Crucifix in the Sanctuary of Saint Catherine, Siena

extend her protection over Italian soldiers and aid an Italian victory.[16] The prayer composed for the occasion – and reproduced as a small printed text – was entitled a 'Prayer for Victory and Peace' and, addressed to Christ, asked that he would grant a list of requests, for the sake and because of the intercession of the Virgin, of Catherine and Francis the patron saints of Italy, and of the other '*santi concittadini*' of Siena. The requests were numerous: the blessing of the armed forces and their glorious victory; the protection of Italian soldiers in body and soul, the sustaining of their courage, and that they might be examples of Christian values; that king, the Duce and the military commanders might lead the nation well; for comfort to the families of soldiers and their safe return; for a spirit of cooperation, discipline and sacrifice among Italians; that other nations might recognize the needs, rights and sacrifices of Italy; and that the nation might emerge from this trial better, stronger and greater, thereby expanding its mission of upholding truth, justice and Christian civilization to the world.[17]

The same themes were again in evidence on 7 December 1940, when the relic of Catherine's head was the focus of a ceremony to move it from its customary position in the chapel dedicated to Catherine on the right hand side of the nave of San Domenico, so that restoration work could be undertaken in the nave of the church. The relic was taken in procession out of the main door of San Domenico, around the small piazza in front of the church and then back into the church through the lateral entrance that led into the left transept. Catherine's head was then placed on the altar dedicated to the *beato* Ambrogio Sansedoni in the right transept where it remained exposed for public veneration and prayer for three days. The announcement of the ceremony in the local Catholic paper explained that it was dedicated to asking the *Patrona d'Italia* for victory for the nation.[18] The ceremonies and procession were conducted in the presence of the civic authorities and representatives of the armed forces and of the Fascist youth groups of the *Gioventù Italiano del Littorio* – the latter having taken their places in the nave of San Domenico. After the procession, once the relic had been installed on the altar of Ambrogio Sansedoni, Archbishop Toccabelli gave an address – directed in particular to the soldiers present – in which he sought the intercession of Catherine, as *Patrona d'Italia*, in favour of God's blessing on Italy's armed forces, in the hope of victory and of a true peace based upon greater justice among the nations. Toccabelli then blessed the troops and the members of the *Gioventù Italiano del Littorio* with the relic of the finger of Saint Catherine. After the ceremony in San Domenico, Toccabelli, together with the Podestà, Luigi Socini Guelfi, and the rest of the civic and religious authorities, then went to the Sanctuary of Saint Catherine where, in the name of the city, the Podestà presented, and lit for the first time, a Votive Lamp to burn in front of the crucifix of

16 *Il Popolo di Siena*, 23/6/1940, p. 3.

17 'Preghiera per la Vittoria e per la Pace letta nell'occasione del Triduo a S. Caterina nei giorni 21–22–23 Giugno 1940 nell'Oratorio della Nobile Contrada dell'Oca', Archivio della Nobile Contrada dell'Oca, copy preserved in the file 'Triduo a Santa Caterina', inventory number XIII B. 12 52.

18 *Il Popolo di Siena*, 8/12/1940, p. 1.

the stigmata.[19] Both ceremonies prefigured important subsequent developments in the cult of Catherine as *Patrona d'Italia*.

In early 1941 there was a further *triduo* of prayer at the Sanctuary of Saint Catherine for Italian soldiers and for the nation, this time prompted by, and linked to, the annual festival in celebration of Catherine's experience of the stigmata.[20] At the end of April the second *Festa Nazionale* in honour of Catherine was held and was stamped firmly with an even more overtly patriotic and military character than the initial festival. As well as the customary presentation of votive candles by the civic authorities to both the Sanctuary of Saint Catherine and the church of San Domenico, and the exposition of the relic of Catherine's head to the faithful, the celebrations – as the local press reported in detail – also included a parade of troops in the piazza in front of San Domenico. The parade was addressed by Mons. Angelo Bartolomasi, the bishop – described in the press simply as the 'Bishop-General' – who headed the *Ordinariato Militare*. Speaking from the turret of an armoured car, Bartolomasi concluded with a blessing, performed with the relic of Catherine's finger, addressed to and intended for all Italian troops – whether fighting in North Africa or part of the occupying forces in '*Dalmazia liberata*' – but physically given to the representative soldiers present before him.[21]

The association of Catherine with Italian participation in the war and with the Italian armed forces was also at the centre of another project initiated in 1941. As the pages of both *Il Telegrafo* and *La Rivoluzione Fascista* reported in late July, an official committee had been founded to organize subscriptions for a Votive Lamp, dedicated to Saint Catherine and to be placed in the Sanctuary dedicated to her in Siena. An initiative of the women of Siena, the lamp was to be a votive offering to Catherine that she might hasten 'the day of victory', restore 'our heroic soldiers' safely to their families and obtain 'peace with justice' for Italy and the world. The initiative had the official blessing of Archbishop Toccabelli and the formal support of the local Federal Secretary of the Fascist party.[22] As the returned subscription lists – now held in the archive of the *Associazzione Internazionale dei Caterinati*

19 *Il Popolo di Siena*, 15/12/1940, p. 2; *La Nazione*, 10/12/1940, p. 4; *S. Caterina da Siena, Patrona d'Italia*, 8, 1940, p. 15.

20 *Il Popolo di Siena*, 15/2/1941, p. 2; *Il Telegrafo*, 16/2/1941, p. 4.

21 *Il Popolo di Siena*, 27/4/1941, p. 1; 3/5/1941, p. 2; *S. Caterina da Siena, Patrona d'Italia*, 8, 1941, p. 90; *Il Telegrafo*, 30/4/1941, p. 4; *La Rivoluzione Fascista*, 4/5/1941, p. 4. The militaristic tone of Bartolomasi's address and his use of an armoured car reflect the adoption by the *Ordinariato Militare* throughout the Fascist period of what Mimmo Franzinelli has described as a 'militarized Catholic creed', for which see Franzinelli (2003b, pp. 640–42). See also Franzinelli (1991, pp. 44–7, 61–6; 1995, esp. pp. 120–318; 2003a, p. 28). In the latter, Franzinelli suggests that 'it was not by chance' that the *Ordinariato Militare* was the most convinced philo-fascist wing of the church during the period of the regime.

22 *Il Telegrafo*, 22/7/1941, p. 4; *La Rivoluzione Fascista*, 28/7/1941, p. 2. A copy of the original appeal to the women of Siena from the 'Comitato Organizzatore per una Lampada Votiva a S. Caterina da Siena', signed by the committee president, Contessa Maria Ugurgieri della Berardenga, and warmly endorsed by Archbishop Toccabelli, is now held in the Archivio dell'Associazione Internazionale dei Caterinati. I am again indebted to Dottoressa Franca Piccini for drawing my attention to this and for providing me with a photocopy of the

in Siena – show, the appeal, which initially sought completed returns by 1 October 1941, prompted responses both from individual women and from various women's groups in Siena, including, for example, the women of particular Sienese *contrade*, and the members of local *Fasci Femminili* within Siena. The lists also show, however, that the appeal went well beyond the city of Siena, initially attracting contributions from *Fasci Femminili* in other communities in the Province of Siena, and subsequently prompting subscriptions not only from elsewhere in Tuscany, but also from other parts of Italy. Catholic associations – such as the women's section of *Azione Cattolica* – also contributed to the appeal.[23]

From mid 1941 onwards the local press and the bi-monthly periodical published by the Dominican community at San Domenico carried reports of particular acts of devotion towards Catherine by Italian soldiers and examples of incidents in which, it was believed, Catherine had miraculously intervened. In mid July, for example, an item in *La Nazione* reported on the faith in Catherine of a particular group of wounded who visited the Sanctuary, escorted by a Red Cross sister, but also observed that, ever since Siena had begun to receive Italian wounded for treatment in the city's hospitals, there had been an almost daily series of visits to the Sanctuary by some of the wounded themselves and by wives and mothers visiting others.[24] In September the paper then reported that the chaplain of the 131st tank regiment had written to Archbishop Toccabelli informing him that, at a service held at a field-altar, the regiment had adopted Catherine as their special patron saint.[25] The May–June and August–September editions of the Dominican periodical *S. Caterina da Siena*, meanwhile, carried pages devoted to testimonies of Catherine's protection of Italian soldiers and sailors, and of a recovery of sight by a wounded soldier after he had been blessed with the relic of Catherine's finger.[26] Also in September, it was reported that very high numbers were attending the services held every Sunday in the Sanctuary of Saint Catherine for a 'victorious peace' and for the protection of 'our soldiers'.[27]

It was not only in Siena, however, that appeals were made to Catherine for such ends. Thus, for example, a devotional image produced in Bologna in 1941 portrayed Catherine of Siena and Francis of Assisi standing above and looking protectively and prayerfully down towards an outline of Italy, including the islands of Sicily and Sardinia, which was in turn superimposed upon a sequence of silhouettes of famous monuments representing major Italian cities (Plate 15) – a device which clearly evoked the imagery of the poster for the first *Festa Nazionale* of 1940 designed by Bruno Marzi. These images were accompanied by the request that these two '*Grandi Santi, Francesco e Caterina, Patroni Principali d'Italia*' would bless and

---

document. Dottoressa Piccini's own brief account is the only other published analysis of the lamp and its origins of which I am aware, for which see Piccini (2004).

23 See the collected 'Scheda di sottoscrizione per l'offerta di una Lampada Votiva a S. Caterina da Siena' which are kept in a red box, decorated with gold and green embroidered thread and bearing the embroidered lettering 'S. Caterina da Siena'. See also Piccini (2004).

24 *La Nazione*, 13–14/7/1941, p. 4.

25 *La Nazione*, 14–15/9/1941, p. 4; *Il Popolo di Siena*, 14/9/1941, p. 3.

26 *S. Caterina da Siena, Patrona d'Italia*, 8, 1941, pp. 84, 130.

27 *La Nazione*, 16/9/1941, p. 4.

defend Italy and make her ever greater and more glorious. On the back of the image was a prayer to the two saints, again seeking their blessing on Italy and asking that they protect the nation from its enemies, inspire Italian soldiers to heroism, and that a victory would result in secure and lasting peace.[28]

As in the previous year, so also in 1942, the annual celebration of Catherine's experience of the stigmata prompted a *triduo* of prayer – in addition to the service held every week since the beginning of the war – for Italian servicemen, for the ending of the war and for peace with victory for Italy.[29] Two months later, the third *Festa Nazionale* for Catherine as *Patrona d'Italia* was again both highly patriotic and also highly military in tone. It is also possible, however, to detect the beginning of a subtle but significant shift in the rhetoric that accompanied the patriotic and military themes. In April 1942, despite the military reverses that Italy had already experienced, there clearly remained both the hope of and a belief in an Italian victory. Setbacks and defeats notwithstanding, it was not yet clear that the war would be lost, or that Italy was to be on the losing side. It was, however, already a longer, harder war than had been anticipated and the language surrounding the festival reflected this: whilst victory was still anticipated – and heavenly support for this end was still requested – there was now also greater emphasis upon the dangers faced and the sacrifices made by the Italian armed forces and upon the request for divine protection and oversight of them. Thus, in announcing the festival, Archbishop Toccabelli explained that its aim was to gather Italy's heroic soldiers, who were making supreme sacrifices on various fronts, under Catherine's protective cloak.[30] On the eve of the festival the front page of *Il Popolo di Siena* carried an editorial recalling that, when Catherine had been proclaimed *Patrona d'Italia* in June 1939, it had been hoped that her intercession would keep the horrors of war far from Italy; but now it was understood that Catherine would not only protect Italy in times of peace, but would also stand militantly by her side in time of war to assure justice and victory. The enemy, the editorial continued, remained powerful despite a series of defeats, whilst the decisive moment in the course of the war was approaching. Therefore, with both Cardinal Giovanni Battista Nasalli-Rocca of Bologna and the Apostolic Nuncio to Italy, Cardinal Francesco Borgongini Duca, present at the festival to represent 'Catholic Italy', all Italy – and especially the

---

28 A copy of the image and prayer may now be found among the pages relating to 1941 in the Notiziario compiled by Don Leopoldo Tuci and now in the Archivio Arcivescovile in Siena.

29 *Il Popolo di Siena*, 8/2/1942, p. 3; *La Nazione*, 7/2/1942, p. 2; 14/2/1942, p. 2; *Il Telegrafo*, 7/2/1942, p. 2; 14/2/1942, p. 2. There were also, it should be noted, other religious events in Siena which included prayers for the nation, for the Italian armed forces and for both peace and victory – as for example in the cathedral for the festival of Domenica in Albis 1942, when the chosen image for the festival was the *Madonna del Voto*, one of the most revered images of Sienese civil religion. On this occasion, too, Archbishop Toccabelli explicitly linked the festival to the fortunes of the nation in arms and its armed forces, for which see *Il Popolo di Siena*, 22/2/1942, p. 3; 12/4/1942, p. 1; 19/4/1942, p. 1; *Santa Caterina, Patrona d'Italia*, 9, 1942, pp. 54–6. In the present context, however, it is services, devotions and religious events specifically associated with Catherine and her cult that are the focus of attention.

30 *Il Popolo di Siena*, 19/4/1942, p. 1.

members of its armed forces – would look to Siena with a living faith and a secure hope. Siena in turn, the editorial affirmed, would proudly represent all Italians in praying to Catherine for her intercession with God for a blessing on Italy's soldiers and for the gift of victory.[31]

In the various reports that followed the festival on 29 and 30 April, the same tone was maintained, particular emphasis and attention being given to the ceremony of the '*solenne Benedizione delle Forze Armate*', given to troops on parade in the piazza at San Domenico – an event which that year was recorded by Italian state radio and subsequently broadcast to Italian forces on the various fronts in the war. In the presence of civil and military authorities, Cardinal Nasalli-Rocca prefaced the blessing with a highly patriotic address, calling upon Italian servicemen to look to Catherine's example, and asking her to bless Italy's soldiers, sailors and airmen, to be close to and aid those who were wounded, and to be present at the graves of the dead and bring them to the light of eternal joy. He asked also that Catherine give her wisdom to those who ruled Italy – the king and the 'condottiere' who, with the Pope, had secured the concordat that had resulted in Catherine's recognition as patron saint of Italy – and help Rome and Italy to live worthily in the present hour. After Nasalli-Rocca, Archbishop Toccabelli added a further blessing, in which he began by affirming again that all of Italy was spiritually present at the event – to which end he read a prayer to Catherine by the Governor of Rome, Giangiacomo Borghese, affirming that Rome and Italy looked to her in hope and faith and with renewed fervour as the nation sought to bring a just, Roman and Christian peace to the world. Toccabelli then added his own request that, in the present struggle for the greatness and liberty of the nation and justice in the world, Catherine would bless the king-emperor, the Duce and the nation's soldiers, sailors and airmen; would sustain them in battle, crown their sacrifice with victory and give peace and glory to the fallen. And finally he asked that, in the hour of the nation's destiny, Catherine would again show that she was the '*Mamma degli Italiani*'.[32]

The *Festa Nazionale* of 1942 was also the occasion for two further initiatives which brought together Catherine, the war and the Italian armed services. The first was the publication – dated 27 April to coincide with the *Festa Nazionale* – of a collection of the thoughts and exhortations of Saint Catherine, chosen and edited especially for the use of Italian soldiers. Entitled *La Patrona d'Italia ai Soldati d'Italia in Guerra* and edited by Luigi Sbaragli – the decorated military chaplain from the First World War who had subsequently become the chaplain to the *Balilla* and the *Piccole e Giovani Italiane* in Siena – the slim volume of 74 pages was designed to fit easily into a serviceman's pocket. Published under the joint auspices of the *Accademia degli Intronati* of Siena and the *Centro Nazionale di Studi Cateriniani* in Rome, the volume was divided into three sections headed '*Credere*', '*Obbedire*' and '*Combattere*', thereby corresponding to the three 'commandments' of Mussolini's slogan, 'Believe, Obey, Fight', each section containing material

31 *Il Popolo di Siena*, 26/4/1942, p. 1.

32 *Il Popolo di Siena*, 3/5/1942, pp. 1–2; *S. Caterina da Siena, Patrona d'Italia*, 9, 1942, pp. 68–72. See also *La Rivoluzione Fascista*, 4/5/1942, p. 3.

drawn from Catherine's letters and her *Dialogue*.[33] With a reproduction of the famous Andrea Vanni painting of Catherine opposite the title page, the volume also included a preface by Luigi Bonelli, a popular Sienese playwright, author and journalist, who had long been an enthusiastic member of the *Società Internazionale di Studi Cateriniani* in Siena and was by then also both rector of the *Accademia degli Intronati* in Siena and president of the *Centro Nazionale di Studi Cateriniani* in Rome.[34] Bonelli's preface was a fiercely patriotic evocation of Catherine's heroic virtues, which he hoped would inspire Italy's armed forces in the present war. Like them, Bonelli asserted, Catherine was born of the people and sacrificed her youth for the idea of Rome and in preaching a crusade. He concluded by asking his readers rhetorically, 'and is not your war a holy crusade?' The book, Bonelli concluded, which was destined to be read in cockpits, ships, tanks and the trenches of all the various fronts, was issued on the day that the troops, assembled at San Domenico and facing the '*sacrario dei martiri*', received a blessing on behalf of all the Italian forces then engaged in a supreme struggle against the enemies of Italy's culture and future.[35] As the reviewer of the book in the *Bullettino Senese di Storia Patria* observed enthusiastically, the collection presented Catherine not as a distant medieval voice, but as a living comrade whose thoughts would appropriately accompany Italian soldiers, sailors and airmen as they fought, on the order of the Duce, to save not only Latin and Roman civilization but also the future of the entire world. In the third part especially, under the heading '*Combattere*', the volume concluded with a series of extracts from Catherine's letters that illustrated her political aims of the liberation of the papacy, the pacification of Italy and the organization of a crusade against the infidels.[36] On the final page, a concluding footnote explained that the political teaching of Saint Catherine was that governments must act for the common good and not as destroyers of the people: rulers are to be fathers, not thieves. This was why, the footnote continued, there was a sad but just necessity to fight the rapacious governments that exploited their subject peoples – as today England typically did.[37]

The second initiative during the *Festa Nazionale* of 1942 was the decision to place a large book – usually described in contemporary sources as an 'Album' – in the Sanctuary of Saint Catherine in the room traditionally known as the '*cameretta*' or the '*celletta della Santa*', in which Catherine had spent years in prayer and devotion. A large and handsome volume, covered in white vellum secured by threaded leather ties, the front cover is embellished with two bands of black decoration ornamented

33 Sbaragli (1942).

34 For Bonelli, see his obituary notice in the *Bollettino Senese di Storia Patria*, 61, 1954, p. 178. The *Centro Nazionale di Studi Cateriniani* in Rome had been founded in 1940 by Mario Felice Bianchi. Its development was limited, however, by the outbreak and circumstances of the Second World War. It was subsequently revived in the 1960s.

35 Sbaragli (1942, pp. 3–7). The '*sacrario dei martiri*' was a reference to the crypt of San Domenico which was restored during the 1930s and inaugurated, in November 1938, as the 'Crypt of the Fascist Martyrs' of the city and province of Siena. For this episode in the history of San Domenico, see Parsons (2007).

36 Prunai (1942). See also *Il Telegrafo*, 2/5/1942, p. 2.

37 Sbaragli (1942, p. 74, n. 2).

with strips of white leather, and the invocation, '*Italiam Protege Tuam*', executed in black letters with red initials, the 'I' of '*Italiam*' being further enhanced by a blue floral design (Plate V).[38] The book also carries an elaborately inscribed frontispiece dated 29 April 1942 (Plate VI). The text of the frontispiece explains that, whilst all of Italy – now engaged in a 'struggle for greatness and liberty' – had joined spiritually with the bishops, Podestà, and other civil leaders of the Province of Siena to honour Catherine at her annual festival, and also in the broadcast blessing of all Italian soldiers, sailors and airmen, this book would now collect the names of individual Italian servicemen who wished to place themselves under the special protection of Catherine of Siena.[39] Archbishop Toccabelli had referred to the Album in his announcement of the details of the *Festa Nazionale* of 1942, when he spoke of drawing Italian soldiers beneath the cloak of Catherine's protection. The Album, he explained, would be available in the '*celletta della Santa*' for individuals to write their names, or for families to do so on their behalf, or for parish priests to do so at the request of soldiers, sailors and airmen serving far from the city.[40]

Despite the date of 29 April on the frontispiece and the reference to the book by Toccabelli in his announcement of the approaching festival of Saint Catherine, more substantial references to the Album in the local newspapers do not occur until September 1942 and, indeed, the opening page of the actual signatures in the Album is headed '*Agosto 1942*'. The two fullest accounts of the Album in the local press occurred in the edition of *La Nazione* of 12 September and the edition of *Il Popolo di Siena* of 27 September. *La Nazione* reported, under the headline, '*Mistica fede di combattenti per la Patrona d'Italia al Santuario di Fontebranda*', that it was notable that so many servicemen were making the 'pilgrimage' to the sanctuary of Saint Catherine to place their names in the Album. The article noted in particular that there were names from all the regions and all the cities of Italy, including the most remote parts of the nation, from 'Brennero' in the far north of Italy to the 'Capo Passero' at the southernmost point of Sicily. Similarly, the article reported, the signatures also represented all the different branches of the Italian armed forces and ranged from the highest ranks to the lowest. And when, the article continued, for obvious reasons, servicemen could not visit the Sanctuary themselves to place their names in the Album, then their mothers, wives, sisters and other relations could do so. The headline in *Il Popolo di Siena*, meanwhile, read '*Al Santuario di Fontebranda: Devozione dei combattenti per la Patrona d'Italia*' and emphasized, again, the comprehensive range of the signatures, in respect of both the various regions and cities of Italy and of the variety of military ranks represented. This article, too, emphasized the way in which relatives could place the names of their sons, husbands or brothers in the Album.[41]

---

38 The 'Album' is now held in the Archivio della Compagnia di S. Caterina, inventory number 128 [177] which, in turn, is kept by the Associazione Internazionale dei Caterinati, Siena.

39 The full text of the frontispiece is reproduced in Bacci (2002, p. 135).

40 *Il Popolo di Siena*, 19/4/1942, p. 1.

41 *La Nazione*, 12/9/1942, p. 2; *Il Popolo di Siena*, 27/9/1942, p. 2.

Examination of the Album itself amply confirms that such descriptions of the range and variety of the signatures were by no means mere rhetoric. From the very first page, names accompanied by a note that the signatory came from the city or province of Siena are mixed with others from elsewhere in Italy. The first page alone includes names of soldiers from Livorno, Empoli, Bologna and Castiglione Fiorentino, for example, whilst page six includes signatories from Livorno, Rome and Lucca, and page seven alone has names from Bari, Pistoia, Grosseto, Palermo, Arezzo, Forli, Verona, Florence and Naples. Some entries include the rank of the signatory and his military unit – and again the range and variety in both categories is, indeed, extensive. A further notable feature of the Album is the inclusion of entire groups of names, entered in the same handwriting, sometimes from a particular parish, and sometimes from a particular military unit. Pages one and two already include groups of names from parishes near Siena such as, for example, the 'Parrochia di Ponte a Tressa' and the 'Parrochia di Vignano', whilst three columns beginning on page 71 are filled by names entered by the parish priest of Vico d'Elsa. As for particular units, between pages 11 and 20, for example, each double column page is filled with the names – entered in meticulous handwriting – of legionnaires of the *97th Battaglione d'Assalto C.C. N.N.*, a local unit of the Fascist blackshirt militia, the *Milizia Volontaria per la Sicurezza Nazionale*.[42] Other entries can clearly be identified as made on behalf of individuals by relatives: thus, for example, on page 33 there is an entry for a soldier who is a prisoner of war and now in a POW camp in England; on page 65 an officer from Pistoia is listed as currently serving in Russia; and on page 69 another soldier is described as a prisoner of war in South Africa. Similarly, as an article in *La Nazione* explained, a military chaplain who was by then serving on the Russian front, Tenente Cappellano Don Flavio Pacchiarotti, had sent to the rector of the Sanctuary, Don Leopoldo Tuci, the names of a number of fellow officers who, 'together with their chaplain', wished to be entered into the Album to 'demonstrate their trust in the protection of Saint Catherine'.[43]

In addition to the weekly services for Italian soldiers and for victory, a further service of veneration of the crucifix of the stigmata was held in the Sanctuary of Saint Catherine, on 14 September 1942 with the particular intention of praying for the protection of Italian soldiers and an Italian victory.[44] In the bi-monthly periodical published by the community at San Domenico, it was reported that, in August, as part of a series of lectures on '*Grandi Senesi*' organized by the local *Istituto di Cultura Fascista*, Archbishop Toccabelli had spoken on Catherine of Siena, applying the 'motto of the New Italy': 'Believe, Obey, Fight' to the life of the saint – and thus clearly also evoking the text of the book of Catherine's thoughts edited by Luigi Sbaragli for Italian soldiers earlier in the year.[45] In November, Toccabelli

42 For this battalion of the MVSN, often described in the local press as the '97.a Legione "Senese"', see also *La Nazione*, 31/1/1943, p. 2; 13–14/6/1943, p. 2; *La Rivoluzione Fascista*, 1/2/1943, p. 2.

43 *La Nazione*, 24/9/1942, p. 2. The name of Tenente Cappellano Pacchiarotti, together with 17 officers from his unit, appears on page 107 of the Album.

44 *La Nazione*, 15/9/1942, p. 2; *Il Telegrafo*, 12/9/1942, p. 2.

45 *S. Caterina da Siena, Patrona d'Italia*, 9, 1942, p. 86.

also gave a series of addresses on Catherine as *Patrona d'Italia* in Calabria and Sicily, the lecture in Palermo being, again, at the invitation of the *Istituto Nazionale Fascista di Cultura*. The same source also published further examples of testimonies from soldiers who claimed to have been saved or healed as a result of Catherine's intervention.[46]

The subtle shift in language that had already begun to be evident in 1942, in invocations of Catherine in relation to Italy's role in the war and the Italian armed forces, became much more pronounced during 1943. By then the tide of the war had evidently turned. After the allied victory at El Alamein in late October 1942 and the subsequent allied landings in French North Africa in November, the German and Italian forces in North Africa faced defeat. That defeat in turn brought the prospect of an invasion of Sicily and then the Italian mainland much closer. In Russia, meanwhile, the failure of the German attack on Stalingrad, followed by the encirclement of the German sixth army within the city, was the prelude to the beginning of the long retreat from the eastern front – a retreat which included the members of the Italian army, numbering some 240,000 in total, that Mussolini had sent to Russia to support the German invasion of the Soviet Union. The changing fortunes of war had already been reflected in the changed tone of the rhetoric that occurred in the publications and official announcements of the *Ordinariato Militare* and its co-ordination of the work of Italian military chaplains. Whereas, during the mid and late 1930s and the early years of the Second World War, the *Ordinariato Militare* had adopted a strongly patriotic, nationalistic and militaristic note, from late 1942 and early 1943 onwards Italy's worsening military position prompted a clear and rapid change of tone. In place of the previous emphasis on the certainty of victory and on ideological support for the Fascist regime, the focus turned decisively to the need for spiritual assistance and support for the faith of Italian servicemen.[47] A similar pattern also occurred in Siena in the language used in relation to Catherine and her cult in the context of the war. Whilst patriotic and overtly militant language and requests that Catherine lend her support to an Italian victory did not disappear altogether, they now became less frequent, whilst emphasis on placing loved ones under the special protection of Catherine assumed new prominence.

Whilst signatures continued to accumulate in the Album at the Sanctuary of Saint Catherine, at the end of January 1943 a second process was initiated whereby individual Italian servicemen could be placed under the special protection of Saint Catherine, again either at their own request or that of their relatives. In the afternoon of 31 January, after delivering an address on the subject of Saint Catherine and the military – in which he discussed Catherine's contact with military leaders and argued that her moral and religious ideals for soldiers were discipline, loyalty and commitment even to the sacrifice of self to one's cause – the new parish priest of San Domenico, Padre Giacinto D'Urso, announced a new initiative, namely, the '*Consacrazione dei Militari alla Patrona d'Italia*'. Noting that, in the present circumstances, it was the courage and sacrifice of Italy's soldiers that would decide the destiny of the nation, D'Urso explained that, beginning that day and continuing

46 *S. Caterina da Siena, Patrona d'Italia*, 9, 1942, pp. 130, 133–4.

47 Franzinelli (1991, pp. 146–7).

on the last Sunday of each month, there would be a ceremony at the altar of Saint Catherine. As parish priest of San Domenico, he would read out the names of members of the military who had either asked personally, or whose families had asked on their behalf, that they be placed under the special protection of Saint Catherine. Their names would then be placed under the reliquary that contained Catherine's head. Each serviceman thus named would also receive a small image of Saint Catherine with, on the reverse side, confirmation that his name had been added to those thus consecrated, the text of a brief popular Sienese prayer to Catherine and a quotation from the words of reassurance from Catherine which Raymond of Capua claimed to have experienced at the moment of her death. Each serviceman would also receive a letter from Padre D'Urso explaining the significance of the '*Consacrazione dei Militari alla Patrona d'Italia*', assuring him of Catherine's mission to protect those dedicated to her, and promising that he would be remembered regularly in San Domenico. The letter also asked recipients to write to D'Urso to request other images of Catherine, to report examples of help received from her, or names of other soldiers who wished to have their names added to the list of those consecrated to the saint. He also asked that the recipients show the letter to their military chaplains so that they might also write to him with further names.[48]

The by now customary *triduo* of prayer again took place in the Sanctuary of Saint Catherine in March 1943 as part of the annual festival to mark Catherine's experience of the stigmata. The tone was, however, significantly changed from previous years. Prayers were still offered to Catherine for the nation and its soldiers but in reports of the *triduo* reference to victory was conspicuous by its absence; instead emphasis fell upon the numbers who visited the *celletta della Santa* to add names to the Album.[49] The *Festa Nazionale* of 1943, on the other hand, represented a combination of the earlier patriotic style and the newer more sombre tone. Thus, in reporting on the *Festa Nazionale* of April 1943, *La Nazione* continued to speak of Italian forces fighting 'like eagles and lions for the defence of the sacred soil of their nation against the barbarism of the east and the arrogance of the west'.[50] Similarly, the address given by Cardinal Adeodato Piazza, at the blessing of the representative members of the armed forces – on this occasion assembled at the new Portico dei Comuni at the Sanctuary (Plate 16) – was notable for its continuing insistence on the possibility of an Italian victory and its continued use of the rhetoric of a victorious Italy which would teach all peoples the examples of the human

48 *S. Caterina da Siena, Patrona d'Italia*, 10, 1943, pp. 38–40. See also *La Nazione*, 31/1/1943, p. 2; 2/2/1943, p. 2; *Il Telegrafo*, 31/1/1943, p. 2. The quotation attributed to Catherine printed on the reverse of the image was her assurance, 'Do not fear; I am in heaven for you; I will protect and defend you', mystically experienced by Raymond at the moment of her death. It was subsequently reported that there had been an enthusiastic response to the *Consacrazione*, particular examples of requests from individual soldiers being cited, for which see *S. Caterina da Siena, Patrona d'Italia*, 10, 1943, pp. 54–6. See also *Il Popolo di Siena*, 21/3/1943, p. 3.

49 *Il Popolo di Siena*, 21/2/1943, p. 2; *La Nazione*, 5/3/1943, p. 2.

50 *La Nazione*, 28/4/1943, p. 2.

and Christian civilization of '*Roma immortale*'.[51] The blessing of the armed forces assembled at the new Portico was, once again, transmitted by radio to the rest of the Italian armed forces. At the same time, however, as the report in *Il Popolo di Siena* observed, those at the festival would offer their prayers to Catherine as '*Mamma*' and present their intercessions to her on behalf of all that Italians held most dear – their families, their relatives serving in the armed forces, their dead and the Italian people suffering under the effects of war.[52]

The *Festa Nazionale* in honour of Catherine in April 1943 also included the culmination of the project for a Votive Lamp dedicated to her. On 29 April, before the blessing of the armed forces, the Lamp was carried in procession by four women, past a parade of troops, into the Sanctuary of Saint Catherine (Plate 17). Taken to the high altar of the Church of the Crucifix in the Sanctuary, the lamp was blessed by Cardinal Piazza and then formally lit by the mother of Marcello Giuggioli, a Sienese airman killed in Spain in 1937 and posthumously awarded a *Medaglia d'Oro*.[53] The work of the sculptor Giovanni Cappelletti, the Votive Lamp – which still burns in the Church of the Crucifix in the Sanctuary of Saint Catherine – consists of a pendant lamp set above a shallow hemispherical bowl for the oil (Plate VII). The outer surface of the bowl is subdivided by a series of mouldings which frame four narrative scenes portraying a series of scenes from Catherine's life, namely: her efforts to pacify hostile civic factions; her presence at the execution of Niccolò di Toldo; the dictation of her letters; and her role in persuading Pope Gregory XI to return to Rome from Avignon. Placed directly above these scenes on the upper rim of the bowl are four statuettes in bronze representing different branches of the Italian armed services: a soldier, an airman, a sailor and a second soldier in colonial uniform. Above the four servicemen and raised on an elaborate plinth is a standing figure of Catherine of Siena with her right hand raised in a gesture of blessing and her left hand holding a lily as a symbol of her purity. A Latin inscription in raised gilt bronze letters, interposed between the four statuettes of servicemen and the scenes from Catherine's life, asserts that the flame of the lamp, lit by the faith of Italian hearts, burns in eternal intercession for the destiny of the nation. The year 1943 is then recorded, both in the form 'MCMXXXXIII' and also in the official Fascist style as 'F.R.XXI'.[54] The lamp thus embodied the profound ambiguity of the

51 *S. Caterina da Siena, Patrona d'Italia*, 10, 1943, pp. 62–5. Cardinal Piazza, it has been noted, was 'universally regarded as a warm friend of the regime', Binchy (1977, p. 625), and still, in May 1943, expressing his solidarity with Italian troops and 'preaching that nations could not die', Bosworth (2005, p. 489), an assertion that he included in his address at the blessing of the armed forces in Siena.

52 *Il Popolo di Siena*, 28/4/1943, p. 1.

53 *Il Popolo di Siena*, 28/4/1943, p. 2; *La Nazione*, 28/4/1943, p. 2; *Il Telegrafo*, 30/4/1943, p. 2; 1/5/1943, p. 2; *S. Caterina da Siena, Patrona d'Italia*, 10, 1943, p. 62. See also Piccini (2004).

54 The Latin quotation reads: CELSAE FORTUNIS PATRIAE PER SAECLA FOVENDIS FULGEAT ITALICUS CONCITA PECTORIBUS SENIS A.D. MCMXXXXIII F.R. XXI. For a detailed analysis and description of the lamp, see Riedl and Seidel (1992a, p. 251). It should be noted, however, that the transcription of the Latin inscription presented in the latter source is not fully accurate.

Festa Nazionale in honour of Catherine in 1943. Bearing a date rendered in Fascist form, and first conceived two years earlier when an Italian victory still seemed a possibility, it was now given by Italian women, not for Italian victory, but for the protection of their husbands, sons and brothers in the Italian armed forces as the tide of war had already turned against Italy.

In June 1943 two articles in the Sienese press eloquently and explicitly linked together the Votive Lamp and the Album of signatures in the Sanctuary of Saint Catherine (Plates V–VII). On 8 June, a brief article in *Il Telegrafo* reported that a military chaplain who was a veteran of the Russian front had recently celebrated mass in the Sanctuary of Saint Catherine. The chaplain in question was Tenente Cappellano Don Flavio Pacchiarotti – who had previously written to the rector of the Sanctuary to ask for his name and those of others in his unit to be entered in the Album. Don Pacchiarotti, the article explained, had celebrated a propitiatory mass for the nation and for the protection of Italian combatants. In his sermon, it was reported, he recalled how, in the hardest battles of the previous winter in Russia, officers and men had prayed with great faith to Saint Catherine as the patron of Italy. He also affirmed that the new Votive Lamp given by the women of Italy symbolized the faith of Italian soldiers, sailors and airmen in the patronage and protection of Catherine – a faith which was also revealed in the signatures, which increased every day, in the book placed in the '*Cella della Santa*'.[55] Subsequently, on 26 June, *La Nazione* carried a longer article contributed by Don Pacchiarotti himself. After evoking the atmosphere of the Sanctuary and reminding readers that it was three years since Pope Pius XII had officially proclaimed Catherine a patron saint of Italy, he asserted that, as all Italian mothers knew well, the *Patrona d'Italia* favoured especially the best of Italy's sons, namely its military forces. He then retold the story of the origins of the Album of signatures, explaining again that families, chaplains and commanding officers had sent lists of names to be included, and describing the pages of the Album and the way in which all ranks and units of the armed forces were represented there. Speaking 'as if to his companions and comrades' of the Russian front, Pacchiarotti explained that he had entered their names, with his own, into the Album and had prayed for them and for all their fellow soldiers who had died in the snows of the Russian steppes. He then gave his own description and celebration of the Votive Lamp, which he described as given to Saint Catherine by the women of Italy, on the initiative of the women of Siena, asking the '*Patrona d'Italia*' to grant victory to Italy's forces and a better tomorrow. Pacchiarotti concluded by assuring Italian soldiers, sailors and airmen that, together with the rector of the Sanctuary, 'Don Poldo', he had prayed for them all, echoing the prayer printed on the posters for the previous national celebration of Saint Catherine: '*S. Catherina, Italiam protege tuam!*'[56]

By mid 1943, however, the course of the war had turned even more decisively against Italy. On 10 July the allies landed in Sicily – and in August the Sienese papers reported a special mass in the Sanctuary of Saint Catherine for the tank regiment that had adopted Catherine as its patron and had recently fought in the

55 *Il Telegrafo*, 8/6/1943, p. 2.

56 *La Nazione*, 26/6/1943, p. 2.

battles for Sicily. At the service, which was attended by the civil and military authorities of Siena, the members of the regiment gave thanks for their deliverance from the battles and remembered especially their dead in Sicily, their wounded and those taken prisoner, whilst Archbishop Toccabelli, in his sermon, encouraged the regiment to renew its commitment to 'Mother Italy'.[57] By the time that mass took place, however, Mussolini had already been deposed for a month, and only two weeks later, on 8 September, the new government led by the king and Marshall Badoglio signed an armistice with the allies, also changing sides in the war. Thus began the traumatic final years of the war in Italy with the nation divided between a south liberated by the allies and a north occupied by the German army, supported by Mussolini's re-established Fascist Republic of Salò and – in the occupied centre and north – a state of de facto civil war between partisans and the continuing Fascist authorities and the Germans.

From autumn 1943 onwards, the Album of signatures in the Sanctuary of Saint Catherine in Siena reflected the changing fortunes and circumstances of the war. From mid September 1943 – after the Italian armistice with the allies on 8 September and the de facto division of Italy – the Italian names in the Album began to be joined by the names of German soldiers who, now part of the occupying German army in central and northern Italy, also wished to place themselves under Catherine's protection. In the pages for the period immediately after 8 September 1943 there also appeared a group of entries which stand out from the rest of the Album because of their highly politicized content. One of the most striking aspects of the Album as a whole is the general absence of ideological statements or sentiments accompanying signatures: usually the most detail that is added is a rank, a unit, a hometown, a detail such as the front the soldier is serving on or a note that he is a prisoner of war. Overt political rhetoric is strikingly absent. It is this which makes three entries on page 150 of the Album so distinctive, for in these cases Italian soldiers still loyal to Mussolini and the continuing Fascist government in the centre and north of the country made a point of adding highly politicized comments to their names. In the first case, members of the 'San Marco' battalion asked for protection of their unit and for support in removing their hated enemy, the English, from the sacred soil of Italy. In the second, the 'M Padova' battalion sought protection as they aimed to 'redeem the honour of the nation by the offer of their young lives', and a third brief entry asked Catherine to protect and watch over Rome that she might regain her authentic and civilizing influence in the world.[58] All three entries clearly reflected the traumatic emotional and psychological impact of Italy's armistice with the allies upon young Italian soldiers still personally committed to the Fascist cause. After these three entries the signatures in the Album again revert to being simply names, with perhaps also name, rank, unit or place of origin, but without other observation. German names become increasingly numerous, especially in April, May and June 1944.

---

57 *Il Popolo di Siena*, 29/8/1943, p. 3; *La Nazione*, 24/8/1943, p. 2.

58 The details in this paragraph are the result of careful inspection of the Album by the author in September 2006. Having examined each page of signatures, these entries were the only ones that I identified as including overt ideological content.

At the end of April 1944 the festival of Saint Catherine was again celebrated in Siena, but in a manner that reflected the critical circumstances of the war. The battles at Anzio and Cassino continued to hold back the allied advance northwards. In the centre and north of Italy – including southern Tuscany – Italian partisans were in conflict with both the German army and the forces of Mussolini's Republic of Salò. Reports of the festival that year are, unsurprisingly, rare but clearly convey both the necessarily reduced nature of the ceremonies and the profound ambiguity that attended them. In March, Archbishop Toccabelli called for a 'crusade of prayer' to Saint Catherine, as '*Patrona d'Italia*', and for offerings for the continued restoration of the Sanctuary and the completion of the Portico dei Comuni.[59] In *Il Popolo di Siena*, the report of the festival itself was headed simply, '*Protegge, o Caterina, la tua Italia*', and included no reference to either the Votive Lamp or the blessing of the armed forces, although it was noted that the civic authorities still offered the customary votive candles at the Sanctuary and San Domenico.[60] A later retrospective account, published in the periodical edited by the Dominicans of San Domenico, in early 1946, supplied some contextualization of the earlier contemporary report. For Siena in April 1944, this brief report noted, the climax of the war was approaching, with central and northern Italy under the '*dominazione nazifascista*', and with Siena more or less cut off from the rest of Italy because of air-raids and disruption of transport. The festival of Saint Catherine was nevertheless held, the account continued, but without any blessing of the armed forces which, it was said, was wisely omitted because the ceremony could have been interpreted as a sign of political approval of Mussolini's Republic of Salò – which the report described as the 'dying neo-Fascist republic'.[61]

Just over two months later, on the morning of 3 July, Siena was liberated by allied forces as they advanced northwards. As the front approached Siena in June the Sienese had rededicated their city to its principal heavenly patron, the Virgin, thereby reviving a practice of the civic authorities of earlier centuries on occasions when Siena had faced severe crises. The rededication had taken place on 18 June and thus on the fifth anniversary of the official proclamation of Catherine as '*Patrona d'Italia*'.[62] On 29 June, in San Domenico, a day of prayer for the salvation of the city was also held to mark the anniversary of Catherine's canonization.[63]

---

59 *Il Popolo di Siena*, 19/3/1944, p. 1.

60 *Il Popolo di Siena*, 30/4/1944, p. 1.

61 *S. Caterina da Siena, Patrona d'Italia*, 11, Jan–Feb 1946, p. 13, '*... la benedizione alle forze armate ... fu sapientemente soppressa perchè la cerimonia non fosse interpretata come un'adesione politica alla moribonda repubblica neofascista*'. The *Bollettino*, which had run, in various formats, since 1922, ceased publication in September 1943 and only resumed in January–February 1946. The first number of the renewed *Bollettino* included a brief review of important events that had occurred in San Domenico in the intervening years.

62 For the origins of the rededication and its subsequent commemoration see Parsons (2001).

63 *S. Caterina da Siena, Patrona d'Italia*, 11, Jan–Feb 1946, p. 14. The same source also notes that, from 14 to 16 July there was a *triduo* of prayer in thanksgiving to Catherine in San Domenico.

The liberation also witnessed the beginning of a further chapter in the history of devotion to Catherine during the Second World War. In the right hand column of page 155 of the Album of signatures held in the Sanctuary of Saint Catherine there appears, inserted as a break within the flow of names, the date '*3 Luglio 1944*', an entry made – almost certainly by Don Leopoldo Tuci – to mark the date on which Siena was liberated by allied forces.[64] The signatures which follow immediately are overwhelmingly French – reflecting the fact that it was French troops that initially liberated Siena.[65] A handwritten entry in the collection of press cuttings and notes relating to the Sanctuary of Saint Catherine compiled by Leopoldo Tuci – placed opposite a page of press cuttings about the annual celebration of Catherine's festival in 1944 – also records that on the morning of 3 July senior officers and four chaplains assisted in a celebration of mass in the Sanctuary.[66] Although not stated explicitly, it seems overwhelmingly probable that the officers and chaplains were members of the French units that had liberated Siena that morning.

Within five pages, however, the signatures of soldiers of other allied nations begin to appear in the Album, including Americans, Britons, South Africans, New Zealanders, Canadians, Mauritians and British officers of the Indian Army.[67] In the front of the Album, there still remains the handwritten notice that clearly accompanied the Album during the war years – both before and after the liberation of Siena in July 1944. On one side appears the simple text, '*Album per i coli militari che vogliono in modo speciale esser protette dalla grande e amabile Mamma*'. On the other side appears a literal English translation: 'Album for the sole use of military personnel who wish especially for the protection of the great and loving mother (St Catherine).' Ink-stained and well-worn, it seems likely that the notice is the original one that accompanied the Album – the Italian version clearly being the original notice for Italian soldiers between 1942 and 1944 and the English version a translation for English-speaking soldiers after July 1944.[68] The signatures of various allied nationalities then continue with increasing variety until the end of the war. They also begin to include Italian names again, presumably now mainly, if not entirely, those of Italian soldiers of the re-constituted Royal Italian Army now fighting alongside allied forces in the campaign to liberate northern Italy.[69] Across

64 The judgement that the entry is by Tuci is based not only on the fact that he was rector of the Sanctuary but also on comparison of the handwriting in this case with that in Tuci's 'Notiziario' in the Archivio Arcivescovile of Siena.

65 They also, however, include the name Wynford Vaughan Thomas together with a note that he was a BBC war correspondent in Italy.

66 Tuci, 'Notiziario', Archivio Arcivescovile of Siena.

67 Similarly, it was also noted that, following the liberation, many allied soldiers visited San Domenico to express their devotion to Catherine, for which see, again, *S. Caterina da Siena, Patrona d'Italia*, 11, Jan–Feb 1946, p. 14.

68 When examined by the author in September 2006, the notice was lodged between the cover and the first decorated page of the Album, before the frontispiece recording the original dedication of the book.

69 Tenente Cappellano Don Flavio Pacchiarotti – who had celebrated mass in the Sanctuary in 1943 and had written of the Album and the Votive Lamp in the local papers – subsequently became a chaplain with these forces. Evidence for this may be found in the

the top of pages 205 and 206 of the Album, again almost certainly in Leopoldo Tuci's hand, there appear the words, '*29 aprile 1945 – Firma della resa a Caserta con termine della guerra in Italia*', thus announcing the German surrender and the end of the war in Italy.

Read superficially, the Album could easily be dismissed as no more than a telling demonstration of the inherent contradictions of intercession in wartime. Initiated in 1942 when – as the local papers in Siena make clear – Italians could still hope that they might be on the winning side, the early signatures were entered into the book when Catherine was still routinely invoked not only as a special heavenly protector of Italian service personnel but also as one who might help Italy secure 'victory and a just peace'. By 1943–44, the context in which names were entered had changed utterly. Now German names joined Italian ones in a context in which, whilst Catherine's special protection was still sought, her aid in securing an Italian victory was no longer a prominent theme. Finally, the names of various allied nationalities came to predominate, as numerous non-Italian soldiers sought the protection of Catherine of Siena as they faced the dangers of the Italian campaign. It is possible, of course, to interpret – or, indeed, merely dismiss – this process of transition as no more than a demonstration of both the essential ineffectiveness of intercession and the convenient mutability of religious devotion in time of war. But it is also possible to interpret the Album more positively – and more humanely – as a religious artefact which transcended its original context and the narrowly patriotic ethos of its origins and became a moving testimony to the desire of soldiers of various nationalities, and on both sides in the war, to place themselves under the special oversight and protection of Catherine of Siena – a point which Don Leopoldo Tuci himself made in an article in *La Voce del Popolo*, the renamed local Sienese Catholic paper, in September 1945.[70]

In the same way that he had noted the German surrender and the end of the war in Italy in the Album of signatures, Don Tuci also placed a similar note on the relevant page of his collection of recollections and cuttings relating to the Sanctuary of Saint Catherine. Dated Sunday 6 May, the entry recorded a solemn Te

---

Archivio Arcivescovile in Siena. Among the papers of Archbishop Toccabelli is a substantial file of letters written to him during the war by military chaplains from the archdiocese of Siena. These include a series of letters from Pacchiarotti, including several from his time on the Russian front; a formal release of Pacchiarotti back to the diocese dated 20 July 1944, signed by the then head of the *Ordinariato Militare*, Angelo Bartolomasi and commending his service in Russia; and then further letters to Toccabelli from Pacchiarotti, sent from northern Italy in the closing days of the war where he was serving with the Royal Italian Army. The letters may be found in the file numbered 2998 in the inventory of the Archivio Arcivescovile.

70 *La Voce del Popolo*, 16/9/1945, p. 2. Despite Don Leopoldo's reflections in 1945, however, the Album of signatures received little subsequent attention. After the pages noting the end of the war in Italy, the book continues with numbered pages, up to page 233 and the date 6 April 1948. During this time Italian signatures mix with further French, British and American ones, not all of them now military. After that, signatures continue to be entered, for a further 14 unnumbered pages, covering the period 1948 to 1952, and then resume briefly for the years 1964 to 1966, the final signatures bearing the date 28/29 April 1966.

Deum in thanks for the surrender signed at Caserta on 29 April, noting specifically that this was the day on which Catherine's death was commemorated each year.[71] The signing of the German surrender had indeed taken place on the middle day of Catherine's annual festival in 1945, which was celebrated in Siena from 28 to 30 April. In mid April Archbishop Toccabelli called upon the Sienese to celebrate the recurrence of Catherine's annual festival, noting that, while parts of Italy remained under enemy oppression and still at war, and while even cities already free could not send representatives to the festival because of inadequate communications and transport, the Sienese must represent all Italians in front of Catherine.[72] With the end of the war now clearly imminent and the front far to the north of Siena, in addition to the offering of candles by the civic authorities at the Sanctuary and San Domenico, the relic of Catherine's head was also restored to its customary place in San Domenico, having been placed in a niche in the crypt of the church since 1942 to protect it from possible damage as a result of bombing. The blessing of representatives of the armed forces – assembled in the piazza at the Portico in the Sanctuary – was also restored to the ceremonies. On this occasion, the blessing and accompanying address was given by the new bishop appointed to head the *Ordinariato Militare* in the post-Fascist era, Carlo Ferrero Cavallerleone. The event was described, retrospectively, as a 'blessing of the resurgent [or resurrected] Italian army'. Once again, however, the Votive Lamp remained unmentioned.[73]

The coincidence of Catherine's festival and the German surrender in Italy was also the subject of a small printed devotional text published and distributed in Siena to mark the sixth anniversary of Catherine's proclamation as '*Patrona d'Italia*'. Anyone who sees the unfolding of a providential design in the events of human history, the text asserted, must see the spiritual significance of the occurrence of the German surrender and the official cessation of hostilities in Italy on the anniversary of Catherine's death and the date of the annual celebration of her festival. (The German forces, meanwhile, were now described as an army that, with 'vindictive, Teutonic stubbornness', had made Italy the theatre of an 'exterminatory struggle'.) Now, however, the text continued, the nightmare that had afflicted Italy for almost five years had been dispelled at the same time as the bishop of the renewed Italian army had blessed the nation's soldiers in Catherine's name. The singular coincidence of the two dates, the text concluded, would strengthen the gratitude and devotion of Italians towards Catherine. As well as being distributed publicly, the text was also reproduced in the first edition of *La Voce del Popolo*, the refounded and renamed local Catholic newspaper in Siena.[74]

The small text produced in June 1945, contrasted markedly with the prayer that had been composed – and reproduced in the same devotional format – in June

71 Tuci, 'Notiziario', Archivio Arcivescovile di Siena.

72 *Corriere del Mattino*, 21/4/1945, p. 2.

73 *Rinascita*, 29/4/1945, p. 2; 3/5/1945, p. 2; *Corriere del Mattino*, 4/5/1945, p. 2; *S. Caterina da Siena, Patrona d'Italia*, 11, Jan–Feb 1946, p. 15.

74 *La Voce del Popolo*, 17/6/1945, p. 2. A copy of the original text may be found in Leopoldo Tuci's 'Notiziario', together with a note in Tuci's hand that a thousand copies were distributed.

1940. The former, entitled a 'Prayer for Victory and Peace', had looked forward to the glorious victory of the Italian armed forces under the leadership of the king and the Duce and in the cause of the nation's mission of upholding truth, justice and Christian civilization. The latter celebrated the deliverance of Italy from the destruction and horror of a ruinous war and the blessing of a 'renewed' Italian army. The contrast between the two texts encapsulated the dramatic transformation that had occurred, within just five years, in the cult of Catherine of Siena as '*Patrona d'Italia*'. It also prefigured the reconstruction of Catherine's image and role as '*Patrona d'Italia*' that was to follow in the post-war era.

Plate 11 Arturo Viligiardi, 1928, Bust of Saint Catherine of Siena, Pincio Gardens, Rome

Plate 12 Festival of Saint Catherine of Siena, 1940, procession with the head of Saint Catherine passing in front of the Palazzo Pubblico

Plate 13 Festival of Saint Catherine of Siena, 1940, laying the foundation stone of the Portico dei Comuni at the Sanctuary of Saint Catherine

Spedizione in abbonamento postale
SIENA - APRILE 1940 XVIII N. 5 Supplemento al N. 15 del "Popolo di Siena"

LA PATRONA D'ITALIA

Solenni Festeggiamenti Nazionali in onore di S. Caterina da Siena Patrona d'Italia
SIENA 4 - 30 APRILE 1940 XVIII

FOGLIO DI INFORMAZIONI

Il presente Foglio viene distribuito gratuitamente. E lasciato alla generosità dei Signori Lettori di far recapitare un'offerta al Comitato Ordinatore delle Feste — Dirigere al Comitato: Palazzo Arcivescovile - Siena.

Nella luce e nel fuoco dei Santi la Chiesa e la Patria innalzano, accanto a S. Francesco d'Assisi, S. Caterina da Siena, Patrona d'Italia, esempio ed auspicio di cristiana italica grandezza.
Le solenni Feste Nazionali, sotto l'alto patronato del DUCE, si sono iniziate domenica gloriosamente, e gloriosamente si svolgono, fra preci e canti, trofei di fiori e di bandiere, musiche ed acclamazioni.
E' un trionfo di gloria, che sfolgora su la Chiesa e su la Patria. E in questa gloria, Cattolici, Italiani, Senesi, eleviamoci, elevando i nostri pensieri ed i nostri cuori per impermearli di tanto amore, per allenarli a tanta grandezza, e renderci ognora più degni di tanta glorificazione, che sfavilla su Roma, su l'Italia, sul Mondo!

Plate 14 Cover of the *Foglio di Informazione issued as a supplement to Il Popolo di Siena,* 14 April 1940

Plate 15 Catherine of Siena and Francis of Assisi as Patron Saints of Italy, devotional image, printed in Bologna, 1941

Plate 16. Festival of Saint Catherine of Siena, 1943, blessing of representatives of the Italian armed forces at the Portico dei Comuni at the Sanctuary of Saint Catherine

Plate 17 Festival of Saint Catherine of Siena, 1943, procession carrying the Votive Lamp in honour of Saint Catherine into the Sanctuary of Saint Catherine for its inaugural blessing

Plate 18 Francesco Messina, 1962, Statue of Saint Catherine of Siena, Castel Sant'Angelo, Rome

Plate 19 Francesco Messina, 1962, Monument to Saint Catherine of Siena, showing scenes from her life, Castel Sant'Angelo, Rome

Plate 20 Francesco Messina, 1962, Monument to Saint Catherine of Siena, rear view showing symbols of institutions that contributed to the monument, Castel Sant'Angelo, Rome

Plate 21 Bruno Burrachini, 1972, Statue of Saint Catherine, Viale dei Mille, Siena

Chapter 4

From '*Patrona d'Italia*' to '*Patrona d'Europa*': the Cult of Saint Catherine of Siena 1946–2007

In April 1946, in the renamed local Catholic paper, *La Voce del Popolo*, Archbishop Toccabelli published a call to the Sienese to celebrate the first *Festa Nazionale* in honour of Catherine of the post-war era. Recalling that a year previously the war in Italy had ended as the festival was celebrated, but also looking forward to the following year and the occurrence of the sixth centenary of Catherine's birth, Toccabelli observed that Italy had particular need of heavenly assistance as it approached the elections for the post-war Constituent Assembly that was to lay the foundations of Italy's post-war political system and define its new democratic constitution.[1] Similarly, in its anticipation of the forthcoming festival, *La Nazione* concluded by affirming that, in the difficult times that Italy then faced, the figure of Saint Catherine stood – high above all their sorrows, afflictions and disagreements – as a symbol of the resurrection of the nation and of unity and peace among Italians.[2]

As *La Voce del Popolo* reported, the *Festa Nazionale* of 1946 took place over three days, from 28 to 30 April, with the offering of votive candles by the civic authorities at both the Sanctuary of Saint Catherine and at San Domenico on the evening of the 28th, celebration of the festival at the Sanctuary on the 29th including the blessing of Italy and representative members of its armed forces in the afternoon, and a further series of celebrations in San Domenico on the 30th – thus at one and the same time repeating the structure of the festival in previous years and establishing its continuity into the post-war period. At the blessing of the armed forces and of Italy at the Portico dei Comuni addresses were given both by Archbishop Toccabelli and by the minister for post, Mario Scelba, who was present as a representative of the Italian provisional government – thereby establishing a precedent that was to become a regular feature of the annual *Festa Nazionale* of the post-war period. Scelba invoked Catherine as an inspiration and comfort for Italians in the task of post-war reconstruction, recalled her mission to the Pope at Avignon as an example of an action that was at once both religious and political, and affirmed that, just as Catherine acted between the two forces of church and state, so the collaboration of

1 *Voce del Popolo*, 27/4/1946, p. 1 The elections were held on 2 June 1946, together with the referendum to decide between a republic or a continuation of the monarchy.

2 *La Nazione, Cronaca di Siena*, 27/4/1946, p. 2.

these two powers was also now the guarantee of prosperity and peace.[3] Toccabelli, meanwhile, in his address before imparting the blessing to the armed forces and to Italy – a task which on this occasion fell to him because Cardinal Nicola Canali, who was to have attended on behalf of the Vatican, was unable to do so due to illness – gave an address which, in its echoes of the language of the festivals of 1940 to 1943, reflected the profound and enduring ambiguity of his own political views and sentiments. Evoking the nation's geographical identity as a country dominated by the Appenines and surrounded by the Alps and the sea, he affirmed that, despite the multiplicity of its regions, Italy nevertheless had a shared history, tradition and purpose, namely, to be the guardian of Rome, because Rome in turn was the defender of truth, justice and peace in the world. In tragic times for the church, he continued, Catherine's mission had, inevitably, been deeply Italian. It had been a religious mission certainly, but also a social one, of love and of peace; and in addition a political one because of the extent to which Italy had suffered from foreign interference in Catherine's day. Now, he continued, Italy again had particular need of Catherine because the social, moral and political miseries that were the tragic inheritance of the war had left Italians disorientated and divided. In the light of their tragic recent history – and at a time when the nation was not yet fully free because its future remained in the hands of the modern foreigners who had been the victors in the Second World War – Italians needed assistance from Catherine as their '*Patrona*' and as the '*grande mamma degli italiani*'. Christian, Catholic Italy, Toccabelli, concluded, which had been the mother and teacher of the nations for 2,000 years, had particular need of Catherine's help now because there was a danger that the light of her traditional faith would be extinguished by the influence of people who knew nothing of the spirit or of God.[4]

The report of the *Festa Nazionale* of 1946 in the periodical published by the community at San Domenico was much shorter and simply emphasized that, in the particularly difficult circumstances that Italy faced in the aftermath of the war, the annual celebration of Catherine once again took on a truly national significance – not least in honouring a figure who embodied the best qualities of the Italian people. In this source too, however, it was emphasized that the following year would see the celebration of the sixth centenary of Catherine's birth.[5] Moreover, the previous edition of the periodical had carried three brief articles which, both individually and collectively, presented Catherine as an exemplar of the values and virtues that post-war Italy most needed. Thus, in an article on '*L'Italianità di S. Caterina*', she was extolled for the way that she had embodied the Italian character, and in particular for her passionate call for unity, peace, harmony and justice. She had therefore courageously and energetically opposed all that divided families, cities and political

3 *La Voce del Popolo*, 4/5/1946, p. 2.

4 *La Voce del Popolo*, 4/5/1946, p. 1. Toccabelli's remarks not only evoke the language of the festivals of 1940 to 1943 but may also be seen as an echo of his practice, in his wartime diaries for 1944–45, of referring to the period immediately after the liberation of Siena in July 1944 as a period of 'occupation'. For this aspect of his diaries see Ciabattini (1991, pp. 399–407); Bocchini Camaiani (1994, p. 89).

5 *S. Caterina da Siena, Patrona d'Italia*, 11, 1946, pp. 60–62.

groups and had visited Pisa, Lucca, Florence and Avignon in the cause of overcoming factions and conflicts. But peace, according to Catherine, the article continued, could not be separated from justice, hence her many injunctions to rulers in her letters to observe this principle.[6] A second article, entitled '*La Croce e l'Ulivo*', began by explaining that Catherine's use of the symbols of the cross and the olive branch symbolized her dual commitment to faith and to peace and her mission to promote these two virtues in the world. Again citing her various missions of peacemaking, the article reflected on the integral relationship between faith and peace in Catherine's thought and action, affirming that, for her, the mission of faith was precisely that of offering the world the promise of peace.[7] The third article, entitled '*Italiani Amatevi!*' – a title that evoked one of Catherine's letters to the Florentines of her day to set aside factional hatreds and love one another – emphasized yet again that, just as Catherine had both travelled and sent letters to urge the virtues of justice, humility, charity and peace, so now Italians had need, above all, of peace both with neighbouring countries and among themselves. In particular, the article continued, for Italians at this time, love of country meant not deepening divisions and exacerbating wounds, but setting aside the desire to dominate and the threat of hatred of each other – despite the fact that such attitudes were being fostered by the 'overheated demonstrations of the masses' in Italy's streets and public spaces, by lies in the press and by 'vulgar threats and insults'.[8]

As the reference to the 'overheated demonstrations of the masses' makes clear, in the politically highly charged context of Italy in 1946, such appeals to unity and the setting aside of faction were themselves by no means objective or politically neutral. On the contrary, they represent an implicit – but nonetheless clear and in fact barely coded – warning against the role and influence of the left in contemporary Italian politics. That Catholic sources should be expressing such views at this time is hardly surprising. Moreover, the conflict between left and right in both the province and the archdiocese of Siena in the post-war period was intense. Locally, the left enjoyed substantial electoral success – the province of Siena often being described as '*la provincia più rossa*'.[9] In response to the left, the support of Archbishop Toccabelli – and thus also of the local clergy – for the Christian Democrats was, predictably, both strong and resolute. Indeed, it has been argued that anti-communism became the defining theme within Sienese Catholicism during the late 1940s and the 1950s, the decade from 1948 to 1958, in particular, being described as 'the years of crusade' (against the political left in general and the influence of the Italian communist party in particular).[10] Toccabelli, it has been noted, had begun to articulate his ferociously anti-communist position even before the end of the war and continued to do so throughout the 1950s, basing his opposition, above all, on the advocacy of the absolute priority

6 *S. Caterina da Siena, Patrona d'Italia*, 11, 1946, pp. 19–21.

7 *S. Caterina da Siena, Patrona d'Italia*, 11, 1946, pp. 25–6.

8 *S. Caterina da Siena, Patrona d'Italia*, 11, 1946, pp. 27–8. For the letter in question, from Catherine to the '*signori priori dell'arti, e al gonfaloniere di giustizia del popolo e del commune di Firenze*', see Meattini (2006, pp. 181–5).

9 For a detailed account of the left in Siena in this period see Nuti (2003).

10 Mirizio (2003, p. 240, and also pp. 240–454, *passim*).

of the three ideals of God, nation and family, in each case conceived, of course, in terms of his own intensely conservative Catholic worldview.[11] The conflict between the Christian Democrats and the left in Siena, meanwhile, reflected at a local level the broader conflict in Italian political life as a whole in the immediately post-war era.[12]

Important as they are, however, these caveats as to the context and precise meaning of articles and speeches such as those preceding and accompanying the *Festa Nazionale* of 1946 should not be allowed to obscure the extent to which – taken as a whole – these texts nevertheless constituted a significant shift from the manner in which Catherine had been presented, interpreted and celebrated in the 1920s, 1930s and early 1940s. Indeed, in place of the overtly patriotic, nationalistic, heroic and often distinctly combative Catherine of the early period, these articles and speeches of 1946 already clearly define the principal features of the Catherine that was to be celebrated and promoted in the post-war era: that is to say, the messenger and ambassador of peace, of justice and of unity – first of all among Italians, but also more broadly in Europe and the wider world. If the *Festa Nazionale* of 1946 thus defined these themes, it was that of 1947 – together with the ceremonies to mark the sixth centenary of Catherine's birth – which ensured that they became firmly established.

The celebrations to commemorate the sixth centenary of Catherine's birth began on 30 March 1947 with a series of ceremonies and events in Siena which – in a manner reminiscent of the *Feste Nazionali* of the post-war era – combined distinctively Sienese traditions with overtly national participation.[13] At 2 p.m. the bell of the Torre del Mangia began to ring, accompanied by all the other bells of the city. At the same time, costumed representatives of Siena's 17 *contrade* left their respective neighbourhoods to process to the Campo from which they then processed together to the University for the official reception of representatives of the city of Rome. The procession then returned to the Palazzo Pubblico where, in the Sala del Mappamondo, the official speaker, the minister of education, Guido Gonella, delivered an address in celebration of Catherine on behalf of the Italian government and in the presence of the civic authorities of Siena and of representatives not only of Rome but also of other Italian cities and of the Constituent Assembly charged with completing the transition to the new Italian constitution. The address was broadcast, not only to the crowd gathered outside in the Campo, but also on Italian national radio. After the address by Gonella in the Palazzo Pubblico, the civic authorities,

11 Barzanti (1997, pp. 345–6); Bocchini Camaiani (1994, p. 90; 1998); Mirizio (2003, pp. 240–454, esp. pp. 455–6). Luchini (2002, pp. 27–36) publishes a number of photographs that convey the intensity of the political engagement between the Christian Democrats and the left in Siena in the post-war period.

12 For the conflict between the Christian Democrats and the left at the national level in the late 1940s – and in particular in relation to the crucial election of April 1948 – see Casella (1992); Ventresca (2003; 2004).

13 The account here is based on the reports in *La Voce del Popolo*, 29/3/1947, p. 1; *Popolo e Libertà*, 19/3/1947, p. 2; 2/4/1947, p. 2; *S. Caterina da Siena, Patrona d'Italia*, 12, 1947, pp. 29–32. *Popolo e Libertà* was a local paper issued, from time to time, by the Sienese Christian Democrats, for which see Balocchi (2004, pp. 426–8).

the various visiting dignitaries, the *contrade* of Siena and representatives of other civic institutions processed in turn to San Domenico and to the Sanctuary of Saint Catherine to place floral tributes at the two sites most closely associated with her cult.

Gonella's address in the Palazzo Pubblico was entitled, significantly, '*La Pace Armata di Amore*' and opened with the bold observation that, whereas at the time of her proclamation as *Patrona d'Italia* – which he described as a time of 'dark anxiety' – Italians had asked Catherine for inspiration and strength to overcome the despair and hopelessness of war, now Italians sought her help to overcome a more insidious form of despair prompted by the circumstances of post-war peace. For that reason, in beginning the celebration of the sixth centenary of her birth, it was fitting that those present should hear, understand and meditate upon Catherine's own message of peace and its meaning.[14] The humanity of Catherine's own political actions, Gonella continued, made her teaching relevant and living for the present, especially her assertion that politics must understand humanity as a totality, combining both the material and the spiritual, and must be put at the service of humanity in a manner that acknowledged the sacred nature of life. For this reason, the end of politics is not the narrow affirmation of the individual or of a party, and its means should not be the passion and vehemence that leads to violence. Above all, politics is not an end in itself but only a means – a distinction that Gonella supported by appeal to Catherine's letters. Quoting Catherine, he emphasized her repeated insistence that only living in fear of God could guarantee to preserve the nation and its cities in peace, and only by removing hate from the soul was is it possible to make peace with God and one's neighbour. Citing further examples of Catherine's repeated emphasis upon peace, Gonella also showed how, in her letters to political figures and leaders, she called, above all, for them to respect truth and observe the requirements of moral law. Catherine, he continued, knew that peace was the reward for obedience to the demands of both truth and justice – and conversely that truth and justice were the instruments of peace. Nevertheless, he conceded, in a passage that reflected the title of his address, Catherine also recognized that in order to eliminate the obstacles to peace, in the name of justice it is sometimes necessary to use force: but the suffering and bloodshed that result are the price to be paid for the re-establishment of the justice that humanity violates from time to time. It was for that reason that Catherine – the apostle of peace – was also the apostle of crusade against the Turks. However, Gonella continued, in calling for a crusade her motives were not so much politically opportunistic – in seeking to bring all Christian forces under the leadership of the papacy – but rather that all might be brought within the rule of Christendom and thus of Christ who is the source of peace with God. Gonella concluded his address with a further reference to the recent Italian experience of war – which he characterized as a form of bloodshed that only stained, but did not redeem – and to the present Italian experience of continuing and destructive factionalism and bitterness. He ended with the hope that, by looking to Catherine and seeking her help, contemporary

---

14 The full text of the speech was subsequently published under the auspices of Gonella's ministry of Public Instruction, for which see Gonella (1947). The passages summarized here may be found on pages 3, 5, 6, 8–14.

Italians would liberate themselves to achieve a genuine Christian peace in which they recognized Catherine's values.

Although Gonella's address reflected the same tensions and ambiguities that had been evident in the speeches at the *Festa Nazionale* the previous year – the appeal to 'Christian' peace and the reference to contemporary factionalism inevitably constituting, in themselves, a highly party political statement in the context of Italy and Italian politics in 1947 – the defining characteristic of the speech was, once again, Catherine as the messenger and apostle of peace and justice, and of politics as a means of serving the general good of society. The same themes were also emphasized in the public notices published for the occasion by the Commune of Siena and by the *Contrada dell'Oca*. The notice published by the Commune referred to Catherine's dedication – by word, action and example – to the pacification of the factional strife of her own society and the fostering of human fellowship in place of self-centredness or party allegiance. It concluded by relating her example to the experience of contemporary Italians, who had only recently escaped from a ruinous war and violent factionalism, in the hope that Catherine's example might teach them in the way of peace and harmony.[15] Similarly, the notice published by the *Contrada dell'Oca* – both in the form of a large poster and in a smaller format for distribution by hand – after celebrating both Catherine herself and the pride of the *Contrada dell'Oca* as the neighbourhood in which she had been born, concluded with the hope that the celebration of the sixth centenary of her birth would signal the beginning of a longed-for rebirth of Italy, in a spirit of justice, work, order and social peace.[16]

The *Festa Nazionale* of 1947, unsurprisingly, reflected the same themes. It also, however, took on an extended form as part of the Sienese celebrations of the sixth centenary of Catherine's birth. Thus, the relic of Catherine's head was chosen for the annual Sienese festival of Domenica in Albis and was taken in procession from San Domenico to the cathedral on 13 April to be placed on the high altar for the duration of the festival. On Sunday 27 April it was then processed from the cathedral via the Campo and the streets of Siena to the Sanctuary of Saint Catherine, the procession stopping in the Campo for a blessing of Italy, with the relic of Catherine's head. Administered by Archbishop Toccabelli, from the Cappella della Piazza, it was accompanied by Toccabelli's explanation that the blessing sought the coming of the peace of Christ in Italy and the world. On 28 April the customary offering of votive candles by the civic authorities at San Domenico and the Sanctuary took place and, on 29 April, after celebrations at the Sanctuary, the relic of Catherine's head was processed back to San Domenico where, the following day, the *Festa Nazionale* concluded with the final blessing of Italy and of representatives of its the armed

---

15 'Il Manifesto del Comune' in *S. Caterina da Siena, Patrona d'Italia*, 12, 1947, p. 30.

16 Original copies of the poster and smaller sized texts may be found in the Archivio of the Nobile Contrada dell'Oca, in a collection of documents entitled 'VI Centenario della nascità di S. Caterina 1347–1947', XIII B. 16 90. The text was also published in *S. Caterina da Siena, Patrona d'Italia*, 12, 1947, pp. 31–2.

forces.[17] On 18 May the Sienese paid a further tribute to Catherine in celebration of the sixth centenary of her birth by running an additional *Palio* in honour of the anniversary. The banner for the *Palio* depicted the figure of Catherine above a montage of Siena's principal buildings. In the foreground appeared the Portico dei Comuni of the Sanctuary, behind which was San Domenico, and behind San Domenico, the Palazzo Pubblico and Torre del Mangia and the dome, campanile and façade of the cathedral – thus combining the four sites that had featured most prominently in the civic celebrations in her honour in late March and April.[18]

At the national level, meanwhile, the sentiments expressed in the festivals and celebrations of 1946 and 1947 in Siena were also evident in the publication, in July 1947, of a study of Catherine's social and political thought entitled *Massime di Reggimento Civile* (*Principles of Civil Government*). The book consisted of seven chapters which presented an account and interpretation of Catherine's social and political teachings and actions – derived from the texts of her letters – together with a long final chapter which presented extracts from the letters, particularly those sent to political figures and rulers.[19] Edited by Anna Maria Balducci, the book was directed especially to Italian women and presented Catherine as the perfect model for the participation of women in Italian public life and in the reconstruction of post-war Italy, not least through the right to vote, which Italian women had been able to exercise for the first time in the referendum and elections for the Constituent Assembly in 1946. The relevance of the publication in this particular context was not only noted at the time. In 1980, in a lecture on 'Catherine of Siena and the women of today' given as part of the celebrations of the sixth centenary of Catherine's death, Senator Rosa Jervolino Russo was careful to refer back to the publication of the *Massime di Reggimento Civile*, relating it specifically to the new political influence that Italian women were able to exercise in post-war Italy, again affirming Catherine's status as the best model for the participation of women in public life, and also noting that in the first speech by a woman in the Italian parliament Catherine had been cited as the highest example of civic virtues.[20]

The seven chapters of exegesis and explanation of Catherine's thought in *Massime di Reggimento Civile* located her in her era, examined her role as a teacher of a particular vision of social life and her concept of society, and focused especially on the two themes of her understanding of the role and responsibilities of those who govern and her view of the relationship between love of country and morality in international affairs. Of the former, it was argued that the heart of Catherine's social and political thought and of her understanding of society and its well-being lay in the insight that the rights and duties of political authorities and those who govern

17 *La Voce del Popolo*, 5/4/1947, p. 1; 19/4/1947, p. 1; 29/4/1947, p. 1; 10/5/1947, p. 1.

18 There are two annual *Palii*, run on 2 July and 16 August respectively. From time to time the Sienese also run an additional *Palio* in honour of a particular event or anniversary. For the banner for the *Palio* in honour of Catherine in May 1947, see Betti (1992b, pp. 36–7).

19 Balducci (1947).

20 Jervolino (1980, pp. 60–61). The speech in question was delivered by Angela Maria Cingolari Guidi.

must be in balance and harmony with the rights and duties of the people governed by them. Only by such cooperation could all contribute to the common good. For those who held political power, this also implied the exercise of self-control – because those who cannot control themselves cannot control others – and the recognition that government in accordance with the divine will did not consist of the power to command but rather the privilege of service. For Catherine, the concept of the perfect city – according to this exegesis of her thought – required the realization of justice. Without justice neither civil nor divine law could be preserved, and justice required that everyone be rendered his or her due. But justice also demanded – and must be regulated by – the exercise of charity. Similarly, when justice required the exercise of punishment, this too must be exercised strictly in the interests of the common good, respecting the equality, liberty and rights of individuals, which in turn were the foundation of civil liberty.

As to the relationship between love of country and morality in international affairs, the penultimate chapter of *Massime di Reggimento Civile* began by affirming that Catherine had been an 'ardent Italian', above all in her desire for the realization of peace and unity in the entire country. Such unity did not, however, exclude the existence of different parties and opinions and those who governed should not abuse their power over those who differed from them lest this create new enmities and ills in the future – a lesson, the author observed, that had a sad resonance for contemporary Italians. But, Balducci continued, in the end, Catherine placed love of humanity and the ideal of universal justice above love of country. Therefore statesmen had a responsibility for the well-being of other nations as well as their own and should avoid interfering in the internal politics of other states. They should seek to resolve problems in accordance with the interests of all humanity and without losing sight of the ideal of universal justice. This did not rule out the possibility of a just war – as Catherine demonstrated by her support for the concept of a crusade – but, in her thought, war must be entered into with right intentions, in a just cause, in the interests of an eventual peace, against evil, and for the triumph of a greater good. Above all, however, international politics must be orientated towards the maintenance of peace between peoples, and the Christian ruler must be willing to subordinate some national aspirations to the greater good of the international community.[21] The Catherine presented in the *Massime di Reggimento Civile* was, therefore, fully consistent with the Catherine that had been presented and promoted at the annual festivals of the first post-war years, espousing the same social and political ideals – most notably of justice, of peace and of government as service of the common good – in both national and international contexts.

Both the rituals and the prevailing tone and sentiments of the speeches and addresses of the *Feste Nazionali* of 1946 and 1947 – and also the interpretation of Catherine set out in *Massime di Reggimento Civile* – established what proved to be an enduring pattern for subsequent celebrations of Catherine's annual festival in the post-war era. The annual speeches and addresses – and especially those given by visiting government ministers before the blessing of representatives of the armed forces – characteristically focused upon Catherine's role as an ambassador and

21 Balducci (1947, esp. pp. 38–9, 41, 44, 69–71, 74, 83–9).

peacemaker, upon her emphasis that the source and guarantee of peace was justice, and therefore also upon the role of the armed forces as the protectors and guarantors of the nation's peace, liberty, justice and prosperity. In the fifteen years from 1948 to 1962, these themes recurred regularly, as the reports of the annual *Festa Nazionale* in both the weekly newspaper *La Voce del Popolo* and the periodical *La Patrona d'Italia, Santa Caterina da Siena* amply testify.[22] Occasionally, a more overtly patriotic note was struck. Thus, in 1952, in addition to his reference to Catherine's two great principles of love of country and love of peace, the speech by the visiting minister, Adone Zoli, also referred to Catherine's desire for the unity of all of Italy's regions and territories and related this to the continuing debate over the future of the city of Trieste, at that time still under the post-war oversight of Britain, France and the United States.[23] Similarly, in 1956, Zoli – who was again the visiting minister at the *Festa Nazionale* and the blessing of the armed forces – celebrated the fact that Trieste was by then returned to Italian rule and sovereignty, suggesting that the participation of civic representatives of Trieste in that year's *Festa Nazionale* in Siena was like a 're-consecration' of Trieste's place among Italy's cities.[24] On other occasions Archbishop Toccabelli's conservative political views were again in evidence. At the *Festa Nazionale* in 1949, for example, in his address at the blessing of the armed forces, he marked the tenth anniversary of Catherine's proclamation as *Patrona d'Italia* by describing that event in 1939 as itself a 'coronation' of the Concordat of 1929, even citing Pius XI's description of the Concordat as an event that gave God back to Italy and Italy back to God.[25] Similarly, in 1951, an article in *La Voce del Popolo* the week before the *Festa Nazionale* evoked Catherine's desire for Italians to live peacefully together and contrasted this with what it described as the attempts of masons, freethinkers and Marxists to spread secularism and disaffection from the church in contemporary Italy.[26] Such examples of more nationalistic sentiments and overtly political conservatism were, however, exceptions to the general rule: the predominant tone of the rhetoric of the *Feste Nazionale* of these years remained that of Catherine the ambassador, messenger and apostle of peace, justice and liberty.

During the 1950s several significant additions and modifications were introduced to the rituals of the annual *Festa Nazionale*. In each case, however, the changes remained in fundamental continuity with the existing liturgical structure as a whole, thus reflecting a process of evolution rather than transformation. In 1952, for the first time since the Second World War, the bronze Votive Lamp, given by the women

22 See for example *La Voce del Popolo*, 6/5/1948, p. 2; 7/5/1949, p. 1; 6/5/1950, p. 2; 5/5/1951, p. 2; 3/5/1952, p. 2; 2/5/1953, p. 2; 6/5/1956, p. 2; 12/5/1957, p. 2; 4/5/1958, p. 2; 10/5/1959, p. 4; 15/5/1960, p. 4; 7/5/1961, p. 4; *La Patrona d'Italia, Santa Caterina da Siena*, 2, May–June 1949, pp. 6–7; 3, May–June 1950, pp. 2–6; 4, May 1951, pp. 1–4; 16, May–June 1961, p. 7. The latter periodical, which varied between being bi-monthly and quarterly, began publication in 1948, was published from San Domenico, Siena, and was the successor to *S. Caterina da Siena, Patrona d'Italia*.

23 *La Voce del Popolo*, 3/5/1952, p. 2.

24 *La Voce del Popolo*, 6/5/1956, p. 2; *La Patrona d'Italia, Santa Caterina da Siena*, 9, May–June 1956, pp. 4–5.

25 *La Voce del Popolo*, 7/5/1949, p. 1.

26 *La Voce del Popolo*, 21/4/1951, p. 1.

of Italy in 1943, was reintroduced to the festival and, indeed, became the focus of a new ritual. On 29 April, during the traditional celebration of Catherine's annual festival at the Sanctuary of Saint Catherine, together with the civic authorities of Siena, the Mayor of Rome presented oil for the flame of the Votive Lamp. He did so, the report of the new ritual in *La Voce del Popolo* explained, because the oil that burned in the lamp would repeat the enduring vow of the Italian people for peace in Italy and the world.[27] He also initiated a new annual ritual in which oil for the Votive Lamp would be offered each year at the *Festa Nazionale* by a different Italian city. This newly 'invented tradition' thus reaffirmed that Catherine was, indeed, *Patrona d'Italia* – patron, that is to say, of the entire nation – and both evoked and annually symbolically renewed the original offerings made, in 1940, by different Italian cities for the building of the Portico dei Comuni at the Sanctuary. It also, clearly, drew upon the precedent of the '*lampada votiva dei Comuni d'Italia*' that had been inaugurated at Assisi in October 1939 in recognition of the proclamation of Francis of Assisi as *Patrono d'Italia* and for which, during the annual *Festa Nazionale* in honour of Francis, oil was annually donated by the cities of one of the regions of Italy.[28] The choice of Rome for the first such presentation once again reflected the fact that, in addition to being the capital of Italy, Siena and Rome were the two principal places of significance in the life of Saint Catherine – the former being the place of her birth and early life, the latter the place of her final years and death.[29]

Two more major innovations to the ceremonies of the festival were introduced in 1958. Firstly, the ceremony in which another Italian city offered oil for the Votive Lamp was now accompanied by a full civic procession from the Palazzo Pubblico to the Sanctuary of Saint Catherine. Secondly, and even more strikingly, for the first time, the blessing of representatives of the Italian armed forces took place as a separate ceremony in the afternoon, not at either the Sanctuary of Saint Catherine or the church of San Domenico, but in the Campo, the central piazza of Siena. Moreover, instead of the armed forces being represented only by members of the regiment of the Italian army that happened to be stationed in Siena, the military presence now included representatives of the various branches of the Italian forces. For the blessing, the relic of the finger of Saint Catherine was to be carried in procession to the Campo, where the visiting cardinal representing the Vatican used it to impart the blessing, after the customary speech by a minister of the Italian government. The ceremonies were also to be recorded and filmed for subsequent transmission on Italian radio and television.[30] These two innovations to the rituals and ceremonies of the annual *Festa Nazionale* of Saint Catherine in 1958 were then followed, in 1959, by the introduction of the practice of moving the date of the *Festa Nazionale* to the

27 *La Voce del Popolo*, 3/5/1952, p. 2.

28 For the Votive Lamp at Assisi see Gatti (1983, pp. 420–26) and also Chapter 3, note 6 of the present book.

29 In the first five years of the new 'tradition', Rome was followed by Florence in 1953, Venice in 1954, Genoa in 1955 and Trieste in 1956 – the latter being the occasion for the suggestion that the ritual amounted to a 're-consecration' of Trieste as an Italian city, for which see note 24 above.

30 *La Voce del Popolo*, 27/4/1958, p. 1; 4/5/1958, p. 2; *La Nazione*, 26/4/1958, p. 4.

Sunday nearest to 29 April (the actual date of Catherine's death in 1380) in order to increase public participation.[31]

During 1961 and 1962, in addition to the annual *Festa Nazionale*, the celebration of two centenaries – namely the first centenary of Italian Unification and the fifth centenary of Catherine's canonization – provided occasions for particular reflection on Catherine and her status and significance as *Patrona d'Italia*. The sequence of events during 1961 and 1962 to celebrate the fifth centenary of Catherine's canonization was initiated in Siena, on Sunday 18 June 1961. With the streets decorated both with the flags of the seventeen *contrade* of Siena and with public notices signed by the Mayor of Siena and the local Dominicans, the official events of the day began in the morning with planes flying over the city and dropping flowers and leaflets in praise of Catherine as *Patrona d'Italia*. This was followed by a mass in San Domenico – where the relic of Catherine's head was on display – in the presence of the local civic and military authorities and of the Italian members of parliament Maria Jervolino and Arturo Viviani. Subsequently, in the evening, in the Sala del Mappamondo of the Palazzo Pubblico, Maria Jervolino gave an address celebrating Catherine as Sienese, as Italian, as a spiritual daughter of the Dominican Order and as a heroine of the church and the papacy. Defining her as the greatest woman in the history of Italy, Jervolino concluded by emphasizing that it was particularly appropriate to celebrate the fifth centenary of Catherine's canonization at the same time as Italy was celebrating the first centenary of its national unity.[32]

The association of Catherine with the celebration of the first centenary of Italian unity had also been evident at the beginning of June 1961 when the Sienese ran an extra *Palio* on 4 June, specifically to celebrate the centenary of Italian Unification. It is an integral part of the ritual of every *Palio* that the unique banner that is painted for each *Palio* and then awarded to the winner of the race is always blessed by the Sienese religious authorities and placed on display in one of the city's major churches. In the case of the *Palio* of 4 June 1961 in honour of the centenary of Italian Unification, the banner was blessed and placed on display in San Domenico, next to the altar that housed the relic of the head of Catherine of Siena.[33] The link between Catherine as *Patrona d'Italia* and the centenary of Italian Unification was also acknowledged and celebrated in an article in the periodical dedicated to Catherine that was published by the Sienese Dominican community. Entitled, '*Santa Caterina e l'unità d'Italia*', it asserted that, whilst the roles of Victor Emmanuel II, Cavour and Garibaldi as architects of Italian unity were well known, Catherine had also contributed to the formation of a national consciousness among Italians. In particular, the article emphasized, once again, on the one hand, Catherine's words and actions in defence and promotion of peace, and on the other, her opposition to

31 *La Voce del Popolo*, 3/5/1959, p. 4; *La Nazione*, 5/5/1959, p. 4.

32 *La Voce del Popolo*, 25/6/1961, p. 4; *La Patrona d'Italia, Santa Caterina da Siena*, 16, July–October 1961, p. 7

33 *La Voce del Popolo*, 4/6/1961, p. 4. The banners for the two annual *Palii* are blessed and displayed in, respectively, the church of Santa Maria di Provenzano and the cathedral. For these rituals and their context within the *Palio* see Parsons (2004a, pp. 130–59). For the banner for the *Palio* of 4 June 1961 see Betti (1992b, pp. 72–3).

factional strife and division. In so doing, the article continued, she had inspired the admiration of both nineteenth-century patriots such as Niccolò Tommaseo and the twentieth-century Pope Pius XII who had made her the heavenly patroness of the nation.[34]

In April 1962 the year-long celebration of the fifth centenary of Catherine's canonization was marked in Siena not only by Catherine's annual festival but also by a major academic conference dedicated to Catherine and her significance, together with an exhibition, in the Palazzo Pubblico, of documents from the Sienese archives relating to her life and cult. The opening ceremony for the conference took place in the Sala del Mappamondo of the Palazzo Pubblico. The Mayor of Siena, Ugo Bartolini, concluded his address by reaffirming that the Sienese celebrated their saint for her commitment to peace – but a peace based on freedom and justice.[35] The first address at the conference was then presented by Professor Igino Giordani on the theme of 'Saint Catherine as a social reformer'.[36] The papers from the conference and the catalogue for the exhibition were subsequently published in a special edition of the influential Sienese historical journal, the *Bollettino Senese di Storia Patria*.[37] In May 1962, the relic of Catherine's head was once again chosen as the focus for the Sienese festival of Domenica in Albis, the exposition of her head in the cathedral then being followed by another translation of the relic to the Oratory of the *Contrada dell'Oca* and a further exposition there for 24 hours before its return to San Domenico.[38] Finally, the banner for the annual *Palio* of 2 July 1962 was also dedicated to Catherine in celebration of the fifth centenary of her canonization. Catherine was portrayed, holding a lily and a book – and in a style that evoked the famous painting of her by Andrea Vanni – looking down benignly on a representation of Siena, and framed by, on one side, the Torre del Mangia of the Palazzo Pubblico, and on the other by the campanile of Siena cathedral.[39]

In Rome, meanwhile, the year of celebration of the fifth centenary of Catherine's canonization was marked by the completion and inauguration, at the end of April 1962, of a major monument to Catherine and her life. Located next to Castel Sant'Angelo, the monument consists of a statue of Catherine (Plate 18) together with two sequences of sculpted reliefs depicting, respectively, scenes from Catherine's life and the symbols of Italian institutions and organizations that had contributed to

34 *La Patrona d'Italia, Santa Caterina da Siena*, 16, May–June 1961, p. 3.

35 Bartolini (1962, p. 6).

36 Giordani, (1962).

37 The volume was subtitled 'Atti del Symposium Catherinianum nel V Centenario della Canonizzazione di Santa Caterina da Siena'.

38 See the correspondence and copy of the 'Avviso Sacro' issued by the *Contrada dell'Oca* in the file 'Solenni Festeggiamenti in occasione del Quinto Centenario della Canonizzazione di Santa Caterina, Maggio 1962' in the Archive of the Nobile Contrada Dell'Oca, XIII B. 18 37.

39 For the banner see Betti (1992b, pp. 76–7). The artist for this banner was Bruno Marzi and it is clear that he re-worked the central feature – namely Catherine above a walled city – of his banner for the *Palio* of August 1939 in honour of Catherine's proclamation as *Patrona d'Italia*. In 1962, however, the city was clearly Siena, whereas in 1939 it had been an idealized city containing monuments from various parts of Italy.

the cost of the project (Plates 19, 20).[40] The work of the Sicilian sculptor Francesco Messina, the monument originated in an idea of a Dominican priest, Cristofaro Bigazzi, and was then progressed by Luigia Tincani, a devotee of Catherine of Siena and the founder, in 1924, of the *Missionarie della Scuola*, a community of Dominican women dedicated to working in schools and universities. The statue of Catherine – which is placed opposite the beginning of the *Via della Conciliazione* leading to Saint Peter's Square – is intended to evoke and commemorate the daily 'pilgrimage' that Catherine undertook during the final months of her life, from the house in which she and followers lived to old Saint Peter's, in order to pray for the restoration of the unity of the church following the schism that had occurred after the election of Pope Urban VI in 1378.[41] Catherine is portrayed in a pose of intense devotion and clasping her traditional symbol of a lily (Plate 18).[42] To the right of the statue, on the front of a low wall, appears a sequence of four sculpted scenes from Catherine's life, each of which is accompanied by a quotation from one of Catherine's letters, inscribed on the relief (Plate 19). The four scenes are: Catherine dictating her letters to an amanuensis; her ministry to Niccolò di Toldo at his execution in 1375; the threat to her life from a mob in Florence in 1378 during the violence associated with the revolt of the Ciompi; and her visit to Pope Gregory XI to call for his return to Rome.[43] At the end of the low wall and sequence of scenes a sculpted inscription dedicates the monument to Catherine as patron of Italy, of Rome and of her followers throughout the world and as Protector of the Dominican Order on the fifth centenary of her canonization. It also records that the monument was blessed by Pope John XXIII.

On the rear of the low wall four further panels portray a series of sculpted emblems, each accompanied by an inscription dedicated to Catherine and each representing one of the major groups or institutions that had contributed to the cost of the monument (Plate 20). The first panel (reading from left to right) portrays the emblem of *Azione Cattolica Italiana* – a circular shield with a cross at its centre – and a dedication describing Catherine as a fearless champion of faith and a martyr for love of the papacy. The second panel portrays a shield bearing a handshake against the background of a generic Italian townscape – the emblem of the *Comitato Civico*, the network of local organizations first set-up, under the leadership of Luigi Gedda and at the specific request of Pope Pius XII, to mobilize Catholic support for the Christian Democrats in the crucial parliamentary elections of April 1948. The

40 For a detailed analysis of this monument, see Parsons (2008b, forthcoming).

41 The route of Catherine's daily 'pilgrimage' is reconstructed in Cavallini and Giunta (2000, pp. 52–64).

42 It is commonly said that the orientation of the figure is towards Saint Peter's as, for example, in Vanni (1975, p. 278); Bianchi and Giunta (1988, p. 137) and Cavallini and Giunta (2000, p. 40). Although an arguable interpretation, it is also the case that the statue is so positioned that Catherine appears to look across the Tiber towards the Via Giulia, the street in which the church of Santa Caterina da Siena in Roma and the confraternity of the same name are located, and which in the late medieval and renaissance periods included the area known as the *Castrum Senensis* in which the Sienese community in Rome lived.

43 For details of the quotations associated with each scene, see Parsons (2008b, forthcoming).

accompanying inscription, in this case, celebrates Catherine's willingness to defy the risk of death in the cause of bringing peace between opposing factions within Italian cities. The third panel represents the cities of Italy, carries an inscription recalling her role as a messenger of peace between Italian cities, and portrays a shield bearing within it a series of famous monuments representing the cities of Venice, Pisa, Rome, Siena and Florence.[44] The final panel portrays the traditional symbol of the famous Sienese bank the Monte dei Paschi and an inscription celebrating the fact that Catherine sent her message of truth and love from Siena.

Despite the scale, complexity and detail of the monument, its inauguration in April 1962 prompted surprisingly little comment – a trend that has also continued in subsequent decades. The reports of the inauguration both in the Sienese press and in Dominican periodicals were not only curiously brief but also remarkably limited in their analysis of the monument and its imagery. Collectively, they did little more than offer brief details of the origins of the monument, of the groups that had contributed to its cost, and of the ceremony for its inauguration, together with short descriptions of the statue and its accompanying panels.[45] The inauguration was attended by leading Christian Democrat politicians, six cardinals and the mayors of Siena and Florence and was preceded by speeches that celebrated Catherine's message of peace to Italy and the world. Why, then, has the monument been thus neglected? Although it cannot be stated with certainty, it seems probable that the monument to Catherine of Siena at Castel Sant'Angelo was neglected at the time of its inauguration, and has continued to be neglected since then, because its imagery reflected a specific interpretation of Catherine and her political significance within Italian society and Italian Catholicism. The interpretation in question, however, was one that reflected the political and ecclesiastical contexts of the late 1940s and early and mid 1950s – contexts that, by 1962, were already in process of transition.

Analysis of the relationship between two of the front panels depicting scenes from Catherine's life and two of the rear panels representing institutions that had contributed to the project suggests that the monument was designed not only as a commemoration of the fifth centenary of Catherine's canonization but also as a celebration of her status as a symbol of the values of the conservative wing of Italian Christian Democracy and of the fiercely anti-communist stance of the papacy of Pius XII during the late 1940s and the early and mid 1950s. The panels in question are those on the front of the monument that depict the scenes of Catherine threatened by the Ciompi and of Catherine urging Pope Gregory XI to return to Rome, and those on the rear of the monument that portray the emblems of the *Comitato Civico* and of *Azione Cattolica Italiana*. All four of the scenes on the front of the monument are, in

44 It thus also recalls the similar use of such representative monuments on the *Palio* banner of August 1939 in honour of Catherine's proclamation as *Patrona d'Italia* (Plate III), on the special supplements of *Il Popolo di Siena* (Plate 14) and the official posters for the first *Festa Nazionale* in 1940, and on the leaflet portraying both Catherine and Francis overseeing Italy produced in Bologna in 1941 (Plate 15).

45 *La Voce del Popolo*, 6/5/1962, p. 4; *Il Campo di Siena*, 11/5/1962, p. 3; *La Patrona d'Italia, Santa Caterina da Siena*, 17, January–February 1962, p. 6; 17, May–June 1962, p. 7; *Memorie Domenicane*, 79, 1962, pp. 138–43.

fact, paired specifically with particular emblems on the rear: the pairings being the scene of Catherine dictating her letters with the emblem and inscription relating to the Monte dei Paschi; the scene of the execution of Niccolò di Toldo with the panel depicting various Italian cities; the scene of Catherine threatened by the Ciompi with the emblem of the *Comitato Civico*; and the scene of Catherine before Pope Gregory with the emblem of *Azione Cattolica Italiana* (Plates 19, 20). It is, however, the latter two pairings that appear to carry the burden of the ideological message of the monument.[46]

The link between the scene of Catherine urging Pope Gregory XI to return to Rome and the emblem of *Azione Cattolica Italiana* not only focused on Catherine's role as a champion of the papacy, but also implicitly related that role to key aspects of the pontificates of both Pius XI and Pius XII. Thus, Pius XI had not only been the 'Pope of the *Conciliazione*' – and it is important to recall that, in 1929, devotees of Catherine were quick to draw a parallel between the return of Gregory XI from Avignon and the 'return' of Pius XI to Rome and Italy through the reconciliation of church and state – but had also, during the Fascist era, made the promotion and protection of *Azione Cattolica* one of the key aims of his pontificate, even expressing the hope that he would be remembered as 'the Pope of Catholic Action'.[47] The pontificate of Pius XII, meanwhile, was renowned not only for the intensity of its anti-communist crusade but also for its promotion of both a Roman Catholic version of *romanità* – in which Rome was conceived as a sacred centre and the fulcrum of world history – and of a veritable cult of the personality and charisma of Pius XII himself.[48] In the post-war period, moreover, it was precisely the well-established local networks and structures of *Azione Cattolica Italiana* that Pius XII ensured were used to facilitate the work of the *Comitati Civici* – the network of local pressure groups organized in the run-up to the crucial Italian elections of April 1948 with the precise aim of promoting the cause of the Christian Democrats and defeating the alliance of left-wing parties in the Popular Front. Thus, in early 1948, Pius XII had entrusted the organization of the *Comitati Civici* to the notoriously conservative figure of Luigi Gedda, already president of the men's section of *Azione Cattolica*, and subsequently to be appointed by Pius XII as vice-president of the entire movement in 1949, and general president in 1952.[49]

It is precisely the *Comitati Civici*, however, that are associated with Catherine in relation to the sculpted scene of her near death at the hands of a mob during the revolt of the Ciompi in Florence in 1378. And it is in this particular linkage of scene and emblem that the political message of the monument at Castel Sant'Angelo is, arguably, at its most acute. In the crucial election campaign of 1948, the *Comitati*

46 For further detailed analysis of all four pairings of front and rear panels see Parsons (2008b, forthcoming).

47 Binchy (1977, p. 6); Koon (1985, p. 122).

48 Logan (1997, pp. 484–5; 1998).

49 For studies of the origins, role and significance of the *Comitati Civici*, see Casella (1992, pp. 79–156); Ventresca (2004, pp. 178–95). For Gedda's own retrospective account of the 1948 election and the importance of the *Comitati Civici* see Gedda (1998), and for a critique of Gedda's account which emphasizes its subjective and politically charged nature see Alberigo (2000).

Civici not only mobilized the Catholic vote on behalf of the Christian Democrats but also sponsored and distributed ferociously anti-Marxist posters and election propaganda, much of which played explicitly and crudely upon fears of socialist and communist violence. Using graphic and often bloodthirsty imagery, such posters and propaganda associated the Popular Front with Stalin, with the threat of social disorder and with the fear of violent revolution and foreign domination.[50] In the mid-twentieth century, the revolt of the Ciompi was often interpreted, especially by Marxist historians, as an early expression of working-class revolutionary action on the part of Florentine proletarian cloth-workers. Subsequently historians have challenged this interpretation and suggested that it is both anachronistic and over-simplified,[51] but even if such revisionism is correct, it nevertheless remains the fact that the interpretation of the Ciompi as proletarian revolutionaries engaged in violent social unrest was one which carried considerable currency when the monument at Castel Sant'Angelo was conceived and executed. In terms of the monument, the implied meaning of the panel and its association with the emblem of the *Comitati Civici* is clear: as Catherine defied a violent revolutionary mob in seeking to bring peace among the factions within Florence, so the *Comitati Civici* defied and overcame the threat of revolutionary violence in post-war Italy.

The imagery of the monument to Catherine of Siena at Castel Sant'Angelo therefore expressed a political message that associated it not only with the Christian Democrats, but with the conservative and resolutely anti-communist wing of the party associated in particular with Luigi Gedda.[52] By 1961–62, however, when the fifth centenary of Catherine's canonization was being celebrated and the monument completed and inaugurated, the political and ecclesiastical context had already been changed dramatically by the death of Pope Pius XII in 1958 and the election of Pope John XXIII. It was precisely during 1961 and 1962 that John XXIII initiated his profound re-evaluation and re-orientation of the role of the church in Italian political life, replacing his predecessor's implacable anti-communism and highly interventionist approach with a policy of 'disengagement' and 'reserve' in respect of direct participation by the church in Italian politics. At the same time, John XXIII also thereby signalled his sympathy, in principle, to the idea of an 'opening to the left' – as proposed by the moderate and centrist sections of the Christian Democratic

50 For examples of such propaganda see the illustrations in Casella (1992, pp. 461–86) and Ventresca (2004, between pp. 210–11).

51 For discussion of the Ciompi and their historiography that challenges the Marxist interpretation, see Brucker (1968, pp. 314–19, 352–6; 1969, pp. 44–8, 66–8, 151–2). For subsequent re-interpretations that re-emphasize the role of lower social classes in the revolt see Cohn (1979, 1980, pp. 130–33, 208–10) and Luongo (2006, p. 199).

52 Gedda himself asserted that the scene on the monument associated with the Comitati Civici showed Catherine's readiness to sacrifice herself to defend justice and bring peace, but he also linked Catherine firmly with Joan of Arc in a manner that was reminiscent of pre-war assertions of their similarity, for which see Gedda (1962). For the extent of Gedda's right-wing sympathies, which led him to defend the race laws of the late 1930s and advocate post-war electoral alliances between the Christian Democrats and neo-Fascist candidates, see Webster (1960, p. 160); Osbat (1981, p. 95); Maggi (1981, p. 208); Hebblethwaite (1984, pp. 254–5); Margiotta Broglio (2000, pp. 1180, 1183).

party – and to the possibility of a process of dialogue with the left. As a consequence the *Comitati Civici* were reined in and *Azione Cattolica* was instructed to focus on spiritual and social issues, not overtly political ones, whilst Gedda was replaced as its president.[53] In May 1961 – shortly before the beginning of the year-long celebration of the fifth centenary of Catherine's canonization – John XXIII had issued his encyclical, *Mater et magistra*, focusing on the social teaching of the church and the need for greater social justice. In July 1962, his final encyclical, *Pacem in terris*, confirmed the new direction of papal policy, replacing the anti-communist Cold War rhetoric of Pius XII with an appeal to all 'men of goodwill' and for cooperation between those of differing ideological beliefs. In October 1962 the beginning of the Second Vatican Council then confirmed the scale of the changes that were taking place in the Catholic church.

In such a context, the lack of attention to the monument at Castel Sant'Angelo – both at the time of its inauguration and later – becomes unsurprising. The Catherine portrayed and celebrated in that monument was representative of the political context of the post-war period – a Catherine who was also reflected in the speeches and addresses that accompanied the annual festivals in honour of Catherine as *Patrona d'Italia*. Whilst the emphasis in the period since 1945 had been upon her role as a messenger and ambassador of peace and social justice, yet during the later 1940s and the 1950s, in discussions of Catherine, there also remained a strong sense of the ongoing conflict between left and right and of Catherine's symbolic significance within that conflict. In the decades after Vatican II, however, the image of Catherine and her role as '*Patrona d'Italia*' was to develop yet again with an even stronger emphasis upon her teaching on peace and social justice and culminating, indeed, in a new role as patron saint not merely of Italy but of Europe.

In Siena, the impact of the ethos and emphases of the post-conciliar church upon the celebration of Catherine and the annual *Festa Nazionale* in her honour was greatly facilitated by the presence of a new archbishop. Archbishop Toccabelli died in April 1961. His successor, appointed in June 1961, was Mario Ismaele Castellano. A member of the Dominican Order and previously closely involved in the national administration of *Azione Cattolica*, Castellano was an enthusiastic participant in the Second Vatican Council, contributing in particular to the preparation of the decrees on social communications, on the role of the laity, and on the church in the modern world. His long tenure of the post of Archbishop of Siena – he did not retire as archbishop until 1990 – was characterized by the application in his archdiocese of the spirit and principles of Vatican II. In marked contrast to the highly political style of his predecessor, Archbishop Castellano sought to avoid political confrontations and focused instead on a strongly pastoral mission that sought to respect and build upon traditional expressions of Sienese culture and devotion such as the *contrade* of Siena.[54] He was also an enthusiastic devotee of Catherine of Siena and, during

---

53 See for example Gorresio (1968); Magister (1979, pp. 258–60, 268–70); Hebblethwaite (1984, pp. 356–63); Ginsborg (1990, pp. 260–61).

54 He was, in consequence, highly regarded in Siena. The extent of the esteem – and also the genuine affection – in which Castellano was held by the Sienese is evident in the articles published in celebration of his 90th birthday in the edition of the fortnightly Sienese

the three decades during which he was Archbishop of Siena, promoted her cult with both skill and dedication. Three themes in particular characterized the development of the cult of Catherine of Siena during Castellano's years as Archbishop of Siena in the 1960s, 1970s and 1980s, namely: the continuing, though also subtly changing, relationship between the figure of Catherine of Siena, in her role as *Patrona d'Italia*, and the Italian armed forces; the revival and renewal of the structure and aims of the organization of and for her devotees; and the promotion of Catherine not merely as a patron saint of Italy, but as a figure of international significance and a potential patron saint of Europe.

During the 1960s, 1970s and 1980s, the annual *Festa Nazionale* in honour of Catherine continued – as, indeed, it still continues – to include a ceremony at the Portico of the Sanctuary of Saint Catherine in which oil was presented for the Votive Lamp dedicated to Catherine, and a parade of representatives of the Italian armed forces later in the day in the Campo where a blessing was delivered by a visiting cardinal representing the Vatican, following an address by a minister representing the Italian government. As reports of the annual festivals frequently show, the speeches and addresses associated with these events continued to emphasize the themes – already established in the late 1940s and the 1950s – of Catherine as an ambassador and messenger of peace, fraternity, truth and social justice, of the armed forces as the guardians of these values in contemporary Italy, and of Italy's commitment to and participation in the new post-war community of European nations.[55] Particular examples of sermons and addresses from the *Feste Nazionali* of these decades that illustrate these themes – and which were subsequently published in full in the series *Quaderni Cateriniani*[56] – include the sermons in San Domenico by cardinals Sebastiano Baggio and Giovanni Benelli, (in 1973 and 1978 respectively), and the speeches in the Campo by government ministers Italo Giulio Caiati, Mario Pedini, Pietro Schietroma, Antonio Gava and Luciano Bausi (in 1973, 1978, 1982, 1985 and

magazine *La Voce del Campo* of 9 October 2003, pp. 9–12, and again in the obituaries that appeared in the local papers following his death in April 2007, for which see *Il Corriere della Provincia di Siena*, 13/4/2007, pp. 6–8; 14/4/2007, pp. 6–7. For Castellano's enthusiasm for the *contrade* of Siena and their contribution to the life of the city see also Parsons (2004a, pp. 99–100, 109–10; 2006, pp. 53, 55–6). For the way in which he avoided political controversy see especially Barzanti (2003, and also his obituary tribute to Castellano in *Il Corriere della Provincia di Siena*, 13/4/2007, pp. 6–7) and for a summary biography of Castellano see Lotti (1992, pp. 108–9).

55 For particular examples, see *La Voce del Popolo*, 7/5/1961, p. 4; 12/5/1963, p. 4; 7/5/1972, p. 4; *Il Campo di Siena*, 20/4/1973, p. 2; *La Casa di S. Caterina* (October 1981): 4–5; (November 1982): 6–7; (August 1985): 4–6; (August 1987): 6–7. Such speeches consistently appealed to Catherine's life and teaching as exemplars of the themes of service, peace and unity, to her role in seeking to end the papal schism and the Avignon papacy, her efforts to persuade warring Italian cities to make peace and her personal commitment to service to others.

56 The *Quaderni Cateriniani* is an occasional series of pamphlets – and sometimes more substantial publications – initiated in 1971 by the newly constituted *Associazione Ecumenica dei Caterinati*, for which see further in the following pages. The series continues to be published and now numbers over 120 items.

and conflicted with Catherine's ideal of peace. In response, the author argued that the blessing was authentic and valid because it was not simply for the members of the armed services themselves but for all of Italy and its social, political and military institutions, which the forces represented and which they defended together with the freedom, peace and prosperity of the Italian people. The author conceded that the description 'blessing of the armed forces' might perhaps be less appropriate now than when the ritual was first introduced. Then it had been in the context of war and it had been appropriate to seek Catherine's blessing upon victory or for a good end to the war without excessive damage to Italy. Now, however, the ritual was better described as a blessing of the youth of Italy currently in military service and of the Italian people – a form of words, it was noted, that was already being used as the title of the ceremony in the Campo. Those responsible for the organization of the *Festa Nazionale* had therefore considered the objections to this part of the annual ceremonies and had rejected them, not least because, whilst it would, perhaps, be easy simply to abolish the blessing it was not clear how it could be reformed. Who, for example, would replace the representative presence that the young members of the forces currently provided, not out of personal or political choice but as an expression of duty and service to their country? The first page of the edition in which the article appeared also carried a full-page colour photograph of the Votive Lamp with its four figures representing the various branches of the Italian forces.[63]

The blessing of the armed forces thus remained part of the *Festa Nazionale*. Moreover, the link between the Italian forces and the figure and cult of Catherine as *Patrona d'Italia* was also maintained in other ways. Not surprisingly, given the role of her cult – and of the Sanctuary dedicated to her – during the war, both cult and Sanctuary became a focus for reunions and pilgrimages by veterans' groups in the post-war period. Thus, for example, at the end of May 1970, veterans of Italian tank units from Lombardy and Tuscany met at the Sanctuary as part of a reunion and presented a gold urn containing sand from the desert of El Alamein in tribute and memory of their dead in the battle of October 1942. The report of the event also noted that Archbishop Castellano's secretary, Monsignor Gino Lotti, had been wounded at El Alamein whilst serving as a military chaplain.[64] Similarly, in October 1981, the programme for an inter-regional reunion in Siena of veterans of the famous *Alpini* units included an opportunity for devotion to Catherine and a mass in San Domenico celebrated by Archbishop Castellano who, it was noted, wore his own *Alpini* hat during the parade that followed the mass. Castellano had served as an officer in the *Alpini* during his military service in the 1930s, before he joined the Dominican Order, and again in 1942–43 as a chaplain with the *Alpini* units among

63 Ancilli (1973).

64 *La Casa di S. Caterina*, 1970, 2 (June), p. 4. Thirteen years later a room at the parish church of 'Santa Caterina Dottore della Chiesa' at Aquacalda, on the outskirts of Siena, was dedicated to Mons. Lotti. At its inauguration his service as a military chaplain in North Africa was a major theme, as was his post-war role as a secretary to both Toccabelli and Castellano, for which see *La Voce del Popolo*, 9/10/1983, p. 8.

the Italian forces sent to Russia in support of the German campaign.[65] In 1984 two groups of veterans of the Second World War participated at the offering of oil for the Votive Lamp at the Portico dei Comuni during the annual *Festa Nazionale*. Representatives of the *Unione Nazionale dei Reduci d'Africa* presented a votive candle, whilst members of the *Unione Nazionale dei Reduci di Russia* presented a framed version of the original design for the public notices to advertise the National Convention of the veterans of the Italian campaign in Russia that was to be held in Siena on 6 and 7 October that year. The design showed the figure of Saint Catherine, a cross in her right hand and a palm and an olive branch in her left hand, portrayed above an icy Russian landscape which included a river, a church and a cemetery. On the left of the design, meanwhile, a portrayal of the Torre del Mangia of the Sienese town hall both 'framed' the image of Catherine and provided a visual reference to the city's role as venue for the veterans' reunion.[66]

As well as serving to publicize the national convention of veterans in October 1984, the imagery also celebrated the fact that the *Reduci di Russia* had recently sought Catherine's assistance in their attempts to identify the location of the graves of Italian soldiers killed in the Russian campaign – an endeavour in which they had been unsuccessful for 40 years – and to have as many as possible of their remains returned to Italy. The initial appeal to Catherine on the part of the veterans of the Russian campaign had taken place in November 1982, in a ceremony in front of Catherine's remains beneath the high altar of the church of Santa Maria sopra Minerva, in Rome during a pilgrimage by the *Unione Nazionale dei Reduci di Russia*. Subsequently, in March 1983, during a reunion in Siena of the Tuscan branches of the *Reduci di Russia*, at a mass celebrated by him in San Domenico, Archbishop Castellano had expressed the hope that progress would soon be made in respect of the location and return of remains. During the mass the field altar of an ex-chaplain, Mons. Enelio Franzoni, had stood in front of the altar, whilst volumes containing the names of the Italian dead in Russia were on the altar of the chapel in San Domenico dedicated to Catherine. Some five months later, in August 1983, as a result of the increasing influence of Mikhail Gorbachev and the beginning of 'Glasnost', an initial list of 64 Italians buried in the cemetery of Kirsanov was indeed released by the Soviet authorities – a coincidence that devotees of Saint Catherine were of course quick to attribute to her miraculous intervention. When the national reunion of Russian veterans took place in Siena in October 1984, Castellano again celebrated mass for the veterans and their families in San Domenico and confirmed Catherine's status as a patron of the veterans and their families.[67]

65 *La Voce del Popolo*, 4/10/1981, p. 6; 11/10/1981, p. 6; *La Casa di S. Caterina*, 1981, 2–3 (October), p. 7; *Il Corriere della Provincia di Siena*, 14/4/2007, 7.

66 *La Voce del Popolo*, 22/4/1984, p. 8; 6/5/1984, p. 8; *La Casa di S. Caterina*, 1984, 2 (August), pp. 4–5, 8; 1992, 1 (April), p. 7. The actual notice for the Reunion repeated this design with the addition of relevant dates, the name of the Unione Nazionali dei Reduci di Russia, and the names of the various military units that had participated in the Russian campaign. The portrayal of Catherine in these instances evoked that of the bronze statue of her inaugurated in Siena in October 1972 (Plate 21).

67 *La Voce del Popolo*, 3/4/1983, p. 9; 9/10/1983, p. 8; 6/5/1984, p. 8; 30/9/1984, p. 6; *Il Campo di Siena*, 4/10/1984, p. 2; *La Casa di S.Caterina*, 1983, 1 (April), p. 6; 1984, 2

The blessing of representatives of the armed forces – and of Italy – in the Campo at the end of the *Festa Nazionale* in April 1984 had also included another significant example of the continuing relationship between Catherine and the Italian military. The speech by Antonio Gullotti, the minister for cultural affairs, representing the government, before the blessing, included a particular tribute to the *Folgore* Parachute Division, one of whose units had been based in Siena since 1978 and who had recently returned from service with the multi-national United Nations peacekeeping force in the Lebanon. Before departing to the Lebanon in 1982 – on the first overseas mission by the Italian armed forces since the Second World War – the *Folgore* had adopted Saint Catherine as their patron saint.[68] Some 25 years later, moreover, in April 2007, the members of the *Folgore* unit based in Siena were again sent to south Lebanon as part of another multi-national United Nations peacekeeping mission. On that occasion, the president of the international society dedicated to Saint Catherine was present at the ceremony in Siena before their departure and presented a statue of Catherine as a symbol of her protection and blessing.[69] The relationship between Catherine and the Italian forces was also commemorated in 1989 in a special edition of the *Rivista Militare*, the journal of the Italian armed services, published to celebrate the 50th anniversary of her proclamation as *Patrona d'Italia*. Dedicated to Italian military chaplains who had received Italy's highest military decoration for bravery, the publication included articles by Gaetano Bonicelli – then the head of the *Ordinariato Militare* and subsequently Archbishop of Siena in succession to Archbishop Castellano – on the theme of Catherine as the heavenly advocate of the Italian forces, and by Patrizia Francescone on the theme of Catherine as an exemplar for the Italian military in their role as defenders of and workers for peace.[70]

Whilst the relationship between Catherine and the Italian armed forces thus exhibited notable continuity, the official proclamation of Catherine of Siena as a Doctor of the Church by Pope Paul VI in 1970 marked a further innovative development in her cult.[71] Principally a matter of significance within the Roman Catholic church, Catherine's elevation to the status of Doctor of the Church was nevertheless not without impact in terms of the civil religious role and function of her cult. The actual proclamation, in Rome on 4 October 1970, included the participation of the Sienese civic and religious authorities, of the *contrade* of Siena, and of more than 5,000 Sienese who travelled to Rome for the occasion. Indeed, the Sienese participation in the events of Sunday 4 October 1970 in Rome demonstrated beyond doubt that Catherine remained a potent symbol and focus of Sienese civil religion and civic devotion. Although now honoured as a Doctor of the Church as well as *Patrona d'Italia*, the Sienese continued to celebrate Catherine as

(August), p. 8; 1992, 1 (April), p. 7.

68 *La Casa di Santa Caterina*, 1984, 1 (April), p. 8; *La Voce del Popolo*, 22/4/1984, p. 8; 6/5/1984, p. 8.

69 *Il Corriere della Provincia di Siena*, 31/3/2007, p. 4; *La Nazione*, 31/3/2007, pp. II–III.

70 Bonicelli (1989); Francescone (1989).

71 Together with Teresa of Avila, also proclaimed a Doctor of the Church by Paul VI, Catherine became one of the first women to be thus recognized.

their principal '*santa senese*' even as they enthused over the latest of the honours accorded to her. Thus, the Sienese participation in the ceremonies in Rome included not only Archbishop Castellano and the other bishops from the archdiocese of Siena, the Mayor of Siena, Roberto Barzanti, the Prefect and the President of the Province of Siena, but also the costumed representatives of all the *contrade* of Siena, present within Saint Peter's for the mass and formal proclamation and subsequently at further ceremonies at the statue of Catherine at Castel Sant'Angelo, in Santa Maria sopra Minerva for a ceremony involving the mayors of Siena and Rome, and finally in the Campidoglio for a ceremony involving further speeches by the mayors of Siena and Rome, another by a cardinal representing the Pope, and a formal address from Giulio Andreotti, the president of the council on behalf of the government.[72] Within Siena, moreover, it was notable that the reports of the event were prominent not only in the religious press but also in the local secular papers.

Archbishop Castellano took the opportunity of Catherine's proclamation as a Doctor of the Church to create a new organization to promote her cult. With a decree issued under his authority as Archbishop of Siena, Castellano instituted the *Associazione Ecumenica dei Caterinati*. The new organization replaced the earlier *Confraternita di Santa Caterina da Siena in Fontebranda*, the activities of which had steadily declined in the quarter century since the end of the Second World War. The new association was to revive the work of disseminating knowledge of Catherine and her significance, promote her cult and devotion to her, and also work for Christian unity and peace according to the spirit of Catherine's teaching and example. As Castellano's founding decree made clear – and as its very title demonstrated – the new association was also intended to embody the spirit and assumptions of the Second Vatican Council.[73] One of the earliest initiatives of the new association was to establish a series of publications devoted to Catherine and her cult under the title *Quaderni Cateriniani*. At the beginning of October 1972 – and thus coinciding with the celebration of the second anniversary of Catherine's proclamation as a Doctor of the Church – a bronze statue of Catherine was also unveiled in Siena. The work of the sculptor Bruno Burrachini, the statue is located at the end of Viale dei Mille, and is so positioned that the figure of Catherine looks towards San Domenico (at the other end of Viale dei Mille) and, beyond that, across the city of Siena (Plate 21). Catherine is shown standing with arms raised above her head in a gesture of blessing, holding in one hand a cross and in the other an olive branch, and the base on which the statue stands originally bore the simple carved inscription: 'A SANTA CATERINA BENINCASA / FIGLIA DI SIENA PATRONA D'ITALIA / DOTTORE DELLA CHIESA'. (Subsequently, after Catherine's proclamation as a co-patron of Europe, the words 'PATRONA D'EUROPA' were added to the inscription.) The inauguration of the statue once again demonstrated the interaction of both Sienese and Italian civil religion. In a ceremony clearly modelled on the annual *Festa Nazionale*, the statue was blessed and formally 'consigned' to Siena. The civic authorities were present,

72 *Il Campo di Siena*, 10/10/1970, pp. 3–4; *La Nazione, Cronaca di Siena*, 5/10/1970, p. 4; *La Voce del Popolo*, 11/10/1970, p. 4; La Casa di S. Caterina, 1990, 3 (December), pp. 4–5.

73 *Statuto* (1981, esp. pp. 1–2); Morandi (1996, pp. 30–31); Bacci (2002, p. 70).

as were the *contrade* of Siena. In addition, the Cardinal Archbishop of Florence, Ermengildo Florit, attended to represent the Italian bishops and the Pope, whilst the minister for public works, Antonio Gullotti represented the Italian government. A contingent of troops was also present, thus further evoking the closing ritual of the annual *Festa Nazionale*.[74] The new statue also became the focus for an additional ritual during each annual *Festa Nazionale*. On the Saturday of the weekend of the annual festival the Sienese civic and religious authorities participate in a brief event in which floral tributes to Catherine are placed at the statue in a ceremony accompanied by a short address and blessing by the Archbishop of Siena.

Unquestionably, however, the single most striking and significant development in devotion to Catherine of Siena and in the promotion of her cult during the three decades that Mario Castellano was Archbishop of Siena was the initiation and growth of the campaign for her to be proclaimed a co-patron saint of Europe. In 1980, in addition to the usual *Festa Nazionale*, the sixth centenary of Catherine's death was marked by two major international conferences dedicated to Catherine and also by Pope John Paul II's interest in her cult. The two conferences were held in April. The first, in Siena from 17 to 20 April, focused jointly on Catherine of Siena and Bernardino of Siena – 1380 being the sixth centenary of Bernardino's birth as well as of Catherine's death. The second conference, held jointly in Siena and Rome from 24 to 29 April, was devoted entirely to Catherine and culminated in a civic celebration at the Campidoglio in the morning of 29 April, at which the vice-president of the Chamber of Deputies, Oscar Luigi Scalfaro delivered an address affirming the contemporary relevance of Catherine's message,[75] and a mass, celebrated by Pope John Paul II in Saint Peter's in the afternoon. Both conferences resulted in major publications containing the very varied papers presented by a wide range of international scholars.[76] In retrospect, however, perhaps the most significant of all the contributions was a brief paper, presented by Adriana Oddasso-Cartotti – a prominent member of the *Centro Nazionale di Studi Cateriniani* that had been re-founded in Rome in the 1960s[77] – at the International Congress in Rome. Entitled '*Caterina Benincasa, Santa Europea*', her contribution drew attention, once again, to Catherine's enduring commitment to peace and unity within the church, within Italy and within the Europe of her day. In addition, however, she linked Catherine's enthusiasm for this cause to the post-war ideal of European unity within a community of nations and linked this, in turn, to Pope Paul VI's proclamation, in 1964, of Saint Benedict as patron saint of Europe in virtue of the unifying effect of his spirituality upon Europe. Playing upon the coincidence in the centenaries of the traditional date of Benedict's birth in 480 and the date of Catherine's death in 1380, Oddasso-

74 *La Voce del Popolo*, 24/9/1972, p. 4; 1/10/1972, p. 4; 8/10/1972, p. 4.

75 Scalfaro (1981).

76 *Congresso Internazionale* (1981); Maffei and Nardi (1982).

77 The *Centro Nazionale di Studi Cateriniani* in Rome had been revived in 1963 under the leadership of Luigi Tincani, who had been one of the originators of the idea of a statue of Catherine of Siena at Castel Sant'Angelo. Adriana Oddasso-Cartotti and Giuliana Cavallini were among the most prominent members and most prolific scholars in the revived organization. For an overview of the (now 'International') group see www.centrostudiocateriniani.it/2/2cenno.html (accessed 27/11/2007).

Cartotti argued that, nine centuries after Benedict, Catherine had dedicated her life to the same unifying ideal. Therefore, she suggested, Catherine and Benedict might also be recognized as co-patron saints of Europe.[78]

In his Apostolic Letter, '*Amantissima Providentia*', issued on 29 April 1980 for the sixth centenary of Catherine's death, Pope John Paul II also affirmed that Catherine's message and example remained relevant not only for Italy but for the world, referring to the civil and religious divisions and disunity of Europe in Catherine's day and to Catherine's efforts to secure peace and unity within the church, within Italy and within Europe.[79] On 14 September 1980, John Paul II visited Siena with the particular intention of making a pilgrimage to the places in the city associated with Catherine and her cult. The various addresses given by him during the visit – which were reported in detail in the next day's edition of *L'Osservatore Romano* – focused, unsurprisingly, upon Catherine and her contemporary significance including, prominently, her call for peace and reconciliation.[80] At the end of 1980, moreover, in his Apostolic Letter, '*Egregiae Virtutis*', John Paul II gave a further clear indication of the importance that he attached to the themes of Europe and its Christian roots, European identity and European unity when he added two further saints to Benedict as co-patrons of Europe, namely, saints Cyril and Methodius, ninth-century evangelists of Eastern Europe, thus affirming the spiritual unity of Europe, east and west.[81]

During the next two decades a concerted campaign was mounted to promote the cause of Catherine's proclamation as *Patrona d'Europa*. Although the ideological context and content of the campaign was quite different, the strategies and tactics deployed were, in many respects, the same as those that had been used in the 1920s and 1930s in the campaign to secure Catherine's proclamation as *Patrona d'Italia*. Articles, addresses and speeches were produced, conferences were held, resolutions were passed and petitions were organized, all with the aim of promoting the idea of Catherine as a patron saint of Europe, and all designed to urge the Pope officially to proclaim her so. A further similarity lay in the appeal – in the 1980s and 1990s, as in the 1920s and 1930s – to the political career and activity of Catherine, to her ambassadorial travels and mediations, to her aims of restoring the papacy to Rome, and unity to both Italy and Europe, and to her many letters to prominent figures in pursuit of these political aims. The crucial difference, however, was in the ideological end to which appeal to these aspects of Catherine's life was directed. In the 1920s and 1930s it was Catherine's Italian-ness that was to the fore, her status as the most authentically Italian of all Italy's female saints and therefore as a '*santa nazionale*', together with her desire to unify Italy and free the 'nation' from foreign domination,

---

78 Odasso-Cartotti (1981, esp. pp. 664–5).

79 For the full text of the Apostolic Letter see the Vatican online resource: www.vatican.va/holy_father/john_paul_ii/apost_letters/documents/hf_jp-ii_apl_29041980_amantissima-providentia_it.html (accessed 27/11/2007).

80 Again, for the full text of John Paul II's addresses in Siena see the Vatican online resource: www.vatican.va/holy_father/john_paul_ii/speeches/1980/september/index.htm (accessed 27/11/2007). For the press report see *L'Osservatore Romano*, 15–16/9/1980, p. 4.

81 www.vatican.va/holy_father/john_paul_ii/apost_letters/documents/hf_jp-ii_apl_31121980_egregiae-virtutis_it.html (accessed 27/11/2007).

whilst also unifying Europe against the external threat posed by contemporary Islamic powers. In the 1980s and 1990s, however, it was Catherine's international significance that was to the fore, her desire for peace and unity not just in Italy but in all of Europe, under the unifying leadership of the papacy. In seeking to advance this understanding of Catherine, moreover, the campaign of the 1980s and 1990s was able not only to adopt the strategies that had proved so successful in the 1920s and 1930s, but also to adapt the predominant themes of the *Feste Nazionali* of the post-war period. It was easy enough to continue to emphasize Catherine's message of peace, social justice and truth, of political authority as a duty and a service, and of the need of all these qualities for the furtherance of good government and the common good – but to do so in a manner that recast these virtues from the Italian to the European context.

For example, Adriana Oddasso-Cartotti followed her paper at the international congress in Rome with a series of lectures in various venues and articles in *L'Osservatore Romano*, all of which emphasized Catherine's efforts to secure peace and unity in varying contexts – in Siena, in Tuscany, in Italy and ultimately in Europe as a whole. In 1984, a collection of 12 such articles and addresses, all originally published or delivered between 1980 and 1983, was issued under the title *Caterina da Siena Santa Europea*.[82] In an article on 'Catherine of Siena and the European community', Oddasso-Cartotti argued that, among all the female saints of Europe, Catherine had been the most intense advocate of the unity of the Continent, thus making her an appropriate female co-patron alongside Benedict, Cyril and Methodius. Catherine's own work for the ideal of European unity – which was now, Oddasso-Cartotti claimed, 'our own ideal' – would thereby inspire contemporary Europeans.[83] Similarly, in a speech on 'Catherine of Siena as a European Saint', she affirmed that the cause of European unity which Catherine had defended was the same cause that inspired contemporary advocates of a united Europe, and in an article on 'Catherine and the rulers of European states' she insisted that, as in Catherine's day, so now, the basis of European moral, political and economic unity was collective faith in Christ – a faith exemplified in the European context by the three official male patron saints of the Continent and also by Catherine.[84] Archbishop Castellano similarly promoted the theme of '*S. Caterina da Siena e l'Europa*', publishing an address devoted to the subject in three different contexts between 1980 and 1983,[85] whilst in 1984 one of the Italian members of the European Parliament, Mario Pedini, added his voice to the growing trend by presenting an address to the *Centro Nazionale di Studi Caterinati*

82 Oddasso-Cartotti (1984a).

83 Oddasso-Cartotti (1984b, pp. 64, 69). The article first appeared in *L'Osservatore Romano* 26–27/4/1982.

84 Oddasso-Cartotti (1984c, p. 29; 1984d, p. 60). The first of these was originally presented at a meeting of the Rotary Eur in May 1980 and the second was originally published in *L'Osservatore Romano*, 29/4/1981.

85 Castellano (1980; 1981; 1983). In the first instance, although the content of the address was the same, the title referred to the modernity of Catherine's thought, especially in respect of international conciliation in a European context. The lecture was also re-published a fourth time in a collection of Castellano's writings during his first 25 years as Archbishop of Siena, for which see D'Urso (1986, pp. 133–48).

in Rome on '*Caterina da Siena e la nostra Europa*', the text subsequently being published in the series of *Quaderni Cateriniani*.[86]

At the close of his much re-published lecture, Castellano had drawn attention to the fact that devotion to Catherine already had a significant European focus outside Italy in Belgium, at Eupen-Astenet, near Liège, where a chapel dedicated to Catherine had been founded in 1968 and had since become established as a centre of her cult located 'in the heart of Europe' close to the borders of Holland, Germany and France.[87] By the second half of the 1980s, moreover, in addition to the now well-established themes of peace, justice and service, the specifically international significance of Catherine and her legacy was also being emphasized in the annual *Feste Nazionali* in her honour in Siena, whilst the festival itself was given a more international dimension and orientation. Thus, for example, in 1987, the festival included not only the customary participation of another Italian city (in this case Sassari, in Sardinia) to present oil for the Votive Lamp, but also the participation of the mayor and other civic representatives of the French city of Avignon, of representatives of the community dedicated to Catherine at Eupen-Astenet, and of a visiting Swiss choir from Geneva. The participation of the civic authorities of Avignon was in celebration of the 25th anniversary of the official twinning of the cities of Avignon and Siena in 1962 – an act which itself commemorated the historical links between the two cities and, especially, the fact that Catherine had gone to Avignon in 1376 to persuade Pope Gregory XI to end the papal exile and return to Rome.[88] The mayors of Siena, Sassari and Avignon all spoke at the ceremony for the presentation of oil for the Votive Lamp at the Portico dei Comuni. The Mayor of Avignon, it was noted, spoke eloquently of the European dimension of Catherine's vocation and of the relevance of her teaching for the unification of contemporary Europe in a single community of states characterized by a Christian spirit and a mission of peace in the world. The markedly international tone of the festival was seen as an appropriate platform from which to call for Catherine to be officially proclaimed a patron saint of Europe, alongside Benedict, Cyril and Methodius.[89]

Two years later, in 1989, the celebrations of the 50th anniversary of the proclamation of Catherine as '*Patrona d'Italia*' became the occasion not simply for retrospection and nostalgia, but rather for the launch of a further stage in the campaign for her proclamation, additionally, as co-patron saint of Europe. Reports of the *Festa Nazionale* in 1989 in the Sienese Catholic press simply asserted – boldly, though without any official justification – that Catherine was already, in reality, not only patron saint of Italy, but also a de facto patron saint of Europe, whose European relevance and significance were increasingly being recognized. At

86 Pedini (1984).

87 Castellano (1981, p. 15). For the origins and history of chapel at Eupen-Astenet see the website of the community at www.caterinavonsiena.be/frameset140203.htm (accessed 27/11/2007).

88 The connection between Catherine, Siena and Avignon was also celebrated on the 30th anniversary of the twinning of the two cities, in 1992, by a major exhibition held in the Grande Chapelle du Palais des Papes in Avignon, for which see *Catherine de Sienne* (1992).

89 *La Casa di S.Caterina*, 1987, 2 (August), pp. 4–7.

the ceremony at the Sanctuary, the Mayor of Siena affirmed that the oil for the Votive Lamp was offered for justice, for fraternity and for peace, not only in Italy but in the world. Interest in the historical figure of Saint Catherine and her cultural and moral message, the local religious press claimed, was increasing year by year, as shown by the flowering of studies of Catherine and her significance, by the growing success of her annual festival and the number of groups and associations that wished to have her protection, and by the number of requests to the Pope for her proclamation as co-patron of Europe. Such a proclamation, it was acknowledged, would be a major event which would require the careful thought of the Pope – but it was also noted by Cardinal Achille Silvestrini, in his sermon at the High Mass for the festival in San Domenico, that it was already clearly seen to be a genuine possibility.[90]

The use of the celebration of the 50th anniversary of the proclamation of Catherine as *Patrona d'Italia* to promote her further claim to be a co-patron saint of Europe continued in October 1989. A conference in Siena at the beginning of October, to commemorate the 50th anniversary of the proclamation of both Catherine and Francis of Assisi as co-patrons of Italy, took as its theme 'Saint Catherine of Siena, from Patron of Italy to Patron of Europe', whilst a General Assembly of the Sienese and other Italian branches of the *Associazione Ecumenica dei Caterinati* formally adopted a motion to appeal directly to Pope John Paul II to proclaim Catherine a co-patron of Europe. Approved unanimously, the motion was supplemented by similar petitions from the Belgian, German and Dutch branches of the *Caterinati*, as well as petitions from the Commune of Siena and the Sienese *contrade* of the Oca and the Drago (both of which have Saint Catherine as their patron saint and whose territories within Siena include, respectively, the Sanctuary of Saint Catherine and the church of San Domenico).[91] Also in 1989, acting on a suggestion from Archbishop Castellano, a petition of signatures of members of the European Parliament at Strasbourg in support of Catherine's proclamation as co-patron of Europe was organized by Roberto Barzanti, a former mayor of Siena, a historian with a long-standing interest in Catherine of Siena and, at that time, president of the Cultural Section of the European Parliament. An avowedly secular politician of the left, Barzanti sought the support of another Italian member of the European Parliament, Rosy Bindi, who was also from the province of Siena but, in addition, was a practising Catholic and a prominent member of *Azione Cattolica*. Together, they sought broadly based support for the petition, from a range of geographical areas and ideological viewpoints, thus seeking to demonstrate the pluralistic appeal of the petition, and to show that it was not essentially confessional or party-politically based.[92] In February 1990, in a

90 *Toscana Oggi*, 16/4/1989, p. 9; 7/5/1989, p. 9; 14/5/1989, p. 9; *La Casa di S. Caterina*, 1989, 2, (August), p. 7.

91 *Toscana Oggi*, 14/5/1989, p. 9; 15/10/1989, p. 9; *La Casa di S.Caterina*, 1989 (August), p. 7; 3 (December), pp. 4–5. The text of the 'Supplica al Santo Padre per la proclamazione di S. Caterina da Siena a Compatrona d'Europa' on the part of the *Associazione Ecumenica dei Caterinati* is reproduced in *Quaderni Cateriniani*, 73, 1993, pp. 12–15.

92 *Toscana Oggi*, 4/3/1990, p. 11; *La Casa di S.Caterina*, 1990, 1 (April), pp. 6–7; *Il Corriere della Provincia di Siena*, 2/10/1999, p. 15; *La Nazione*, 2/10/1999 (Siena section), p. 3. The text of the petition is included in *La Casa di S. Caterina*, 1990, 1 (April), p. 6 and also in *Quaderni Cateriniani*, 73, p. 16.

private audience with the Pope, Castellano presented John Paul II with the petition signed by Barzanti, Bindi and 77 other members of the European Parliament. Pope John Paul II was reported to have responded by indicating that, pending further study by the appropriate offices within the Vatican, he was disposed to favour such a proclamation, not least because contemporary Europe had need of heavenly patrons, and in particular of a female patron who might guide the 'home of the European community like a mother'.[93]

The momentum created in 1989 was maintained in the early 1990s. At the *Festa Nazionale* in April 1990, the visiting cardinal, Roger Etchegarry, president of the Pontifical Council for Justice and Peace, focused upon Catherine's European significance in his addresses at the High Mass in San Domenico and again at the official lunch held afterwards. The reports of the festival in the local press, meanwhile, spoke of the *Festa Nazionale* already moving 'towards a European festival' and of the importance, as a 'Europe without frontiers' drew nearer, of placing Saint Catherine alongside the existing three male patron saints of Europe in order to emphasize the importance of the role of women in the Continent of Europe and in the church.[94] The international significance of Catherine and her cult was also reaffirmed in the change of name of the *Associazione Ecumenica dei Caterinati*. In 1991 the General Council of the *Associazione* decided to petition the Vatican for official recognition, presenting evidence of the success of their organization over more than two decades, including its development outside Italy and in particular in Belgium where, in addition to the predominantly German-speaking group at Eupen-Astenet, there was now also a predominantly French-speaking branch in Liège. The initial request signed by Mario Castellano – who remained honorary president of the *Associazione* although he had retired as Archbishop of Siena in 1990 – was subsequently supported by his successor as Archbishop of Siena, Gaetano Bonicelli and by Albert Housiau, the Archbishop of Liège. In August 1992 the Vatican granted the desired official recognition and the title of the organization became the *Associazione Internazionale dei Caterinati*. In addition to the previous aims of the existing *Associazione* the new statute now also included the further specific aim of contributing to 'the reconstruction of the spiritual unity of Europe by bringing it back to its Christian roots'.[95] By this time, moreover, the Europe which the *Associazione Internazionale dei Caterinati* hoped to see restored to its Christian roots already included countries of the former Soviet bloc. In April 1991, for example, Giuliana Cavallini, the director of the *Centro Nazionale di Studi Cateriniani* in Rome, and Aldo Bernabei, the president of the Roman branch of the *Caterinati*, had visited Poland to establish a branch of the *Associazione* there and to gather Polish signatures in support of Catherine's proclamation as a co-patron

---

93 The theme of Saint Catherine as a 'spiritual mother of Europe' ('una vera mamma spirituale per tutta l'Europa') was subsequently reasserted with particular emphasis at the *Festa Nazionale* of 2002, for which see *Il Corriere della Provincia di Siena*, 29/4/2002, p. 15.

94 *Toscana Oggi*, 8/4/1990, p. 9; 6/5/1990, p. 9; *La Casa di S.Caterina*, 1990, 2 (July), pp. 4–6.

95 *Statuto* (2005, esp. pp. 3–4, 7–8). For the development of both German- and French-speaking groups in Belgium, see the preface by Castellano to Deraedt (1992, p. 3).

saint of Europe. At the Catholic university of Lublin, Cavallini delivered a lecture – subsequently published both in the series of *Quaderni Cateriniani* and also in the journal *L'Arbore della Carità* – on the importance of Catherine and her message for the construction of the '*casa comune europea*'.[96] Rehearsing once again the much repeated theme of Catherine's vision of a Europe in which factional disputes between Christians were set aside in favour of a united Christian response to the threat posed by Turkish ambitions in Eastern Europe and the Balkans, Cavallini made a point of referring to the letter on this subject addressed by Catherine to Queen Elizabeth of Hungary, pointing out that Elizabeth was the mother of the then reigning king of both Hungary and Poland, Louis I – known as Louis the Great.[97] Having acknowledged that contemporary circumstances were very different from those of Catherine's day, she nevertheless concluded her lecture with a reaffirmation of Catherine's relevance to the task of constructing a new European home, namely, her conception of the spiritual unity of Europe and the Christian roots of its culture and civilization.[98]

The other dramatic political contexts of the early 1990s – both in Italy, with the major political crisis that began in 1992 and witnessed the dissolution of the major parties that had dominated Italian politics since the war, and in Europe with the conflicts that accompanied the break-up of the former Yugoslavia – were also inevitably reflected in the annual *Feste Nazionali* in honour of Catherine. Thus, the theme of the significance of Catherine for the political crisis within Italy was particularly evident in 1993 when, moreover, the *Festa Nazionale* was celebrated on 25 April, thereby coinciding with the annual *Festa della Liberazione* in which Italians commemorate the end of the Second World War. The Mayor of Siena, Pierluigi Piccini, in his address at the Portico dei Comuni during the presentation of oil for the Votive Lamp, asserted that the ideal of peace – understood not just as the absence of war but as the improvement of the quality of life for all on the basis of social justice – was the focal point of Catherine's political creed and reminded his listeners of the pressing contemporary need for peace in the former Yugoslavia, especially in Bosnia, in the Middle East, in Central America, in Eastern Europe and in Africa. Turning to Italy, he noted that the nation was living through difficult moments of institutional crisis, of violence from organized crime and of corruption in public life. In this context, too, he appealed to Catherine's teaching on the duties and appropriate attitudes of those with a responsibility for government.[99] Later in the day, the minister for social affairs, Adriano Bompiani, in his address in the Campo, having reviewed aspects of Catherine's life, drew attention to her emphasis upon the relationship between personal and social responsibility and the need to sacrifice self-interest to the common good, referring as he did so to key publications and speeches

96 Cavallini (1991; 1992).

97 Cavallini (1991, pp. 11–12). For the text of the letter to Elizabeth see Meattini (2006, pp. 60–64). Louis the Great was the son of the Angevin king, Charles I of Hungary and Elizabeth, the daughter of King Vladislas I of Poland. Louis inherited the throne of Hungary in 1342 and that of Poland in 1370. He died in 1382. Elizabeth died in 1380. For their complex dynastic history see Klaniczay (2002, p. 444).

98 Cavallini (1991, pp. 17, 20).

99 Piccini (1993a, esp. pp. 5–6).

of the post-war era which had similarly appealed to her example – most notably to the publication of *Massime di Reggimento Civile* in 1947, to Guido Gonnella's speech the same year in the Palazzo Pubblico at the opening of the celebration of the sixth centenary of Catherine's birth, and to Oscar Luigi Scalfaro's speech at the International Congress devoted to Catherine in 1980.[100] Significantly, the edition of the *Quaderni Cateriniani* in which both these addresses were published (together with the other speeches and sermons delivered that day) was entitled '*La Santa Patrona Caterina e la rinascita morale e politica d'Italia*'.

The urgency of the domestic political crisis in Italy in the early 1990s did not, however, impede the continuing emphasis upon the international – and in particular the European – significance of her cult. In 1991, for example, as the process of the dissolution of Yugoslavia descended into outright war, the notices announcing the *Festa Nazionale* for Catherine that year carried the message that the consolidation of peace was the greatest need of the hour, and asserted that Catherine would ensure that Italy and Europe were clear-sighted and courageous in the pursuit of this aim.[101] In her speech in the Campo at the end of the festival, the visiting minister, Rosa Russo Jervolino, subsequently affirmed that many people in Eastern Europe hoped that Catherine would be made an official co-patron of the 'new Europe' because she was the saint most suited to address the political problems of the Continent.[102] The following year an edition of the *Quaderni Cateriniani* was dedicated to the theme of Catherine as the de facto patron of Christian voters in Europe – a lecture given by a Belgian devotee of Catherine and originally published in the journal of the '*Gruppo Elettori Cristiani*',[103] whilst the Mayor of Siena, speaking in the Campo, again expressed the hope that Catherine would be named a patron saint of Europe.[104] In 1993, two further editions of the *Quaderni* were then devoted to Catherine as a potential exemplar for and co-patron of Europe. The first consisted of two articles by Adriana Oddasso-Cartotti, both of which originally appeared in *L'Osservatore Romano* on 29 April in, respectively, 1992 and 1993. Now combined under the overall title, '*Principii politici di S. Caterina da Siena*', they focused on the need for unity and peace and on the principles of good government according to Catherine, again urging the relevance of these themes to the cause of European unity in peace – itself understood as an example of the potential for world peace.[105] The second edition of the *Quaderni* – entitled '*La nuova Europa*' – consisted principally of two addresses given in Siena in early October 1993 by the Mayor of Siena, Pierluigi Piccini, and by Roberto Barzanti, who was by then vice-president of the European Parliament. Originally given at a conference held in the Palazzo Pubblico of Siena, the addresses by Piccini and Barzanti – both politicians of the left – again emphasized the political and social relevance of the teaching and example of

100 Bompiani (1993, esp. pp. 26–7).

101 A copy of the notice is bound into the copy of the March 1991 edition of *La Casa di S. Caterina* held in the Biblioteca Comunale degli Intronati in Siena.

102 *La Casa di S. Caterina*, 1991, 2 (July), pp. 4–5.

103 Deraedt (1992).

104 *Toscana Oggi*, 3/5/1992, p. 9.

105 Oddasso-Cartotti (1993, esp. p. 5).

Catherine in the context of a Europe in which the high hopes for a new era of peace that had accompanied the fall of the Berlin Wall had been replaced by a resurgence in particularism and an aggressive nationalism that had resulted in crisis and war in the Balkans following the dissolution of Yugoslavia.[106] The same conference also included the presentation of a re-issue of the critical edition of the prayers of Saint Catherine edited by Giuliana Cavallini, the director of the *Centro Nazionale di Studi Cateriniani* in Rome, in which she concluded her brief chronology of Catherine's life with the assertion that Europe had need of the values that Catherine represented and restated, yet again, the hope that Catherine would indeed be proclaimed co-patron of Europe, together with Benedict, Cyril and Methodius.[107]

The international significance of Catherine and the desirability of her proclamation as a co-patron saint of Europe continued to be pressed in subsequent *Feste Nazionali* during the mid and late 1990s,[108] even to the extent that the blessing imparted in the Campo at the conclusion of the festival was already, on occasion, described, pre-emptively, as a blessing not only of Siena and Italy, but also of Europe.[109] Similarly, the themes of reconciliation, justice and peace in contemporary Europe assumed an increasingly prominent place in the addresses, sermons and speeches that accompanied each festival – especially as the successive Balkan crises and wars unfolded in the wake of the collapse of the former Yugoslavia.[110] Just as the campaign in the 1930s for Catherine to be proclaimed *Patrona d'Italia* had included a petition from the Sienese, so the campaign for her to be made a co-patron of Europe also now included a popular petition. On this occasion, however, as befitted the international nature of the new campaign, the signatures were to reflect the range of European support for Catherine as *Patrona d'Europa*. Thus the petition – which was available for signature in San Domenico, Siena – was available in Italian, English, French, German and Spanish.[111] Beyond Siena, meanwhile, the case for Catherine's formal recognition as *Patrona d'Europa* also continued to be pressed in the pages of *L'Osservatore Romano* where Adriana Oddasso-Cartotti regularly marked the saint's annual festival with articles that included enthusiastic references to her role as an inspiration for the reconciliation and union of the various peoples of Europe; to the relevance of her message for the spiritual unity of Europe and the construction of a European community based upon the specifically Christian roots of its civilization;

106 Piccini (1993b); Barzanti (1993, esp. pp. 7, 9–11).

107 Cavallini (1993, p. 151). For the conference in Siena see *Toscana Oggi*, 26/9/1993, p. 11.

108 See for example Bacci (1996, p. 9); *Toscana Oggi*, 3/5/1992, p. 9; 7/5/1995, p. 12; *La Casa di S. Caterina*, 1995, 2 (September), pp. 4–5.

109 *Toscana Oggi*, 25/4/1993, p. 9; *La Casa di S. Caterina*, 1993, 2 (September), pp. 4–5; 1999, 2 (July), p. 5.

110 *Il Corriere della Provincia di Siena*, 26/4/1999, p. 15; *Toscana Oggi*, 7/5/1995, p. 12; 2/5/1999, p. 10; *La Casa di S. Caterina*, 1994, 3 (December), pp. 4–5; 1999, 2 (July), pp. 4–5.

111 For the text of the petition see Castellano (2000, p. 32).

and to the importance of her teaching on peace and justice at a time of war in Kosovo and in the wider Balkan context.[112]

Finally, 60 years after her proclamation as co-patron of Italy, Catherine of Siena was also proclaimed a co-patron of Europe, on 1 October 1999, by Pope John Paul II, at the opening of the Synod of European Bishops. Although Catherine was only one of three female Saints proclaimed co-patrons of Europe at this Synod – the other two being Saint Bridget of Sweden and Saint Teresa Benedetta della Croce – this did nothing to diminish the predictable celebration and enthusiasm of the Sienese for this long-awaited announcement. By midday on 1 October, the chapel in the church of San Domenico that houses the relic of Catherine's head already had the flag of the European Union placed by it, in addition to the Italian flag. The bells of the cathedral, of San Domenico and of the Sienese town hall were rung in celebration, and in the evening Archbishop Bonicelli presided at a mass of thanksgiving in the chapel dedicated to Catherine in San Domenico.[113] The following year, Sienese recognition and celebration of this latest honour to be bestowed upon Catherine found further expression. Firstly, just as in 1939 the banner for the August *Palio* had been dedicated to Catherine's proclamation as *Patrona d'Italia*, so the banner for the *Palio* of August 2000 was dedicated to her proclamation as *Patrona d'Europa*. There, however, the similarities ended. The banner painted for the *Palio* of August 1939, it will be recalled, portrayed Catherine casting a protective cloak over a fictive city which contained within its walls portrayals of monuments representing major Italian cities. The banner also bore the symbols of the Fascist regime (Plate III). The banner for the *Palio* of August 2000, by contrast, showed Catherine standing, gesturing welcomingly towards the viewer whilst, in place of the overt political symbols included in the 1939 banner, there appeared a more discreet political message: at the top of the banner for August 2000 there appeared 12 stars against a blue background, thus representing the 12 states that then constituted the European Union and evoking the flag of the European Union (Plate IV).[114]

A second Sienese celebration of Catherine's new status occurred in October 2000. To mark the first anniversary of her proclamation as *Patrona d'Europa*,

---

112 See respectively *L'Osservatore Romano*, 28–29/4/1997, p. 10; 27–28/4/1998, p. 3; 29/4/1999, p. 4.

113 *Il Corriere della Provincia di Siena*, 2/10/1999, p. 15; *La Casa di S.Caterina*, 1999, 3 (December), pp. 4–5.The text of the introduction to the Apostolic Letter in which Pope John Paul II proclaimed the three new co-patron saints of Europe was reproduced as a supplement to this edition of *La Casa di S. Caterina* and also in *L'Osservatore Romano*, 2/10/1999, pp. 1, 4–6.

114 Betti (2007, pp. 36–7). This image is also now used on the website of the *Centro Internazionale di Studi Cateriniani* on the page which gives a chronology of Catherine's life and also lists the principal moments in the history of her cult. Each entry is accompanied by an image of Catherine and the banner for the *Palio* of August 2000 accompanies the entry in the chronology for the proclamation of Catherine as *Patrona d'Europa*, for which see www.centrostudicateriniani.it/1/1cronologia (accessed 8/1/2008). Alberto Positano, the artist responsible for the banner for the *Palio* of August 2000, also subsequently completed six stained-glass windows for the crypt of San Domenico, Siena. Each of the windows portrays one of the six co-patron saints of Europe.

a marble statue of Catherine by the French sculptor Eric Aman was unveiled in Rome. Placed in an external niche of the Basilica of Saint Peter's, facing the Piazza Santa Marta, the funds for the statue were given by the archdiocese of Siena, by Sienese institutions such as the Monte dei Paschi bank and the university, by the *Associazione Internazionale dei Caterinati* and through public subscription. As in 1970, on the occasion of Catherine's official recognition as a Doctor of the Church, again in 2000, numerous Sienese went to Rome for the inauguration of the statue which was blessed by Pope John Paul II following a mass in Saint Peter's Square. At the blessing and inauguration of the statue there were not only representatives of the civic and ecclesiastical authorities of Siena but also of other towns in the province of Siena and of devotees of Catherine from elsewhere in Italy and Europe.[115] There were again speeches at the inauguration, and also a commemorative publication containing essays in honour of the occasion. The consistent theme, in both cases, was of Catherine as a messenger and ambassador of peace, of social justice and of European unity and cooperation.[116]

Following the formal proclamation of Catherine as a co-patron of Europe, the annual festivals in her honour assumed an even more self-consciously international and European tone. Thus, whilst the festival itself has been formally and officially redefined as an 'International Celebration in Honour of Saint Catherine of Siena, Patron of Italy and of Europe' and as a '*Festa Internazionale*', several of the visiting cardinals at the festival have been from other European countries. In 2000, for the first *Festa Internazionale*, the visiting cardinal was Gottfried Danneels, the Archbishop of Brussels, whilst the oil for the Votive Lamp was presented by the Belgian branches of the *Associazione Internazionale dei Caterinati* – an act which, it was observed, confirmed the now truly international dimension of the celebrations.[117] In 2001 Cardinal Josè da Cruz Policarpo of Lisbon presided at the festival, followed in 2002 by Cardinal Vinko Pulijc, the Archbishop of Sarajevo, and in 2003 by Cardinal Zenon Grocholewski, a Polish cardinal and the Prefect of the Congregation for Catholic Education in the Vatican, whilst in 2005, a Swiss cardinal, Georges Marie Martin Cottier presided.[118]

The tone and content of the speeches, sermons and addresses at the *Feste Internazionali* since 2000 have similarly been consistently and overtly internationalist, so that the festival has become at once a celebration not only of Catherine as patron saint of both Italy and Europe, but also of European unity across national frontiers and, in turn, of European commitment to international cooperation. In April 2002, for example, with the Archbishop of Sarajevo as visiting cardinal, and with events

115 Bonicelli (2000); *Il Corriere della Provincia di Siena*, 30/10/2000, p. 12; *La Nazione* (Siena section), 29/10/2000, p. 10; *Toscana Oggi*, 29/10/2000, pp. 1, 11; *La Casa di S. Caterina*, 2000, 3 (December), pp. 4–6, 8.

116 Bonicelli (2000, p. 28); Piccini (2000); Durand (2000).

117 *Toscana Oggi*, 7/5/2000, p. 12; *Il Corriere della Provincia di Siena*, 26/4/2000, p. 15; 1/5/2000, p. 9; *La Casa di S.Caterina*, 2000, 1 (April), p. 8.

118 *Il Corriere della Provincia di Siena*, 30/4/2001, p. 11; 28/4/2002, p. 18; 29/4/2002, p. 15; 3/5/2003, p. 16; 4/5/2003, p. 16; 5/5/2003, p. 13; *La Nazione*, 30/4/2001, p. 16; *Toscana Oggi*, 6/5/2001, p. 12; 5/5/2002, pp. 12, 15; 4/5/2003, p. I; 11/5/2003, p. I; 24/4/2005, p. I; *La Casa di S.Caterina*, 2001, 1 (April), p. 8; 2002, 2 (August), pp. 4–5; 2003, 2 (July), pp. 4–5.

in Israel and the Palestinian Authority dominating news headlines, all the speeches, sermons and blessings at the various ceremonies, and all the reports in the local press, referred to Catherine's relevance to the themes of peace, justice, community and reconciliation in Bosnia, in the rest of the Balkans, in the Middle East and in the world.[119] The international orientation of the annual festivals is also expressed and symbolized in other elements of the rituals of the festival and its ceremonies. The flags displayed at the various ceremonies routinely include not only those of Siena and Italy, but also that of the European Union, whilst the final blessing in the Campo at the conclusion of the entire festival is now habitually described as a blessing not only of Siena and of Italy through representative members of its armed forces, but also of Europe. Indeed, the international nature and orientation of the annual festival has also prompted further reaffirmations of the fact that the principle role of the Italian forces is now that of peacekeepers and participants in international and multi-national missions, whether with the United Nations, the European Union, or Nato – a theme given particular prominence and poignancy in 2006 when the *Festa Internazionale* took place shortly after the death of further Italian soldiers in Iraq, at Nassiriya where previously, in November 2003, 17 Italian military personnel and two Italian civilians had been killed while serving with the multinational forces stationed there.[120]

It is not only, of course, in the annual *Feste Internazionali* that Catherine continues to be presented and promoted as co-patron of Europe. That process has also continued in, for example, the pages of *L'Osservatore Romano*,[121] in lectures, articles and books that advocate and explore her significance in and for contemporary Europe, and in the work of both the *Associazione Internazionle dei Caterinati* based in Siena and the *Centro Internazionale di Studi Cateriniani* based in Rome.[122] How, exactly, Catherine and her cult will be interpreted, promoted and deployed in debates about European identity and values in the future remains to be seen. It is already clear, however, that her function as *Patrona d'Europa* is not necessarily limited to that of a figure whose teaching on peace, social justice and the priority of the common good is a straightforwardly unifying and inclusive influence and symbol. Alongside this role – which can and often does unite speakers and authors of different political and ideological viewpoints, as in the petition from members of the European Parliament in 1989 or in many of the speeches by successive left-wing mayors of Siena at *Feste Nazionali* over several decades – Catherine, in her capacity as *Patrona d'Europa*, is also sometimes presented as a source and symbol of a particular religious, social and political vision and agenda for Europe, as for example in the debates over a draft constitution for the European Union.

119 *Il Corriere della Provincia di Siena*, 28/4/2002, p. 18; 29/4/2002, p. 15; *La Nazione*, 29/4/2002, p. 7; *Toscana Oggi*, 5/5/2002, 12, p. 15.

120 *Il Corriere della Provincia di Siena*, 1/5/2006, p. 16; *La Nazione*, 1/5/2006, p. 22; *Toscana Oggi*, 7/5/2006, p. I. For previous emphasis on the peacekeeping role of the Italian forces, see also *Il Nuovo Cittadino Oggi*, 4/5/2003, p. 8; *Toscana Oggi*, 9/5/2004, p. II.

121 See for example *L'Osservatore Romano*, 29/4/2001, p. 7; 2–3/5/2001, p. 6; 28/4/2002, p. 4; 30/4/2003, p. 6; 9/5/2003, p. 8.

122 Examples of such publications include Boccardi (2003); Minnucci (2003). The *Centro Nazionale* in Rome changed its name to become *Internazionale* in 2006.

Thus, for example, when the first drafts of the preamble to a proposed constitution for the European Union did not include a reference to the specifically Christian roots of Europe, Pope John Paul II and the Roman Catholic church – as well as other Christian churches and some member states of the European Community – urged the inclusion of such a reference. The *Associazione Internazionale dei Caterinati* took up this cause, seeking to rouse support for the view that the proposed Constitution of the European Union should recognize the explicitly Christian roots of Europe, that these roots constitute the surest foundation of European identity, and that they provide the best – and arguably the only secure – basis for a spiritual, ethical and cultural unity founded on the dignity of all persons and communities.[123] Similarly, speeches at the annual festivals in 2001, 2002 and 2003 asserted that Europe was founded, above all, upon Christian roots and the shared Christian values of all the peoples of Europe and that only the Church could be relied upon to maintain human dignity, justice and peace, which neither socialism nor the free market could do.[124] The *Associazione Internazionale dei Caterinati* is also now a participant in the organization *Anima Europae* – a group formally constituted in 2003 by members of the religious orders and lay societies associated with the six patron saints of Europe. The stated aim of *Anima Europae* is the commitment to promoting the spiritual, ethical and cultural unity of Europe, specifically on the foundation of its common Christian roots – a commitment that also involves defending a particular Catholic understanding of the family; resisting both materialism and secularization; opposing the hedonistic individualism that it perceives to be characteristic of much of modern European life; and promoting the Christian and spiritual values that the organization sees as the principal historical forces for the progress of civilization.[125]

Participation in such groups and the advocacy of such values does not necessarily imply divisive or narrowly sectional attitudes towards contemporary Europe and its future. It does, however, locate Catherine and her social, cultural and political legacy at least in tension with – and arguably in opposition to – other strands in the development of modern and contemporary Europe, most notably those secular and liberal traditions derived from the Enlightenment.[126] Within the recent and contemporary Italian context, for example, it places Catherine and her significance as *Patrona d'Europa* on the side of those politicians, Catholic interest groups and Catholic institutions – such as the Conference of Italian Bishops – who assert the claims of Catholic social and moral teaching and the relevance of the public role of religion within contemporary Italian life and who therefore oppose what are

123 *Il Corriere della Provincia di Siena*, 4/7/2003, p. 15; *La Casa di S.Caterina*, 2003, 2 (July), p. 7.

124 *Il Corriere della Provincia di Siena*, 30/4/2001, p. 11; 29/4/2002, p. 15; *La Nazione*, 29/4/2002, p. 7; *Toscana Oggi*, 5/5/2002, p. 12; 11/5/2003, p. I; *La Casa di S.Caterina*, 2002, 2 (August), pp. 4–5.

125 For the 'Manifesto' of *Anima Europae*, which includes a clear statement of its aims, see Boccardi 2003, pp. 213–18) or the official website of the organization: http://animaeuropae.org (accessed 27/11/2007).

126 See for example Avogadro (2005, pp. 11–12) where the author blames the Enlightenment, especially in France, for the rise of an ideology that asserts the primacy of human reason and rejects divinely revealed dogma.

perceived to be 'secular' policies in relation to a variety of issues – such as the official recognition of civil partnerships (especially, but not only, in the case of gay couples), abortion and the 'morning-after pill', stem-cell research, medically assisted fertilization, euthanasia and a range of other issues associated with 'the family' and with 'Christian values'. It is significant, moreover, that the Conference of Italian Bishops and other Catholic lobbying groups became more assertive in such matters during the pontificate of John Paul II, especially in the aftermath of the collapse of the Christian Democratic party in the early 1990s – precisely the period, that is to say, during which Catherine was being promoted as *Patrona d'Europa*. As recent studies have demonstrated, the political preferences and allegiances of Italian Catholics in the post-Christian Democrat era are complex and certainly do not lend themselves to simple alignments between Catholic belief and particular political loyalties. Nevertheless, it is clear that, in recent years, there has been increasing tension between the church and the centre-left, especially on issues of public and private morality.[127] Of particular note in the present context is the suggestion that, especially since the election of Pope Benedict XVI, the church has not only sought to increase its presence in Italian public debate but has also shifted 'from social themes (solidarity, peace) to areas of public and private ethics'.[128] It is, however, precisely large 'social themes' – such as 'solidarity', 'peace', 'justice' and 'the common good' – that have characterized the majority of the speeches, articles, books and other expressions of support for Catherine as both *Patrona d'Italia* and *Patrona d'Europa* during the last 60 years. Moreover, the fact that the organization *Anima Europae* seeks to apply a similar political-moral agenda in a European context – again focusing not only on 'social' issues such as 'solidarity and peace' but also on 'family values' and issues of personal/public morality – serves further to demonstrate that the figure of Catherine, in her role as *Patrona d'Europa*, could have the capacity to become a divisive rather than solely a unifying figure.[129]

That possibility is a useful reminder that, in the first decade of the twenty-first century, Catherine of Siena and her cult therefore remain potentially ambiguous and contested subjects – especially in terms of their significance for civil religion in both Italian and European contexts. It is not, of course, inevitable that such ambiguity will become more pronounced, or that her significance as *Patrona d'Europa* will prove divisive, but these are at least possible outcomes. This in turn constitutes an appropriate caution against superficial readings of the history of Catherine's cult in the last hundred years. It can be tempting, in reviewing the development of Catherine's cult during the twentieth century, to read it simply as a history of steady advancement – of 'progression' through successive and successful campaigns on the

---

127 For discussion of these themes see Garelli (2007); Diamanti and Ceccharini (2007); Melloni (2007).

128 Diamanti and Ceccarini (2007, pp. 51–2). See also Garelli (2007, pp. 33–4).

129 See for example Avogadro (2005, esp. pp. 11–12), where the author argues that in western democracies there is now an emptiness in relation to ethical and moral values and a rampant individualism which results in the 'sad consequences' of the overturning of the notion of the family, the legal recognition of homosexual relationships, the lack of respect for life from conception to death by natural cause and the abandonment of all moral limits to biological experimentation in the name of scientific research.

1986 respectively). Thus, Cardinal Baggio devoted his entire sermon to the theme of Catherine as an 'ambassador of peace', whilst Cardinal Benelli used the approaching sixth centenary of the end of the war between Florence and the papacy to focus upon Catherine's repeated advocacy of peace in her letters.[57] In his speech in the Campo in 1973, Italo Caiati, minister with responsibility for young people, having noted that the restoration of peace – between families, opposing factions, cities and states – was Catherine's principal ideal, concluded by affirming that fellowship, justice and concord are now the fundamental elements of democracy, and that the armed forces are the custodians of democratic freedom and the defenders of the values of the entire community.[58] Five years later, Mario Pedini, minister of education, again emphasized Catherine's message of peace and her role as a mediator relating it not only to contemporary Italy, but also to the development of a new and united Europe.[59] The address by Senator Pietro Schietroma in 1982 took as its very title Catherine's role as the bearer of truth, justice and peace, and concluded with an affirmation that the role of Italy's armed forces was precisely the defence of these values.[60] In 1985 – at the annual *Festa Nazionale* that coincided with the fortieth anniversary of the end of the Second World War in Italy – Antonio Gava, minister for post and telecommunications, contrasted political doctrines that, 'in recent times', had viewed the armed forces as a means of resolving international disagreements and of attacking the liberty of others, with the vision of the role of the armed forces that was embodied in Catherine's letters. Whereas the former had plunged Europe and much of the world into a bloody conflict, the latter understood the armed forces to be the defenders of independence and liberty – a concept, Gava asserted, that was explicitly endorsed by the constitution of the Italian republic.[61] The following year Luciano Bausi, an undersecretary at the ministry of justice, constructed his address around the three themes of authority (interpreted as a duty and service), justice (as the indispensable foundation of good government) and peace (as the potential result of a universal application of justice).[62]

Moreover, the blessing in the Campo at the end of the *Festa Nazionale* increasingly came to be described not simply as a 'blessing of the armed forces', but as 'a blessing of Siena and of Italy', often with the further explicit gloss that it was a blessing of Italy 'through its representative young people in military service'. The rationale for this interpretation – and also the extent of the transition from the militaristic tone of the original national festivals of Saint Catherine, just before and during the early years of the Second World War, to the re-invented and re-orientated festivals of the post-war era – was acknowledged with particular clarity in an article in 1973. Published in an early edition of *La Casa di S. Caterina* – a magazine published under the auspices of the Sanctuary of Saint Catherine between 1970 and 2003 – the article was prompted by criticism that the military presence at the festival was inappropriate

57 Baggio (1974); Benelli (1978, esp. p. 5).
58 Caiati (1974, esp. pp. 14–16).
59 Pedini (1978, esp. pp. 15–16).
60 Schietroma (1983, esp. pp. 18–19).
61 Gava (1985, esp. p. 14).
62 Bausi (1986).

part of her devotees and of various interest groups – resulting in her proclamation first as *Patrona d'Italia* and then as *Patrona d'Europa*. Behind and within this apparently straightforward narrative, however, there is a more complex history involving the adoption of Catherine and her cult by different interest groups and by the exponents of widely divergent ideological positions. It will be the task of the conclusion to the present book to consider some of the implications of this more complex history and, in particular, its significance for the concept of 'civil religion'.

Conclusion

Catherine of Siena and the Varieties of Civil Religion

This book has surveyed the history of the cult of one Sienese saint over a period of more than six centuries. It has done so, moreover, from the particular perspective of the significance of that saint and her cult for a succession of types of civil religion: firstly Sienese, subsequently Italian and, most recently, European. It is the task of this conclusion, firstly, to look again at these three types of civil religion, to ask how they relate to each other and to consider briefly what they may indicate about the concept of civil religion itself. Secondly, the conclusion must also ask what, if anything, the use of Catherine and her cult in these three types of civil religion reveals about the 'historical Catherine' and her significance.

At first glance, the structure of the present book might appear to suggest that in terms of Sienese civil religion Catherine and her cult were of great importance in earlier centuries but have subsequently left their Sienese significance behind as, during the twentieth century, Catherine became, successively, *Patrona d'Italia* and *Patrona d'Europa*. Thus, Chapter 1 is devoted, firstly, to the way in which the Sienese promoted Catherine's cult and sought her canonization, and, secondly, to the way in which Catherine became a member of the Sienese civic pantheon of '*santi cittadini*', then became one of the elite group of saintly advocates and defenders of the city, and finally assumed a pre-eminent place within the civic pantheon and community of '*santi cittadini*'. In subsequent chapters, however, although Siena continues to be the location for many of the key moments in the development of her cult, and although the Sienese continue to be prominent players in the promotion of her claims to be both *Patrona d'Italia* and *Patrona d'Europa*, yet her significance for Sienese civil religion might be thought to be diminishing. Although understandable, however, in at least two ways, such a reading of the history of the last century and a half of Catherine's cult would, in fact, be seriously misleading.

Firstly, the very enthusiasm of the Sienese, during the twentieth century, for the promotion of Catherine as an Italian and then a European patron saint was also an expression of Sienese civic pride and civil religion. It was precisely as the pre-eminent '*santa senese*' that the Sienese advanced the claims of their historic co-citizen for recognition as an exemplar and heavenly patron of national and then international stature. Again and again in twentieth-century Sienese celebrations of Catherine and in publications and addresses advocating her suitability as both *Patrona d'Italia* and *Patrona d'Europa*, she is referred to as '*concittadina*', as '*la vergine senese*' or as the sometime resident of the Sienese neighbourhood of Fontebranda.

Secondly, even as they promoted Catherine as a saint of national and international significance, the Sienese also invented new ways to celebrate her cult within Siena itself. Thus, after the official proclamation of Catherine as *Patrona d'Italia* in 1940, the Sienese invented a new annual *Festa Nazionale* in her honour. Over the ensuing decades the Sienese then developed that festival, steadily increasing the level of civic involvement and participation so that by the late 1950s it had come to include civil religious ceremonies not only at the Sanctuary of Saint Catherine and in the church of San Domenico, but also in the Campo – the location of the Palazzo Pubblico and the civic heart of Siena. From the early 1970s the rhythm of the weekend of the annual festival also included a distinct contrast between its two days: the first being geared to a more domestic Sienese celebration of Catherine at the statue of her near to San Domenico, and the second being devoted to the national celebration of her status as *Patrona d'Italia* – but a national celebration in Siena and led by the Sienese civic authorities who, without fail, would recall and emphasize her Sienese origins. By the turn of the millennium, the annual festival had become international – but again still retained its Sienese character, including the participation not only of the mayor and other civic officials, but also of the Sienese *contrade* and their costumed representatives – indeed, the final act of the ceremony in the Campo at the climax of the annual festival, after the blessing of Siena, Italy and Europe, remains a performance of the traditional formal display by the flags of Siena's seventeen *contrade* as a salute to the civic and national authorities present.

In the second half of the twentieth century, the Sienese thus not only successfully contributed to the promotion of their pre-eminent civic saint as a national and international figure, but also created a new annual festival within the calendar of Sienese civil religion. The two annual celebrations of the *Palio* – in early July and mid August – undoubtedly remain the most important expressions of Sienese civic identity and civil religion[1] – but the annual festival in honour of Catherine is now a major subsidiary date in the cycle of Sienese civil religion.[2] Moreover, Catherine's continuing status within Sienese civic identity and civil religion was also demonstrated by the number of occasions during the twentieth century that an image or relic relating to her was used for the annual Sienese festival of Domenica in Albis and by the number of times that a *Palio* banner was dedicated to her. Thus, during the twentieth century, an image of Catherine or a relic associated with her was the focus for Domenica in Albis on eight occasions. No other member of the Sienese civic pantheon of '*santi cittadini*' came near to this frequency, the next most favoured member of the pantheon being Bernardino, but on only two occasions.[3] Similarly, between 1939 and 2000, Catherine was celebrated on *Palio* banners on no less than seven occasions – in 1939 in honour of her proclamation as *Patrona*

1 Parsons (2004a, esp. pp. 130–63).

2 It is a moot point whether, in terms of Sienese civil religion, the annual festival in honour of Catherine is more or less prestigious than the annual festival of Sant'Ansano on 1 December, but that it is one of the two principal annual expressions of Sienese civil religion other than the *Palio* is not in doubt. For the festival of Sant'Ansano see Parsons (2006).

3 This, in turn, reflected Catherine's status as the member of the civic pantheon most frequently represented in the festival of Domenica in Albis throughout its entire history. An image or relic associated with her was chosen 28 times between 1567 and 2000. Bernardino was again the second most favoured civic saint, but with only nine instances. For a full list of the relics and images chosen, see Gianni (2002).

d'Italia (Plate III), in 1947 for the sixth centenary of her birth, in 1962 for the fifth centenary of her canonization, in 1971 in celebration of her status as a Doctor of the Church, in 1976 for the sixth centenary of her visit to Pope Gregory XI in Avignon to seek the return of the papacy to Rome, in 1980 on the sixth centenary of her death, and in 2000 in honour of her proclamation as *Patrona d'Europa* (Plate IV).[4] Again, this far exceeds the number of portrayals of any other member of the Sienese civic pantheon on such banners.[5] It also serves to underline the extent to which Catherine remains a central figure within recent and contemporary Sienese civil religion. In their promotion of Catherine as 'the most Italian of Italy's female saints', and then as a figure of European stature, the Sienese did not stop celebrating her as Sienese. Nor did they perceive there to be any conflict between Catherine's role within the civil religion of Siena and her roles as *Patrona d'Italia* and *Patrona d'Europa*. Rather, they themselves asserted her national and international significance whilst also simultaneously celebrating her increasing national and international prominence as an endorsement of Sienese history, of Sienese civic values and, above all, of the pre-eminent '*santa senese*'.[6]

In turning to Catherine of Siena as a focus of Italian 'national' civil religion, a much more complex picture emerges. As early as 1859–60, Catherine was associated with the national aspirations of the war of independence and, indeed, with the provision of material and spiritual assistance to Italian soldiers. By the early twentieth century, she was associated with the Italian military campaign in Libya in 1911–12, and again with the Italian war effort during the First World War. In both cases, appeal was made to her own 'national' consciousness of the reality of a united Italy, and also to her European perspective in calling for a crusade on the part of European Christians to regain 'the Holy Land' from occupation by Muslim powers. Even before the advent of the Fascist period, therefore, Catherine and her cult had been associated not only with Italian national identity, but also with an assertive Italian nationalism and a foreign policy that included the use of military power and the vocabulary of the crusade.

During the Fascist *ventennio* such associations became much more pronounced. The origins of the campaign for Catherine to be proclaimed *Patrona d'Italia* and recognized as a '*santa nazionale*' did not lie in the regime and its propaganda. The impetus for Catherine to be thus honoured lay with her devotees, in Siena and elsewhere, and of course with the Dominican Order. The initiatives that were to result, almost two decades later, in Catherine's proclamation as *Patrona d'Italia* by Pius XII, began in the early 1920s, before the Fascist seizure of power and well before the beginning of the regime's attempt to secure the thoroughgoing 'fascistization' of

4 For details of each of these banners see Betti (1992a, pp. 113, 129; 1992b, pp. 36–7, 76–7; 1993, pp. 46–7, 58–9, 68–9; 2007, pp. 36–7).

5 For the other members of the civic pantheon portrayed in *Palio* banners from the mid-twentieth century onwards see Parsons (2004a, p. 95; 2006, p. 60).

6 Contemporary Siena, it should be noted, is a city which at once retains a strong sense of its own distinctiveness and uniqueness and immense pride in its history, culture and traditions, but is also, at the same time, strongly European and internationalist in outlook and attitudes. The city is, for example, proud of its status as a UNESCO world heritage site.

Italian society. Nevertheless, the development of the campaign during the 1920s and 1930s for Catherine to become *Patrona d'Italia* coincided with the rise of Mussolini's regime and with the years of its dominance. Perhaps inevitably, given the history of relations between church and state during the *ventennio*, the promotion of Catherine's claim to be both *Patrona d'Italia* and a '*santa nazionale*' increasingly drew upon, echoed, and exploited the vocabulary of the regime. Conversely, supporters and representatives of the regime readily recruited Catherine to their cause. Thus, Piero Misciattelli was an early advocate of the '*romanità*' of Catherine, whilst Pietro Fedele was quick to associate the inspiration that Catherine might bring to new generations with that offered by the Fascist renewal of Italy. Similarly, from as early as the inauguration of the bust of Catherine in the Pincio Gardens (Plate 11), a link was suggested between the 'national' and 'Roman' vision of Catherine and the rebirth of Italy under Mussolini – a parallel that was to be made even more explicit, and indeed taken to fanciful extremes, in much of the rhetoric that followed the *conciliazione*. Catherine and her cult were also recruited by the regime to assist the overtly nationalistic and militaristic aims of its youth movements and its imperial ambitions. Thus, Catherine was adopted as the patron saint of the *Piccole e Giovane Italiane*, whilst images of the saint were sent to Somalia and Ethiopia as part of the spiritual support for the Italian invasion of the latter – an event which also prompted cycles of prayer to Catherine for an Italian victory over a people perceived to be barbarous and uncivilized.

When Catherine was eventually proclaimed *Patrona d'Italia* in 1939, the event was accompanied by further rhetoric associating her with the achievements of the new Italy and its imperial ambitions, and the first *Festa Nazionale* in her honour was marked by the presence of Fascist dignitaries and the performance of Fascist ritual and oratory (Plates 12, 13). Within months of that event, however, Italy was at war. Whilst the *Feste Nazionali* of 1941 and 1942 exhibited continued support for the regime and hopes for victory, from 1943 onwards a new, more chastened and more tentative tone began to emerge in relation to the war – not least in respect of the relationship between Catherine's cult and the fate of ordinary Italian servicemen. With the crisis of 1943, the ambiguities surrounding the relationship between Catherine and her cult and the war became even more acute. By mid 1944 Catherine's role in relation to service personnel had come to encompass not only Italians, but also Germans and then additionally members of varied allied armies. And by 1945, the *Festa Nazionale* in her honour had already assumed a distinctively post-fascist tone which prefigured the 'reconstruction' of her cult as *Patrona d'Italia* in – and for – the post-war era.

In the post-war period Catherine – in her role as *Patrona d'Italia* – was emphatically re-fashioned. In place of the emphasis upon '*romanità*' and the spiritual rebirth and renewal of Italy in militantly nationalistic terms, Catherine was now portrayed and invoked as the protector of the Italian people as they engaged in the material and spiritual reconstruction of the nation upon the basis of democratic principles and social justice. Catherine now became the exponent of the principles of good government and the common good, of peace and social justice, of the responsibilities of those who govern, and of constructive and cooperative co-existence within a newly emerging European community of nations. At the same time, the celebration of this version of Catherine as *Patrona d'Italia* showed, from time to time, a continuing tension between the new rhetoric of cooperation, peace and the common good and the tensions between left and right in post-war Italy. Such tensions were, arguably, most clearly evident in some of the speeches at the *Feste Nazionali* of the immediately post-war era, and again in the iconography of the monument to Catherine at Castel Sant'Angelo that was inaugurated in April 1962 (Plates 18–20). Subsequently, however, after the Second Vatican Council, such tensions became less obvious and the emphasis upon Catherine as a patron saint who was, above all, a messenger and an ambassador of peace and social justice became even more predominant. This change of emphasis also applied, moreover, to Catherine's continuing role in relation to the Italian armed forces. Thus, although the blessing of representatives of the armed forces continued to form the climax to each *Festa Nazionale*, the act was firmly re-interpreted as a blessing of Italy and its young people through these representatives, whilst the role of Italy's forces was consistently presented as that of peacekeeping and the protection of democratic values and principles. In the final two decades of the twentieth century Catherine then steadily became re-interpreted yet again, this time in an international context and in the service of an internationalist and thoroughly European vision. From 1980 onwards, Catherine was presented as a messenger and ambassador of peace and social justice on an international scale, culminating in the successful campaign to have her proclaimed as an official co-patron saint of Europe.

In the space of barely three-quarters of a century, therefore, Catherine of Siena was proclaimed and celebrated as both a national patron saint – initially, moreover, in the context of a fiercely and uncompromisingly nationalistic and militaristic regime – and also as a patron saint of an international and multi-national community of nations committed to mutual cooperation. The tensions and contradictions within this process are clear – even if they often remain implicit rather than explicitly stated. The *Patrona d'Italia* of the Fascist era was presented as the patron of and model for the girls and young women of the Fascist youth organizations. She was invoked on behalf of the nation's armed forces, not only for protection of individual soldiers, sailors and airmen, but also for her heavenly endorsement of the justice of Italian war aims and her assistance in a hoped-for Italian victory. And in speeches, articles and press reports both Catherine and her festival were regularly associated with the regime and its values. From 1945 onwards, however, Catherine was presented as the patron saint of a nation firmly committed to democratic values and to international cooperation. Similarly, whilst Catherine and her cult continued to be closely associated with the Italian armed forces in the post-war era, the nature and meaning of the association changed. Building upon a transition that had already begun to occur during the Second World War – as Catherine and her cult increasingly became the focus for personal requests for the protection of individual members of the armed forces – in the post-war era her association with the Italian forces focused increasingly on the themes of the nation's commitment to the defence of democratic values and to participation in peacekeeping missions in an international context. The conflict between the two sets of values and political ideals associated with Catherine in her role as *Patrona d'Italia* in the pre-war and post-war eras is manifest. It also, however, remained largely implicit. The shift away from the pre-war and wartime association between Catherine and the Fascist regime was not presented or expressed explicitly as an overt rejection of Fascism and its values. Rather, the rejection remained implicit, although also decisive: the ethos and ideology of the campaign for Catherine to be proclaimed *Patrona d'Italia* and of the early *Feste Nazionale* in her honour were simply dropped and forgotten, and a different set of values, focused on issues of peace, justice and service, was introduced in their place.

What, however, does this sequence of interpretations of Catherine of Siena as a patron saint – or, it could even be said, this 'sequence of Catherines' – suggest, firstly, about civil religion as a concept, and secondly, about civil religion in twentieth-century Italy? It is still sometimes assumed that 'civil religion' will inevitably tend to promote the celebration of narrowly national and even militaristic interests. Thus, for example, writing with particular reference to Eastern Europe and the Balkans in the post-communist era, Stjepan Mestrovic has asserted that civil religion is neither 'bona fide religion nor ordinary patriotism, but a new alloy formed by blending religion with nationalism'. Moreover, Mestrovic continued, if civil religions were genuinely inspired by bona fide religions, then 'one would expect to find a soft side' to them, teaching love of neighbour and upholding peace and compassion. But this, he claims, is not the case.[7] That civil religion can function as Mestrovic argues is hardly to be doubted. Clearly, it can be the means of fostering and sustaining narrowly and aggressively sectarian interests, either at national or communal level. His own work demonstrates this clearly, especially in relation to Serbian and Croat civil religion in post-communist Yugoslavia, but also more generally in respect of post-communist nations in Eastern Europe.[8] 'Far from leading to the desired end of tolerance', he observes, 'thus far, at least, civil religions in post-communist lands have led to extreme intolerance, up to and including genocide' as Russian, Serbian and Croat nationalisms have adopted 'sacrosanct language concerning the alleged holiness and spirituality of the Russian soil, Serbian blood, Croatian history and so on'.[9] Following the fall of communism, therefore, Mestrovic concludes, it was the 'disintegrative, barbaric, and ethnocentric aspects of civil religion' that became evident.[10] Similarly, the work of Liz Fawcett on the relationship between religion, ethnicity and community in both Northern Ireland and apartheid-era South Africa has demonstrated the role of civil religion in maintaining the distinctive identities of particular Protestant communities and in defining boundaries between these communities and respective 'Others' – not least through highly discriminatory policies and overtly aggressive demonstrations.[11] It is not clear, however, that civil religion must always function in this way. It should not be forgotten, for example, that Robert Bellah concluded his seminal essay of 1967 on 'Civil Religion in America' – a text that still remains highly relevant to discussion of civil religion as a concept – with the hope that, in time a 'vital international symbolism' might be incorporated

7 Mestrovic (1993, pp. 125–31, 142, esp. pp. 125, 130–31).

8 Mestrovic (1993, pp. 135–44; 1994, p. 146).

9 Mestrovic (1994, pp. 147, 152). On Serbia and Croatia in particular see also Perica (2005).

10 Mestrovic (1993, p. 144).

11 Fawcett (2000, pp. 9–10, 81–114, 181–3).

into American civil religion, or even that American civil religion might become 'one part of a new civil religion of the world'.[12] Moreover, as Bellah argued in his famous essay, and as Thomas Hase has more recently reaffirmed, American civil religion can indeed be a means of sustaining and fostering forms of pluralism.[13]

What does the history of the cult of Catherine of Siena during the twentieth century contribute to this debate? It suggests, firstly, that civil religion, like other forms of religion, possesses a striking capacity for change – amounting, indeed, to transformation – over time. Secondly, it suggests that, whilst certainly open to exploitation in narrowly nationalistic and militaristic terms, civil religion is by no means bound to support such ideological ends. The capacity of civil religion to change over time is amply demonstrated by the transitions that occurred in the understanding of Catherine and her role as a patron saint in the course of the twentieth century. In the 1920s, 1930s and early 1940s Catherine was presented and promoted as the patron saint of a nation dominated by a highly nationalistic and militaristic regime. The portrayal of Catherine during these years duly reflected this cultural and political context. It would be excessive and exaggerated to describe the Catherine of the 1920s, 1930s and early 1940s as 'a Fascist saint', but it is entirely appropriate to describe her a 'a national saint in a Fascist state'. The emphasis upon her *romanità*, the close association that was developed between her cult and the Italian armed forces – not only during the Second World War but also in the mid 1930s in relation to the Italian conquest of Ethiopia – and the highly patriotic, nationalistic and militaristic ethos of the early *Feste Nazionali* in her honour all provide vivid illustration of the way in which, at that particular historical point, the history of the cult of Catherine of Siena provides support for Mestrovic's argument that civil religion constitutes 'a new alloy formed by blending religion with nationalism'.

By contrast, however, the post-war history of Catherine and her cult – specifically in relation to her status as *Patrona d'Italia* – decisively refutes Mestrovic's assertion that civil religions are an alloy of nationalism and religion and do not incorporate a 'soft side' teaching love of neighbour and upholding peace and compassion. As the final chapter of this study reveals, it was precisely as a messenger and ambassador of peace, teaching the value of compassion for one's neighbour and affirming the principles of good government in the interests of social justice and the common good, that Catherine was re-interpreted in her role as *Patrona d'Italia* in the period after the Second World War. Moreover, by the end of the century, in one sense, it was no longer Catherine's status as a national patron saint that held centre stage, but rather her international significance and her claim to be a co-patron saint of Europe. Indeed, the development of Catherine of Siena's cult from a national to a European expression of civil religion might well be cited as a demonstration of the fact that – as Bellah once hoped in relation to American civil religion – it is in principle possible to incorporate 'international symbolism' into more specific versions of civil religion. Indeed, in language which could almost be an echo of Bellah's desire that American civil religion might become 'part of a new civil religion of the world', in the early 1990s, one Italian commentator on Catherine's significance for politics

12 Bellah (1967, p. 19).

13 Hase (2001).

went so far as to hope that Catherine might be elected as '*Patrona della umanità intera*' and specifically of the United Nations.[14] There is also a not inconsiderable irony in the fact that, whilst Mestrovic appeals above all to the examples of Serbian and Croatian civil religion to demonstrate his thesis that civil religion is apt to result in an ethnocentric and potentially violence-prone blending of religion and nationalism, in the 1990s it was precisely the violence in the former Yugoslavia that prompted some of the most passionate advocacy of Catherine of Siena as an exemplar of international peace at successive *Feste Nazionali*.

At the same time, however, the very Europeanism and internationalism now associated with Catherine as *Patrona d'Europa* also reflects an important aspect of the national identity and outlook of recent and contemporary Italy. As well as retaining a deep-rooted tendency to value intensely local and regional identities, since 1945 Italy has been, and continues to be, highly pro-European and strongly committed to the European ideal, the European community and union, and to European integration – an outlook that can traced back to the immediately post-war period and to the desire to redeem its reputation within Europe by decisively repudiating its Fascist past.[15] Similarly, the 'reconstruction', in the post-war period, of the relationship between Catherine and her cult and the Italian armed forces – especially as described in many of the speeches in the Campo at the final ceremony of the annual festival in honour of Catherine – also reflects the dominant understanding of the role and purpose of the armed forces in recent and contemporary Italy. Thus the Italian armed forces are now seen – and see themselves – as especially committed to participation in international peacekeeping and other humanitarian missions.[16]

The development of the cult of Catherine of Siena since 1945 indeed demonstrates, therefore, that civil religion is not necessarily narrowly nationalistic but can, in principle, support collaborative and internationalist ideals. At the same time, however, the history of Catherine's cult from the 1920s until the present also stands, less positively, as a warning that civil religion can easily manipulate the same figure to profoundly different ends. In one respect there is a striking strand of continuity in the civil religious 'use' of Catherine and her cult which extends throughout the period from the 1920s to the present. Although applied in support of markedly different political ideologies and values, in both pre- and post-war contexts, those concerned to promote Catherine as a patron saint – whether of Italy or of Europe – all appealed predominantly to the public, politically involved Catherine of the period from 1374 until her death in 1380. It each case, it was the Catherine who addressed letters

14 Pajardi (1993, p. 137).

15 Doumanis (2001, pp. 157, 161–2); Dunnage (2002, pp. 1, 237–8).

16 See for example Ridolfi (2003, pp. 283–4) who draws attention to the reintroduction, in 2000, of a military parade in Rome for the annual celebration of the foundation of the Republic on 2 June. The reintroduced parade, he notes, was not a celebration of military force itself, but of service personnel whose role was to preserve and maintain peace. He notes also that the following year the parade specifically included women serving in the Italian forces, and also military units from other nations, thus emphasizing the European context of the event. For the official self-understanding of the contemporary Italian forces see the pages dedicated to the Italian army on the website of the Italian Ministry of Defence at www.esercito.difesa.it (accessed 27/11/2007).

– especially to persons in authority, such as popes, cardinals and bishops, civic officials, kings and queens, and the leaders of mercenary forces – that was promoted as potential patron saint and exemplar. It was the Catherine, that is to say, who also engaged in visits to the pope and to various cities in an ambassadorial role, and who devoted the last six years of her life to the furtherance of a particular set of political aims. It is hardly surprising that advocates of her potential as a national or European patron saint should choose to appeal to these aspects of Catherine's life – they are, after all, the ones most relevant to such patronal roles. But it is also striking that three distinct types of civil religion can all draw upon the same historical figure, and focus largely on the same aspects of that figure's life, in order to promote such markedly different – and, indeed, sometimes sharply conflicting – ideologies and ideals. In each phase of her promotion as a focus of Italian or European civil religion, the image of Catherine has been adopted and adapted to the political, social and cultural context and aims of those who wished to press her claim to be a patron saint.

In this process, moreover, it is not only secular political groups but also representatives of the Catholic church, of the Dominican Order and of Catherine's lay devotees who have shown a tendency to recruit Catherine and her legacy in support of strikingly different – and even conflicting – ideological positions. Thus, in the 1920s, 1930s and early 1940s it was not only prominent members of the Fascist regime – such as Pietro Fedele, Cesare de Vecchi or Giangiacomo Borghese – who celebrated Catherine and invoked her as an example of the values of Mussolini's Italy. This view was also advanced by various members of the *Società Internatzionale di Studi Cateriniani*, and by prominent members of the Dominican Order, such as the Master General Martin Gillet, and of the Catholic church, such as cardinals Nasalli-Rocca, Salotti and Piazza, or locally in Siena by archbishops Scaccia and Toccabelli. In the 1940s and 1950s, Catherine was then recruited, by some, to the cause of Italian Christian Democracy – whether by Archbishop Toccabelli, once again, in Siena, or by Luigi Gedda and those sympathetic to the activities of the *Comitati Civici* at the national level. Similarly, in the latter decades of the twentieth century, Catherine was presented as the exemplar of a quite different vision of peace, social justice and the common good, not only in an Italian context, but also in a European and international one – a position again espoused by politicians at both local and national level, by prominent representatives of the Catholic church, by members of the Dominican Order and by members of groups such as the *Associazione Internazionale dei Caterinati*.

It is also true that such use of Catherine's public and political life, and of her Letters, has often been profoundly ahistorical and even fanciful, involving the assertion of historical precedents and parallels that owe much to contemporary political persuasion and little or nothing to sober historical analysis. For example, the alleged parallels drawn between the political visions of Catherine and Mussolini – especially in 1929, but also more generally during the 1920s and 1930s – and the extended comparisons often made between Catherine and Joan of Arc during this period will not bear critical analysis in terms of historical accuracy. Similarly, the parallel apparently implied – on the monument to Catherine at Castel Sant'Angelo (Plates 19, 20) – between Catherine's near martyrdom at the hands of rebellious Florentine woolworkers in 1378 and the defeat of the left in the Italian election in

April 1948 owes everything to contemporary political propaganda and nothing to genuine historical similarity. Or again, most recently, the suggestion that Catherine's own vision of a form of European cooperation actually corresponds to contemporary concepts of European unity and community lacks historical credibility – however effective it may be politically as a means of promoting both the European ideal itself and Catherine's relevance as a symbol of that ideal.

Here, however, there is, perhaps, a final irony. Despite the ahistorical nature of many of the appeals to her during the twentieth century, such use – and sometimes abuse – of Catherine and her legacy nevertheless presents a significant contrast to the way in which her sanctity has more usually been celebrated and promoted. As noted in the introduction to the present book, in the interests of successfully promoting her cult and seeking her canonization, Catherine's early hagiographers created a tradition which played down her high-profile public activities and portrayed her as primarily a contemplative and mystic – thereby conforming to the highly gendered nature of late medieval and early modern expectations regarding the appropriate modes of female behaviour, including the behaviour of female religious, mystics and candidates for sainthood. Thus, even the earliest hagiographical accounts of her life presented Catherine pre-eminently by appeal to the ascetic, mystical, 'supernatural' and 'miraculous' aspects of her life, showing her above all as a visionary saint, and emphasizing her experience of the stigmata in establishing her claim to sanctity. The tendency thus established by her early hagiographers was then reinforced in the sixteenth century when the 'mystical Catherine' became a model for nuns in enclosed communities and the Counter-Reformation insistence on monastic enclosure for all religious women further ensured that only the ascetic and mystical aspects of Catherine's life were referred to as models of female sanctity. However anachronistic and ahistorical the twentieth century appeals to Catherine's life may have been, her promotion and celebration as *Patrona d'Italia* and *Patrona d'Europa* has, nevertheless, resulted in the restoration of her identity as an active, public and political figure. To that extent, at least, a more 'historical Catherine' has been reclaimed through this process – one whose sanctity was, indeed, 'not something separate from her engagement in worldly affairs'.[17]

17 Luongo (2006, p. 206).

Bibliography

Unpublished Archival Sources

Archivio Arcivescovile, Siena

2995
2998
3962
4033
4073
6546

Archivio della Compagnia di S. Caterina (1792–1970)

[now held by the Associazione Internazionale dei Caterinati, Siena]

97 [5]
98 [71]
128 [177]

Archivio della Nobile Contrada dell'Oca, Siena

XII B. 11 92
XIII B. 4 95
XIII B. 9 168
XIII B. 12 52
XIII B. 16 90
XIII B. 14 98
XIII B. 18 37

Archivio di Stato, Siena

ASS, Conventi, 1150, *c.*77–84

Newspapers and Periodicals

Secular Newspapers

Il Libero Cittadino
La Nazione
Il Telegrafo

Il Popolo Senese
La Rivoluzione Fascista
Foglio d'ordine della federazione senese dei Fasci di Comabattimento
Corriere del Mattino
Rinascita
Popolo e Libertà
Il Campo di Siena
Il Corriere della Provincia di Siena
Il Cittadino
Il Nuovo Cittadino Oggi

Religious Newspapers

Il Popolo di Siena
La Voce del Popolo
Toscana Oggi
L'Osservatore Romano

Religious Periodicals

Studi Cateriniani
Memorie Domenicane
S. Caterina da Siena, Bollettino Mensile della Chiesa [or] *Basilica di San Domenico*
Rassegna Cateriniana
S. Caterina da Siena, Bollettino Domenicano
S. Caterina da Siena, Patrona d'Italia
La Patrona d'Italia
La Patrona d'Italia e d'Europa
La Casa di S. Caterina

Books and Articles

Alberigo, G. (2000), 'Gedda ieri … e anche oggi?', *Cristianesimo nella storia*, 21, pp. 687–94

Ancilli, B. (1973), 'Soldatini di bronzo e soldati veri a S.Caterina,' *La Casa di S.Caterina*, 2 (June), p. 2

Angiolini, T. (1683, reprinted 1856), *Breve relazione del modo come fu portata da Roma a Siena la Sacra Testa della Serafica S. Caterina Senese*, Siena

Argenziano, R. (1996), 'La Beata Nobiltà: Itinerario iconografico' in M. Ascheri (ed.), *I Libri dei Leoni: La nobiltà di Siena in età medicea (1557–1737)*, Siena, pp. 284–327

Argenziano, R. (2003), 'Corpi santi e immagini nella Siena medievale: i santi patroni', *Bullettino Senese di Storia Patria*, 110, pp. 214–39

Ascheri, M. (1990), 'Quando la fede si misurava a peso', *Il Carroccio di Siena*, 32, pp. 38–9

Ascheri, M. (ed.) (1993), *L'ultimo Statuto della Repubblica di Siena (1545)*, Siena

Ascheri, M. (2000), *Siena nella storia*, Milan

Ascheri, M., Cornice, A., Ricceri, E. and Santini, A. (2004), *Memorie della Compagnia di San Salvatore Contrada dell'Onda (Siena 1524–1764)*, Siena

Avogadro, R. (2005), 'Le radici cristiane nella costruzione dell'unità etica e culturale dell'Europa' in *I sei compatroni d'Europa e la carità intellettuale: Atti del Seminario di studio Roma, LUMSA, 15 marzo, 2003*, Rome

Bacci, A. (1996), 'I caterinati offrono l'olio per la lampada votiva di S. Caterina', *Quaderni Cateriniani*, 91–2, pp. 5–10

Bacci, S. (2003), *L'Archivio della Compagnia di S. Caterina (1792–1970) conservato presso l'Associazione Internazionale dei Caterinati*, Siena

Baggio, S. (1974), 'Santa Caterina da Siena ambasciatrice di pace', *Quaderni Cateriniani*, 12, pp. 3–11

Bagnoli, A. (1980), 'Francesco Rustici' in *L'arte a Siena sotto i Medici 1555–1609*, Rome, pp. 185–7

Bähr, I. (1984), 'Das Katharinenfresko in San Domenico in Siena: Eine Stiftung aus dem Shülerkreis der Heiligen?', *Mitteilungen des Kunsthistorischen Institutes in Florenz*, 27, pp. 385–8

Balducci, A. (1947), *Santa Caterina da Siena. Massime di Reggimento Civile*, Rome

Balocchi, E. (2004), 'Un periodico democristiano: L'avventura di "Siena Cronache – Nuove Cronache" 1966–1970', *Istituto Storico Diocesano di Siena Annuario, 2003–2004*, Siena, pp. 423–39

Barbieri, C. (ed.) (1940), *Solenni Feste Nazionali a Gloria di Santa Caterina da Siena Patrona d'Italia*, Siena

Bartoli, M. (2002), 'Caterina da Siena e le armi della pace' in G. Minnucci (ed.), *Lecturae Catharinae 2001: Santa Caterina da Siena e la pace*, Siena, pp. 5–15

Bartolini, U. (1962), 'Saluto del Sindaco di Siena', *Bollettino Senese di Storia Patria*, 69, pp. 5–6

Barzanti, R. (1993), 'L'Europa ora. Le parole di Caterina Benincasa', *Quaderni Cateriniani*, 73, pp. 5–11

Barzanti, R. (1997), 'Dalla ricostruzione a ieri' in R. Barzanti, G. Catoni and M. De Gregorio (eds), *Storia di Siena: L'età contemporanea*, Siena, pp. 339–66

Barzanti, R. (2003), 'Laicità che esalta la spiritualità', *La Voce del Campo*, 2003, n. 34, p. 11

Barzanti, R., Cornice, A. and Pellegrini, E. (2006), *Iconografia di Siena: Rappresentazione della Città dal XIII al XIX secolo*, Città di Castello

Bausi, L. (1986), 'Giustizia santa', *Quaderni Cateriniani*, 44, pp. 6–10

Bell, R. (1985), *Holy Anorexia*, Chicago

Bellah, R. (1967), 'Civil Religion in America', *Daedalus*, 96, pp. 1–21

Benelli, G. (1978), 'Festa di S. Caterina da Siena', *Quaderni Cateriniani*, 21, pp. 3–11

Betti, L. (1992a), *Pallium: evoluzione del drappellone dalle origini ad oggi – dall'unità d'Italia all'ultimo conflitto mondiale*, Siena

Betti, L. (1992b), *Pallium: evoluzione del drappellone dalle origini ad oggi – dal dopoguerra alla conquista della luna*, Siena

Betti, L. (1993), *Pallium: evoluzione del drappellone dalle origini ad oggi – il drappellone verso il XXI secolo*, Siena

Betti, L. (2007), *Pallium: evoluzione del drappellone dalle origini ad oggi – 1994–2007*, Siena

Bianchi, L. (1988), 'Il sepolchro di S. Caterina da Siena nella basilica di S. Maria sopra Minerva' in L. Bianchi and D. Giunta, *Iconografia di Santa Caterina da Siena, I. L'Immagine*, Rome, pp. 15–62

Bianchi, L. (1990), 'Il Movimento per la proclamazione di S. Caterina a Patrona d'Italia' in *S. Francesco e S. Caterina Patroni d'Italia: Atti del cinquantenario*, Siena, pp. 59–75

Bianchi, L. and Giunta, D. (1988), *Iconografia di Santa Caterina da Siena, I. L'Immagine*, Rome

Bianco, M. (2002), 'Caterina maestra di pace' in G. Minnucci (ed.), *Lecturae Catharinae 2001: Santa Caterina da Siena e la pace*, Siena, pp. 45–58

Binchy, D. (1977, originally published 1941), *Church and State in Fascist Italy*, Oxford

Bisogni, F. and Bonelli Conenna, L. (eds) (1988), *L'Oratorio di S. Caterina nella Contrada del Drago: La storia e l'arte*, Siena

Bisogni, F. (1988), 'La costruzione e la decorazione del monastero e delle due chiese delle monache del Paradiso' in F. Bisogni and L. Bonelli Conenna (eds), *L'Oratorio di S. Caterina nella Contrada del Drago: La storia e l'arte*, Siena, pp. 71–88

Bitelli, G. (1938), *La Santa degli Italiani (Caterina da Siena)*, Turin

Boccardi, G. (2003), *Caterina da Siena: Una Santa degli Europei*, Siena

Boccardi, G. (ed.) (2006), *Lavorando in tre vigne: Cinquecento anni di storia dell'Arciconfraternita di S. Caterina da Siena in Roma*, Rome

Bocchini Camaiani, B. (1994), 'Devozione e cristianità. Chiesa e cattolici a Siena nel periodo fascista', *Passato e presente*, 12, pp. 69–90

Bocchini Camaiani, B. (1998), '"È l'ora di Dio! Dio lo vuole": Contrapposizioni politiche e ripercussioni ecclesiali nell'azione pastorale di Mons. Toccabelli a Siena e nella provincia senese', *Rivista di Storia e Letteratura Religiosa*, 34, pp. 279–304

Boesch-Gajano, S. and Redon, O. (1982), 'La *Legenda maior* di Raimondo da Capua, costruzione di una santa' in D. Maffei and P. Nardi (eds), *Atti del Simposio Internazionale Cateriniano-Bernardiniano, Siena, 17–20 Aprile 1980*, Siena, 1982, pp. 15–35

Bompiani, A. (1993), 'Messaggio all'Italia', *Quaderni Cateriniani*, 70–71, pp. 20–29

Bonicelli, G. (1989), 'Celeste avvocata dei militari italiani', *Rivista Militare, Numero Unico, 'Le Due Patrie'*, Rome, pp. 5–7

Bonicelli, G. (2000), 'Omaggio a Santa Caterina' in S. Soldini (ed.), *Santa Caterina da Siena: Una nuova statua di Eric Aman nella Basilica Vaticana*, Perugia, pp. 21–9

Borghini, G. (1983), 'La Decorazione' in C. Brandi (ed.), *Palazzo Pubblico di Siena: Vicende costruttive e decorazione*, Siena, pp. 145–349

Borghini, G. (1984), 'S. Caterina da Siena a Via Giulia (1766–1776): passaggio obbligato per la cultura figurativa del secondo Settecento romano', *Storia dell'Arte*, 52, pp. 205–19

Borgia, L, et al. (1984), *Le Biccherne: tavole dipinte delle magistrature senesi (secoli XIII–XVIII)*, Rome

Bornstein, D. (1998), 'Spiritual Kinship and Domestic Devotions' in J. Brown and R. Davis (eds), *Gender and Society in Renaissance Italy*, London, pp. 173–93

Bosworth, R. (2005), *Mussolini's Italy: Life Under the Dictatorship*, London

Breve Compendio della Vita della Serafica Vergine S. Caterina da Siena esposta in rima da A.I.P.A. e dai Sigg. della Contrada dell'Oca dedicate alla Quattro Compagnie Deputate dalla Domenica in Albis dall'anno MDCCLXXVII (1777), Siena

Brucker, G. (1968), 'The Ciompi Revolution' in N. Rubinstein (ed.), *Florentine Studies: Politics and Society in Renaissance Florence*, Evanston, pp. 314–56

Brucker, G. (1969), *Renaissance Florence*, London

Caciorgna, M. and Pierini, M. (eds) (1995), *Bruno Marzi*, Siena

Caiati, I. (1974), 'Attualità del messaggio Cateriniano', *Quaderni Cateriniani*, 12, pp. 12–16

Calamati, E. (1988), 'Le monache in Paradiso' in F. Bisogni and L. Bonelli Conenna (eds), *L'Oratorio di S. Caterina nella Contrada del Drago: La storia e l'arte*, Siena, pp. 25–30

Calisse, C. (1895), *S. Caterina da Siena*, Siena

Campanini, G. and Rossi, C. (1988), 'Nel Convento di S. Caterina detto del Paradiso' in F. Bisogni and L. Bonelli Conenna (eds), *L'Oratorio di S. Caterina nella Contrada del Drago: La storia e l'arte*, Siena, pp. 31–8

Cannistraro, P. (ed.) (1982), *Historical Dictionary of Fascist Italy*, Westport

Cannon, J. (2000), 'Founders and Followers (II): The burial and commemoration of "santi" and "beati" among the Dominicans of Central Italy', unpublished paper given at the Association of Art Historians Conference, Edinburgh, 2000

Cantelli, G., Pacchierotti, L. and Pulcinelli, B. (2005), *Il segreto della civiltà: La mostra dell'Antica Arte Senese del 1904 cento anni dopo*, Siena

Carli, E. (1963), 'Le Pitture' in A. Cairola and E. Carli, *Il Palazzo Pubblico di Siena*, Siena, pp. 69–253

Carli, E. (1979), *Il Duomo di Siena*, Genoa

Carrara, G. (1929), 'La Corporazione dei Caterinati – come si afferma', *Rassegna Cateriniana*, 8, pp. 89–92

Casella, M. (1992), *18 Aprile 1948. La Mobilitazione delle Organizzazioni Cattoliche*, Galatina

Castellano, M. (1980), *Modernità del pensiero cateriniano: conciliazione internazionale ed Europa – discorso pronunciato a Roma, il 29 ottobre 1980, sotto gli auspici del Centro italiano di studi per la conciliazione internazionale*, Rome

Castellano, M. (1981), 'S. Caterina da Siena e l'Europa', *Quaderni Cateriniani*, 30

Castellano, M. (1983), 'S. Caterina da Siena e l'Europa', *Studi economici e sociali*, 18, 2, pp. 133–48

Castellano, M. et al. (1990), *S. Francesco e S. Caterina Patroni d'Italia: Atti del cinquantenario (1939–1989)*, Siena

Castellano, M. (2000), 'Mamma e maestra del continente' in S. Soldini (ed.), *Santa Caterina da Siena: Una nuova statua di Eric Aman nella Basilica Vaticana*, Perugia, pp. 31–5

Catherine de Sienne (1992), Avignon

Cavallini, G. (1991), 'Santa Caterina da Siena e la costruzione della casa comune europea', *Quaderni Cateriniani*, 61

Cavallini, G. (1992), 'Santa Caterina da Siena e la costruzione della casa comune europea', *L'Arbore della Carità*, 43, pp. 41–55

Cavallini, G. (ed.) (1993), *Caterina da Siena, Le Orazioni*, Siena

Cavallini, G. (1998), 'Caterina da Siena nei suoi scritti' in *Catharina: Testi ed immagini di S. Caterina da Siena nelle raccolte casanatensi*, Rome, pp. 17–25

Cavallini, G. (2005), *Catherine of Siena*, London

Cavallini, G. and Giunta, D. (2000), *Luoghi Cateriniani di Roma*, Rome

Cavazza, S. (1997), *Piccole Patrie: Feste popolari tra regione e nazione durante il fascismo*, Bologna

Ceppari Ridolfi, M. and Turrini, P. (2002), 'Il movimento associativo e devozionale dei laici nella Chiesa senese (secc. XIII–XIX)' in A. Mirizio and P. Nardi (eds), *Chiesa e Vita Religiosa a Siena: dalle origini al grande giubileo*, Siena, pp. 247–303

Chavin de Malan, E. (1846), *Histoire de Sainte Catherine de Sienne (1347–1380)*, 2 vols, Paris

Ciabattini, P. (1991), *Siena fra la scure e la falce e martello: cronaca e memorie dal 1926 al 1950*, Sovicille

'Cinquantenario dei Patroni d'Italia San Francesco d'Assisi e Santa Caterina da Siena' (1989), *Quaderni Cateriniani*, 54–5

Cohn, S. (1979), 'Rivolte popolare e classi sociali in Toscana nel Rinsacimento', *Studi Storici*, 20, pp. 747–58

Cohn, S. (1980), *The Labouring Classes in Renaissance Florence*, New York

Coiro, G. (1929), 'S. Caterina da Siena e l'avvenimento dell'11 Febbraio 1929', *Rassegna Cateriniana*, 8, pp. 28–9

Colucci, I. (2005), 'Rutillio Manetti, Cocifisso' in *Siena e Roma: Raffaello, Caravaggio e i protagonisti di un legame antico*, Siena, pp. 507–9

Congresso Internazionale di Studi Cateriniani: Siena–Roma, 24–29 Aprile 1980, (1981), Rome

Consolino, F. (ed.) (1991), *I Santi Patroni Senesi*, Siena

Cordovani, M. (1939), 'Santa Caterina da Siena, Patrona Primaria d'Italia', *Memorie Domenicane*, 56, pp. 195–201

Corner, P. (2002), 'Italian Fascism: Whatever Happened to Dictatorship?', *The Journal of Modern History*, 74, pp. 325–51

Cornwall, M. (2000), *The Undermining of Austria–Hungary: The Battle for Hearts and Minds*, London

D'Accone, F. (1997), *The Civic Muse: Music and Musicians in Siena during the Middle Ages and the Renaissance*, Chicago

Dalla Torre, G. (1939), 'I Primarî Patroni d'Italia', *Vita e Pensiero*, 30, pp. 307–13

De Grazia, V. (1992), *How Fascism Ruled Women: Italy, 1922–1945*, Berkeley

Deraedt, M. (1992), 'Santa Caterina da Siena patrona degli elettori cristiani d'Europa', *Quaderni Cateriniani*, 68

Diamanti, I. and Ceccarini, L. (2007), 'Catholics and politics after the the Christian Democrats: the influential minority', *Journal of Modern Italian Studies*, 12, pp. 37–59

Dizionario biografico degli italiani (1960–ongoing), Rome

Doumanis, N. (2001), *Italy*, London

Drane, A. (1914), *The History of St. Catherine of Siena and Her Companions*, 2 vols, London

Dunnage, J. (2002), *Twentieth Century Italy: A Social History*, London

Dupré Theseider, E. (1979), 'Caterina da Siena, santa', *Dizionario Bibliografico degli Italiani*, 22, Rome, pp. 361–79

Durand, J. (2000), 'Santa Caterina da Siena, le nazioni e l'Europa' in S. Soldini (ed.), *Santa Caterina da Siena: Una nuova statua di Eric Aman nella Basilica Vaticana*, Perugia, pp. 93–9

D'Urso, G. (1986), *M. Castellano, Raccolta di Scritti nei venticinque anni di episcopate senese 1961–1986*, Siena

Falassi, A. (1980), *La Santa dell'Oca: vita morte e miracoli di Caterina da Siena*, Siena

Fatini, G. (1929), 'La Santa degli Italiani', *Rassegna Cateriniana*, 8, 1929, pp. 128–32

Fawcett, L. (2000), *Religion, Ethnicity and Social Change*, Basingstoke

Fecini, T. (1931–39), 'Cronaca Senese' in A. Lisini and F. Iacometti (eds), *Rerum Italicarum Scriptores*, 15, part 6, pp. 837–74

Fiume, M. (1940), 'S. Caterina da Siena e le virtù eroiche della stirpe', *Memorie Domenicane*, 57, pp. 203–9

Flury-Nencini, B. (1929), 'S. Caterina da Siena aralda di pace', *Studi Cateriniani*, 6, pp. 4–19

Fortini, A. (1937), *Il Ritorno di San Francesco: Cronaca del Settimo Centenario Francescano 1926–1927*, Milan

Francescone, P. (1989), 'Difensori della pace, operatori di pace', *Rivista Militare, Numero Unico, 'Le Due Patrie'*, Rome, pp. 21–61

Franzinelli, M. (1991), *Il rearmo dello spirito: I cappellani militare nella seconda guerra mondiale*, Treviso

Franzinelli, M. (1995), *Stellate, Croce e Fascio Littorio: L'assistenza religiosa a militarei, balilla e camice nere 1919–1939*, Milan

Franzinelli, M. (ed.) (2003a), *Il volto religioso della guerra: Santini e immaginette per i soldati*, Faenza

Franzinelli, M. (2003b), 'L'Ordinariato militare dal fascismo alla guerra fredda', *Italia Contemporanea*, 233, pp. 637–55

Freuler, G. (1987), 'Andrea di Bartolo, Fra Tommaso d'Antonio Caffarini, and Sienese Dominicans in Venice', *The Art Bulletin*, 69, pp. 570–86

Fusai, L. (1999), *Storia di Siena: dalla caduta della repubblica all'età contemporanea (secoli XVI–XX)*, Siena

Gagliardi, R. (1996), 'Girolamo Gigli' in R. Barzanti, G. Catoni and M. De Gregorio (eds), *Storia di Siena: dal Granducato all'Unità*, Siena, pp. 137–52

Garelli, F. (2007), 'The public relevance of the church and Catholicism in Italy', *Journal of Modern Italian Studies*, 12, pp. 8–36

Gatti, I. (1983), *La Tomba di S. Francesco nei Secoli*, Assisi

Gava, A. (1985), 'Santa Caterina parla all'Italia di oggi', *Quaderni Cateriniani*, 40, pp. 11–16

Gedda, L. (1962), 'A Santa Caterina Patrona d'Italia', *Tabor*, 16, pp. 293–4

Gedda, L. (1998), *18 aprile 1948: Memorie inedite dell'artefice della sconfitta del Fronte Popolare*, Milan

Gentile, E. (1990), 'Fascism as Political Religion', *Journal of Contemporary History*, 25, pp. 229–51

Gentile, E. (1996), *The Sacralization of Politics in Fascist Italy*, Cambridge, Massachusetts

Gentile, E. (2001), *Le religioni della politica: Fra democrazie e totalitarismi*, Rome–Bari

Gentile, E. (2006), 'New idols: Catholicism in the face of fascist totalitarianism', *Journal of Modern Italian Studies*, 11, pp. 143–70

Gianni, A. (2002), 'Le immagini portate nella processione della Domenica in Albis' in A. Mirizio and P. Nardi (eds), *Chiesa e Vita Religiosa a Siena: dalle origini al grande giubileo*, Siena, pp. 323–73

Gigli, G. (1854, originally published 1723), *Diario sanese*, vol.1, Siena

Gillet, M. (1930), 'Santa Caterina da Siena e Santa Giovanna d'Arco – Le Due Sante della Patria', *Studi Cateriniani*, 7, pp. 1–25

Giordani, I. (1962), 'Santa Caterina Riformatrice Sociale', *Bollettino Senese di Storia Patria*, 69, pp. 16–31

Ginsborg, P. (1990), *A History of Contemporary Italy 1943–1980*, London

Giunta, D. (1988), 'L'immagine di S. Caterina da Siena dagli ultimi decenni del trecento ai nostri giorni' in L. Bianchi and D. Giunta, *Iconografia di Santa Caterina da Siena, I. L'Immagine*, Rome, pp. 63–148

Giunta, D. (1999), 'La questione delle stimmate alle origine della iconografia cateriniana e la fortuna del tema nel corso dei secoli' in L. Trenti and B. Klange Addabbo (eds), *Con l'occhio e col lume: atti del corso seminarile di studi su S. Caterina da Siena (25 settembre – 7 ottobre 1995)*, Siena, pp. 319–47

Giunta, D. (2002), 'Il tema della pace nella iconografia cateriniana' in G. Minnucci (ed.), *Lecturae Catharinae 2001: Santa Caterina da Siena e la pace*, Siena, pp. 59–78

Gonella, G. (1947), *La Pace Armata di Amore: Commemorazione di Santa Caterina da Siena tenuta in Siena per l'inaugurazione del VI centenario cateriniano*, Rome

Gorresio, V. (1968), *La nuova missione*, Milan

Grassi, V. (1939), 'Antiche cerimonie per la festa di S. Caterina', *Studi Cateriniani*, 17, pp. 3–5

Grassi, V. (1940), *Ricordi Cateriniani nel territorio della Contrada del Drago*, Siena

Grassi, V. (1972), *Le Contrade di Siena e le loro feste – Il Palio attuale*, vol. 2, Siena

Grassi, V. (1991), 'La visita di Pio IX a Siena' in G. Catoni, P. Leoncini and R. Leoncini (eds), *Virgilio Grassi: Palio ed altro per 'Il Telegrafo'*, Siena, pp. 94–8

Grygiel, L. (2004), *San Benedetto il primo Europeo*, Siena

Hase, T. (2001), *Zivilreligion: Religionswissenschaftliche Überlegungen su einem theoretischen Konzept am Beispiel der USA*, Würzburg

Hebblethwaite, P. (1984), *John XXIII: Pope of the Council*, London

Heusinger, S. von (2000), 'Catherine of Siena and the Dominican Order' in M. Ascheri (ed.), *Siena e il suo territorio nel rinascimento*, Siena, pp. 43–51

Jackson, P. (2007a) 'The Patronage of Pandolfo the Magnificent' in L. Syson et al., *Renaissance Siena: Art for a City*, London, pp. 60–73

Jackson, P. (2007b) 'Chronology' in L. Syson et al., *Renaissance Siena: Art for a City*, London, pp. 74–7

Jemolo, A. (1960), *Church and State in Italy 1850–1950*, Oxford

Jenkins, M. (1972), 'The Iconography of the Hall of the Concistory in the Palazzo Pubblico, Siena', *The Art Bulletin*, 54, pp. 430–51

Jervolino, R. (1980), 'S. Caterina e le donne d'oggi' in *Il sesto centenario del transito di S. Caterina da Siena (1380–1980)*, Siena, pp. 55–73

Jorgensen, J. (1938), *Saint Catherine of Siena*, translated from the Danish by I. Lund, London

Kearns, C. (1980) 'Introduction' in *The Life of Saint Catherine of Siena by Raymond of Capua*, translated, introduced and annotated by Conleth Kearns, Dublin, pp. xiii–lxxxix

Kieckhefer, R. (1997), 'Foreword' in A. Vauchez, *Sainthood in the later Middle Ages*, Cambridge, pp. xix–xi

Kirwin, C. (1972), 'The Oratory of the Sanctuary of Saint Catherine in Siena', *Mitteilungen des Kunsthistorischen Institutes in Florenz*, 16, pp. 199–220

Klaniczay, G. (2002), *Holy Rulers and Blessed Princesses: Dynastic Cults in Medieval Central Europe*, Cambridge

Koenig, J. (2001), 'Prisoner Offerings, Patron Saints and State Cults, at Siena and other Italian Cities from 1250 to 1550', *Bullettino Senese di Storia Patria*, 108, pp. 222–96

Koon, T. (1985), *Believe, Obey, Fight: Political Socialization of Youth in Fascist Italy, 1922–1943*, Chapel Hill

La Pira, G. (1939), 'Spiritualità Italica', *Vita cristiana*, 11, pp. 284–8

Lasansky, D. (2007), 'Political Allegories: Redesigning Siena's *Palio* and Patron Saint during the Fascist Regime' in C. Baskins and L. Rosenthal (eds), *Early Modern Visual Allegory: Embodying Meaning*, Aldershot, pp. 109–31

Laurent, M-H. (1942), *Il processo Castellano, Fontes Vitae S. Catherinae Senensis Historici*, vol. IX, Milan

Lisini, A. (1892), 'S. Caterina e un Capitano del Popolo', *La Vergine Benincasa, S. Caterina da Siena*, 7, pp. 3–5

Logan, O. (1997), 'Christian Civilization and Italic Civilization: Italian Catholic Theses from Gioberti to Pius XII' in R. Swanson (ed.), *The Church Retrospective*, Woodbridge, pp. 475–86

Logan, O. (1998), 'Pius XII: *romanità*, prophesy and charisma', *Modern Italy*, 3, pp. 237–47

Lombardelli, G. (1593), *Ragguaglio della Traslazione della sacra Testa di Santa Caterina da Roma a Siena sua patria*, Siena

Lotti, A. (1992), *La chiesa di Siena a i suoi vescovi*, Siena

Luchini, L. (1987), *Siena dei bisnonni*, Siena

Luchini, L. (1994), *Siena dei nonni*, vol. 2, Siena

Luchini, L. (2002), *Immagini d'Italia: Siena*, vol. 2, Stroud

Luongo, F. Thomas (2006), *The Saintly Politics of Catherine of Siena*, Ithaca and London

Lusini, V. (1901), *Il San Giovanni di Siena e i suoi restauri*, Florence

Maffei, D. and Nardi, P. (eds) (1982), *Atti del Simposio Internazionale Cateriniano-Bernardiniano, Siena, 17–20 Aprile 1980*, Siena

Maggi, G. (1981), 'Comitati Civici' in F. Traniello and G. Camparini (eds), *Dizionario Storico del Movimento cattolico in Italia, 1860–1980*, vol.1.2, Turin, pp. 207–9

Magister, S. (1979), *La politica vaticana e l'Italia 1943–1978*, Rome

Malgeri, F. (1994) 'Chiesa cattolica e regime fascista', *Italia Contemporanea*, 194, pp. 53–63

Margiotta Broglio, F. (2000), 'Dalla Conciliazione al giubileo 2000' in L. Fiorani and A. Prosperi (eds), *Storia D'Italia, Annali 16, Roma, la città del papa*, Turin, pp. 1151–209

Matteucci-Serpieri, I. (1940), 'S. Caterina da Siena e la Società di Studi Cateriniani', *Studi Cateriniani*, 18, pp. 1–21

Matthews Grieco, S. (1994), 'Modelli di santità femminile nell'Italia del Rinascimento e della Controriforma' in L. Scaraffia and G. Zarri (eds), *Donna e Fede: Santità e Vita Religiosa in Italia*, Rome–Bari, pp. 303–25

Meattini, U. (ed.) (2005), *Caterina da Siena: Le Lettere ai papi e ai vescovi,* Milan

Meattini, U. (ed.) (2006), *Caterina da Siena: Le Lettere alle autorità politiche, militari e civili*, Milan

Melloni, A. (2007), 'The politics of the "Church" in the Italy of Pope Wojtyla', *Journal of Modern Italian Studies*, 12, pp. 60–85

Mestrovic, S. (1993), *The Road from Paradise: Prospects for Democracy in Eastern Europe*, Lexington, Kentucky

Mestrovic, S. (1994), *The Balkanisation of the West: The Confluence of Postmodernism and Postcommunism*, London

Minnucci, G. (ed.) (2002), *Lecturae Catharinae 2001: Santa Caterina da Siena e la pace*, Siena

Minnucci, G. (ed.) (2003), *Lecturae Catharinae 2002: Santa Caterina da Siena e l'Europa*, Siena

Mirizio, A. (1993), *I Buoni Senesi: cattolici e società in provincia di Siena dall'Unità al Fascismo*, Brescia

Mirizio, A. (2002), 'Chiesa e cattolici a Siena dal Fascismo al secondo Dopoguerra' in A. Mirizio and P. Nardi (eds), *Chiesa e Vita Religiosa a Siena: dalle origini al grande giubileo*, Siena, pp. 469–511

Mirizio, A. (2003), *Per la religione e per la patria: Chiesa e cattolici a Siena dalla Conciliazione al Centrismo*, Siena

Misciattelli, P. (1911), *Mistici Senesi*, Siena

Misciattelli, P. (1913a), *Pensieri di S. Caterina da Siena*, Siena

Misciattelli, P. (1913b), *Mistici Senesi*, Siena

Misciattelli, P. (1913–21), *Lettere di Santa Caterina da Siena*, 6 vols, Siena

Misciattelli, P. (1922), 'Prefazione' in N. Tommaseo, *Lo spirito, il cuore, la parola di Caterina da Siena*, ed. P. Misciattelli, Siena, pp. vii–xi

Misciattelli, P. (1923), 'Il B. Giovanni Dominici e S. Caterina', *Studi Cateriniani*, 1, pp. 6–10

Misciattelli, P. (1924), *Facsisti e Cattolici*, Milan

Misciattelli, P. (1926a), 'La romanità di Santa Caterina', *Studi Cateriniani*, 3, pp. 15–21

Misciattelli, P. (1926b), 'La romanità di Santa Caterina', *Rassegna italiana politica letteraria e artistica*, 9, pp. 307–16

Misciattelli, P. (1933), 'L'Idealismo civile di Santa Caterina da Siena', *La Diana*, 8, pp. 33–50

Moerer, E. (2003), 'Catherine of Siena and the Use of Images in the Creation of a Saint, 1347–1461', Ph.D. thesis, University of Virginia

Moerer, E. (2005), 'The Visual Hagiography of a Stigmatic Saint: Drawings of Catherine of Siena in the *Libellus de Supplemento*', *Gesta*, 44, pp. 89–102

Morandi, U. (1996), 'La Casa e la Compagnia di S. Caterina', *Quaderni Cateriniani*, 91–2, pp. 11–32

Mostra Cateriniana di documenti, manoscritti ed edizioni (secoli XIII–XVIII) nel Palazzo del Comune di Siena: Catalogo, (1962), *Bollettino Senese di Storia Patria*, 69, pp. 263–367

Mussolin, M. (2006), 'The rise of the new civic ritual of the Immaculate Conception of the Virgin in sixteenth century Siena' in P. Jackson and F. Nevola, *Beyond the Palio: Urbanism and Ritual in Renaissance Siena*, Oxford, pp. 117–39

Nardi, P. (2005), 'Per un profile di Alessandro Toti: cultura e impegno pastorale di un sacerdote senese del XIX secolo' in *Istituto Storico Diocesano Siena Annuario 2004–2005*, Siena, pp. 341–63

Nencini, T. (1932), 'Santa Caterina, Santa Nazionale!', *Studi Cateriniani*, 9, 1932, pp. 39–47

Nencini, T. (1941), 'Noi Cateriniani, nel Culto della Santa, nell'amore di Siena', *Studi Cateriniani*, 17, pp. 45–56

Nevola, F. (2005), 'L'architettura tra Siena e Pienza: Architettura civile' in A. Angelini (ed.), *Pio II e le arti: La riscoperta dell'antico da Federighi a Michelangelo*, Milan, pp. 183–213

Nevola, F. (2006), 'Ritual geography: housing the papal court of Pius II Piccolomini in Siena (1459–60)' in P. Jackson and F. Nevola (eds), *Beyond the Palio: Urbanism and Ritual in Renaissance Siena*, Oxford, pp. 65–88

Nevola, F. (2007a), *Siena: Constructing the Renaissance City*, London

Nevola, F. (2007b), 'Civic Identity and Private Patrons in Renaissance Siena' in L. Syson et al., *Renaissance Siena: Art for a City*, London, pp. 17–29

Noffke, S. (ed.) (1980), *Catherine of Siena: The Dialogue*, London

Noffke, S. (ed.) (2000), *The Letters of Catherine of Siena*, vol. 1, Tempe, Arizona

Norman, D. (1999), *Siena and the Virgin: Art and Politics in a Late Medieval City State*, London

Norman, D. (2003) *Painting in Late Medieval and Renaissance Siena*, London

Norman, D. (2006), '"Santi Cittadini": Vecchietta and the Civic Pantheon in Mid Fifteenth Century Siena', unpublished paper given at the College Art Association of America Conference, Boston

Norman, D. (2007), 'When charity fails: Andrea Gallerani and memory of the Misericordia in Siena' in D. Stathakopoulous (ed.), *The Kindness of Strangers: Charity in the Pre-Modern Mediterranean*, London, pp. 91–118

Norman, D. (2008), 'The Chapel of Saint Catherine in San Domenico: A Study of Cultural Relations between Renaissance Siena and Rome' in M. Ascheri, G. Mazzoni and F. Nevola (eds), *Siena nel Rinascimento: l'ultimo secolo della repubblica, II. Arte architettura e cultura*, Siena

Norman, D. (forthcoming), '"Santi Cittadini": Vecchietta and the Civic Pantheon in Mid Fifteenth Century Siena' in T. Smith and J. Steinhoff (eds), *Art as Politics in Late Medieval and Renaissnace Siena*, Aldershot

Nozzoli, G. (1928), 'L'Arciconfraternita di Santa Caterina da Siena in Roma', *Studi Cateriniani*, 5, pp. 3–9

Nozzoli, G. (1930), 'Carattere nazionale della Confratenita di Santa Caterina da Siena in Roma', *Studi Cateriniani*, 6, pp. 63–6

Nuti, A. (2003), *La provincia più rossa: la costruzione del partito nuovo a Siena (1945–1956)*, Siena

O'Brien, A. (1971), 'The *Osservatore Romano* and Fascism: The Beginning of a New Era in Church–State Relations, October 1922–July 1923', *Journal of Church and State*, 13, pp. 445–63

Odasso-Cartotti, A. (1981), 'Caterina Benincasa, Santa Europea' in *Congresso Internazionale di Studi Cateriniani*, Rome, pp. 664–9

Odasso-Cartotti, A. (1984a), *Caterina da Siena Santa Europea*, Vatican City

Odasso-Cartotti, A. (1984b), 'Santa Caterina da Siena e la Comunità europea' in A. Odasso-Cartotti, *Caterina da Siena Santa Europea*, Vatican City, pp. 63–9

Odasso-Cartotti, A. (1984c), 'Caterina da Siena Santa Europea' in A. Odasso-Cartotti, *Caterina da Siena Santa Europea*, Vatican City, pp. 21–9

Odasso-Cartotti, A. (1984d), 'Santa Caterina da Siena ai Capi di Stato Europei' in A. Odasso-Cartotti, *Caterina da Siena Santa Europea*, Vatican City, pp. 59–61

Odasso-Cartotti, A. (1993), 'Principii politici di S. Caterina da Siena', *Quaderni Cateriniani*, 72

Osbat, L. (1981), 'Movimento Cattolico e Questione Giovanile' in F. Traniello and G. Camparini (eds), *Dizionario Storico del Movimento cattolico in Italia, 1860–1980*, vol.1.2, Turin, pp. 84–96

Paganucci, A. (1962), 'Cento anni fa Siena celebro solennemente la storica ricorrenza', *La Patrona d'Italia*, 17, July–October 1962, pp. 4–5

Pajardi, P. (1993), *Caterina La Santa della Politica: Ricerche e riflessioni sul pensiero etico, giuridico, sociale e politico di Santa Caterina da Siena*, Milan

Pallavicino, C. (1996), 'La decorazione dei Libri dei Leoni' in M. Ascheri (ed.), *I Libri dei Leoni: La nobiltà di Siena in età medicea (1557–1737)*, Siena, pp. 363–8

Pallavicino, C., Ceppari Ridolfi, M. and Turrini, P. (1996), 'Schede delle tavole' in M. Ascheri (ed.), *I Libri dei Leoni: La nobiltà di Siena in età medicea (1557–1737)*, Siena, pp. 369–502

Palmerio, G. and Villetti, G. (1989), *Storia Edilizia di S. Maria sopra Minerva in Roma 1275–1870*, Rome

Parsons, G. (2001), 'O Maria, la tua Siena difendi: The Porta della Riconoscenza of Siena Cathedral', *Zeitschrift für Kunstgeschichte*, 64, pp. 153–76

Parsons, G. (2002), *Perspectives on Civil Religion*, Aldershot

Parsons, G. (2004a), *Siena, Civil Religion and the Sienese*, Aldershot

Parsons, G. (2004b), 'From Nationalism to Internationalism: Civil Religion and the Festival of Saint Catherine of Siena, 1940–2003', *Journal of Church and State*, 46, pp. 861–85

Parsons, G. (2006), 'Civil Religion and the Invention of Tradition: The Festival of Saint Ansano in Siena', *Journal of Contemporary Religion*, 21, pp. 49–67

Parsons, G. (2007), 'Fascism and Catholicism: A Case Study of the *Sacrario dei Caduti Fascisti* in the Crypt of San Domenico, Siena', *Journal of Contemporary History*, 42, pp. 469–84

Parsons, G. (2008a), 'A National Saint in a Fascist State: Catherine of Siena, *c.*1922–1943', *Journal of Religious History*, 32, pp. 76–95

Parsons, G. (2008b), 'A Neglected Sculpture: The Monument to Catherine of Siena at Castel Sant'Angelo', *Papers of the British School at Rome*, 76 (forthcoming)

Pastor, L. (1894), *The History of the Popes from the close of the middle ages*, ed. F. Antrobus, vol. 3, London

Paterna, M. (1989), *Bibliografia Analitica di S. Caterina da Siena, 1976–1985*, Rome

Paterna, M. (2000), *Bibliografia Analitica di S. Caterina da Siena, 1986–1990*, Rome

Paterna, M. (2003), *Bibliografia Analitica di S. Caterina da Siena, 1991–2000*, Rome

Pedini, M. (1978), 'Caterina anticipa i tempi', *Quaderni Cateriniani*, 21, pp. 12–17

Pedini, M. (1984), 'Santa Caterina da Siena a la nostra Europa', *Quaderni Cateriniani*, 49

Perica, V. (2005), 'The Sanctification of Enmity: Churches and the construction of founding myths of Serbia and Croatia' in P. Kolstø (ed.), *Myths and Boundaries in South-Eastern Europe*, London, pp. 130–57

Piccini, F. (2004), 'Una Lampada per la fine della guerra', *La Patrona d'Italia e d'Europa*, 56, October–November, pp. 17–18

Piccini, P. (1993a), 'Forte azione civile e politica', *Quaderni Cateriniani*, 70–71, pp. 4–7

Piccini, P. (1993b), 'La presenza di S. Caterina nell'Europa di oggi', *Quaderni Cateriniani*, 73, pp. 3–4

Piccini, P. (2000), 'Caterina – Pellegrina della luce' in S. Soldini (ed.), *Santa Caterina da Siena: Una nuova statua di Eric Aman nella Basilica Vaticana*, Perugia, pp. 49–55

Pierard, R. and Linder, R. (1988), *Civil Religion and the American Presidency*, Grand Rapids

Pollard, J. (1985), *The Vatican and Italian Fascism, 1929–32*, Cambridge

Prunai, G. (1942), Review of L. Sbaragli, *La Patrona d'Italia ai Soldati d'Italia in guerra*, *Bulletino Senese di Storia Patria*, 49, pp. 214–16.

Rattazzi Papka, C. (1995), 'The Written Woman Writes: Caterina da Siena Between History and Hagiography, Body and Text', *Annali d'Italianistica*, 13, pp. 131–49

Raymond of Capua (1866), *Legenda Sancti Catherine Senensis* in *Acta Sanctorum* 3, Paris, pp. 862–967

Raymond of Capua, (1980), *The Life of Saint Catherine of Siena by Raymond of Capua*, translated by C. Kearns, Dublin

Redon, O. (1992), 'L'image de Catherine dans l'iconographie communale' in *Catherine de Sienne*, Avignon, pp. 169–74

Redon, O. (2004), 'Costruire una famiglia nel medioevo. Banchieri, cavalieri e un santo' in F. Gabbrielli (ed.), *Palazzo Sansedoni*, Siena, pp. 19–55

*Relazione della Solenne Processione fatta in Siena nella Domencica in Albis l'anno MDCCXXVII dedicata all'illustrissimo e reverendissimo monsignore Antonio Felice Zondadori dei Marchese Chigi eletto inquisitore di Malt*a (1777), Siena

Riciotti, R. (2004), *La Ferita Sanata: I Patti Lateranensi e l'accordo di Villa Madama fra storia, politica e diritto*, Rimini

Ridolfi, M. (2003), *Le feste nazionali*, Bologna

Riedl, P. (ed.) (1990), *L'Oratorio di Santa Caterina in Fontebranda: Le vicende costruttive, gli affreschi, gli argenti*, Siena

Riedl, P. (ed.) (1990), 'L'Oratorio della Contrada dell'Oca: Affreschi' in P. Riedl (ed.), *L'Oratorio di Santa Caterina in Fontebranda: Le vicende costruttive, gli affreschi, gli argenti*, Siena, pp. 45–88

Riedl, P. and Seidel, M. (eds) (1985), *Die Kirchen von Siena, Band 1.1, Abbadia all-Arco – S. Biagio*, Munich

Riedl, P. and Seidel, M. (eds) (1992a), *Die Kirchen von Siena, Band 2.1.1, Oratorio della Carità – San Domenco*, Munich

Riedl, P. and Seidel, M. (eds) (1992b), *Die Kirchen von Siena, Band 2.1.2, Oratorio della Carità – San Domenco*, Munich

Riedl, P. and Seidel, M. (eds) (1992c), *Die Kirchen von Siena, Band 2.2, Band 2.2, Oratorio della Carità – San Domenco*, Munich

Righi, M. (1934), *Santa Caterina da Siena e la Conciliazione*, Rome

Ronci, E. (2005), *Arnaldo Fortini e la 'Nova Vita di San Francesco d'Assisi'*, Assisi

Rossi, G. (2002), 'Feste, Cacce e Sacre Rappresentazione' in R. Ferri and G. Vannuchi (eds), *Siena a Teatro*, Siena, pp. 19–39

Rossi, P. (1928), 'Il busto di S. Caterina offerta dai senesi a Roma', *Studi Cateriniani* 5, pp. 10–19

Sabelli, R. (ed.) (2002), *Il Santuario-Casa di Santa Caterina da Siena: conoscenza del monumento attraverso i restauri*, Florence

Sbaragli, L. (1942), *La Patrona d'Italia ai Soldati d'Italia in guerra – esortazioni e pensieri di Santa Caterina da Siena scelta da p.Luigi Sbaragli*, Siena

Sbaragli, L. (1943), 'Il pellegrinaggio della Confraternita Romana di S. Caterina da Siena alla Madonna di Provenzano (1595)', *Bullettino Senese di Storia Patria*, 50, pp. 23–34

Scalfaro, O. (1981), 'Il Messaggio di Santa Caterina agli uomini di oggi' in *Congresso Internazionale di Studi Cateriniani: Siena–Roma, 24–29 Aprile 1980*, Rome, pp. 699–712

Schietroma, P. (1983), 'S. Caterina, portatrice di verità, di giustizia e di pace', *Quaderni Cateriniani*, 35, pp. 17–19

Scott, K. (1992), 'St. Catherine of Siena, "Apostola"', *Church History*, 61, pp. 34–46

Scott, K. (1993), '"Io Caterina": Ecclesiastical Politics and Oral Culture in the Letters of Saint Catherine of Siena' in K. Cherewatuk and U. Wiethaus (eds), *Dear Sister: Medieval Women and the Epistolary Genre*, Philadelphia, pp. 87–121

Scott, K. (1994), 'Urban Spaces, Women's Networks, and the Lay Apostolate in the Siena of Catherine Benincasa' in E. Matter and J. Coakley (eds), *Creative Women in Medieval and Early Modern Italy: A Religious and Artistic Renaissance*, Philadelphia, pp. 105–19

Scott, K. (1999), 'Mystical Death, Bodily Death: Catherine of Siena and Raymond of Capua on the Mystic's Encounter with God' in C. Mooney (ed), *Gendered Voices: Medieval Saints and Their Interpreters*, Philadelphia, pp. 136–67

Slattery, M. (1989), 'Holy Anorexia? Catherine of Siena's Spirituality', *Église et Théologie*, 20, pp. 195–224

Snowden, F. (1989), *The Fascist Revolution in Tuscany 1919–1922*, Cambridge

Soldini, S. (ed.) (2000), *Santa Caterina da Siena: Una nuova statua di Eric Aman nella Basilica Vaticana*, Perugia

Southard, E. (1978), 'The Frescoes in Siena's Palazzo Pubblico, 1289–1539: Studies in Imagery and Relations to other Communal Palaces in Tuscany', Ph.D thesis, Indiana University

Spezzaferro, L. (2005), 'L'omogeneità di una situazione complessa. Vicende della chiesa di Santa Caterina da Siena in Via Giulia' in *Siena e Roma: Raffaello, Caravaggio e i protagonisti di un legame antico*, Siena, pp. 439–53

Statuto (dell'Associazione Ecumenica dei Caterinati) (1981), Siena

Statuto (dell'Associazione Internazionale dei Caterinati) (2005), Siena

Steinhoff, J. (2006), *Sienese Painting after the Black Death: Artistic Pluralism, Politics and the New Art Market*, Cambridge

Steinz-Kecks, H. (1990), 'Santa Caterina in Fontebranda: Storia della costruzione' in P. Riedl (ed.), *L'Oratorio di Santa Caterina in Fontebranda*, Siena, pp. 1–44

Strehlke, C. (1988a), 'Art and Culture in Renaissance Siena' in K. Christiansen, L. Kanter and C. Strehlke, *Painting in Renaissance Siena 1420–1450*, New York, pp. 33–60

Strehlke, C. (1988b), 'Giovanni di Paolo' in K. Christiansen, L. Kanter and C. Strehlke, *Painting in Renaissance Siena 1420–1450*, New York, pp. 168–269

Syson, L. et al. (2007), *Renaissance Siena: Art for a City*, London

Toccabelli, M. (1940), 'La Parola di Mons. Toccabelli' in C. Barbieri (ed.), *Solenni Feste Nazionali a Gloria di Santa Caterina da Siena Patrona d'Italia*, Siena, pp. 22–4

Tommaseo, N. (1860), *Le lettere di S. Caterina da Siena: ridotte a miglior lezione e in ordine nuove disposte, con proemio e note di Niccolò Tommaseo*, 4 vols, Florence

Tommaseo, N. (1922), *Lo spirito, il cuore, la parola di Caterina da Siena*, ed. P. Misciattelli, Siena

Tommaseo, N. (1979), *Lo spirito, il cuore, la parola di Caterina da Siena*, ed. A. Pecchioli, Rome

Tommaso di Antonio Caffarini (1942), *Sanctae Catherinae Senensis Legenda Minor*, ed. E. Franceschini, *Fontes Vitae S. Catherinae Senensis Historici*, vol. X, Milan

Tommaso di Antonio Caffarini (1974), *Libellus de Supplemento Legende Prolixe Virginis Beate Catherine de Senis*, ed. G. Cavallini and I. Foralosso, Rome

Toncelli, D. (1909), *La Casa di Santa Caterina a Siena*, Rome

Torriti, P. (1982), *La Casa di Santa Caterina e la Basilica di San Domenico a Siena*, Genoa

Torriti, P. (1988), *Tutta Siena: Contrada per Contrada*, Florence

Torriti, P. (1993), 'L'iconografia del Beato Ambrogio da Siena', *Bullettino Senese di Storia Patria*, 100, pp. 212–383

Toti, A. (1870), *Atti di votazione della città di Siena e del Senese alla SS. Vergine Madre di G.C. pubblicata per la prima volta pella festa di Agosto dell'anno 1870*, Siena

Toti, A. (1880), *La Casa di S. Caterina in Siena ed il nuovo prospetto della Chiesa di S. Maria sopra Minerva in Roma*, Siena

Tozzi, F. (1913), *Antologia d'antichi scrittori senesi (Dalle origini fino a Santa Caterina)*, Siena

Tozzi, F. (1918), *Le cose più belle*, Lanciano

Trenti, L. and Klange Addabbo, B. (eds) (1999), *Con l'occhio e col lume: Atti del corso seminariale di studi su S. Caterina da Siena (25 settembre – 7 ottobre 1995)*, Siena

Trifone, P. (2004), 'Il "Vocabolario cateriniano" di Girolamo Gigli', *Accademia dei Rozzi*, 11, pp. 15–20

Trifone, P. (2006), 'Gli ingegnosi capricci di un linguaiolo. Appunti sul "*Vocabolario cateriniano*" di Giroloamo Gigli' in L. Leonardi and P. Trifone (eds), *Dire L'Ineffabile. Caterina da Siena e il linguaggio della mistica*, Florence, pp. 189–203

Turrini, P. (1998), 'Religiosità e spirito caritativo a Siena agli inizio della reggenza lorenese: luoghi pii laicali, contrade e arti', *Istituto Storico Diocesano di Siena Annuario, 1996–97*, Siena, pp. 145–293

van Os, H. (1974) *Vecchietta and the Sacristy of the Siena Hospital Church: A Study in Renaissance Religious Symbolism,* The Hague

Vanni, A. (1930), 'Il Patto Lateranense e S. Caterina da Siena', *Studi Cateriniani*, 6, pp. 53–62

Vanni, T. (1975), *Caterina da Siena: 'luce intellettual piena d'amore'*, Rome

Vauchez, A. (1997), *Sainthood in the later Middle Ages*, Cambridge

Vegni, A. (1928), 'L'offerta del Busto di S. Caterina da Siena a Roma', *La Balzana: Rassegna di Attività Municipale*, 2, pp. 26–9

Ventresca, R. (2003), 'The Virgin and the Bear: Religion, society and the Cold War in Italy', *Journal of Social History*, 37, pp. 439–56

Ventresca, R. (2004), *From Fascism to Democracy: Culture and Politics in the Italian Election of 1948*, Toronto

Vigni, G. (1937), *Lorenzo di Pietro ditto il Vecchietta*, Florence

Villani, C. (1940), 'A Santa Caterina da Siena Patrona d'Italia', *Memorie Domenicane*, 57, pp. 199–202

Volpato, A. (2002), 'Divisione e unità della Chiesa nelle lettere di santa Caterina' in G. Minnucci (ed.), *Lecturae Catharinae 2001: Santa Caterina da Siena e la pace*, Siena, pp. 17–43

Walker Bynum, C. (1987), *Holy Feast and Holy Fast: The Religious Significance of Food to Medieval Women*, Berkeley

Walsh, M. (1987), *Butler's Lives of the Patron Saints: edited with additional material*, Tunbridge Wells

Webb, D. (1996), *Patrons and Defenders: The Saints in the Italian City-states*, London

Webster, R. (1960), *Christian Democracy in Italy 1860–1960*, London

Wegner, S. (2005), 'The Rise of Saint Catherine of Siena as an Intercessor for the Sienese' in A. Jenkens (ed.), *Renaissance Siena: Art in Context*, Kirksville, Missouri, pp. 173–93

Zaggia, M. (2006), 'Varia fortuna editoriale delle Lettere di Caterina da Siena' in L. Leonardi and P. Trifone (eds), *Dire L'Ineffabile. Caterina da Siena e il linguaggio della mistica*, Florence, pp. 127–87

Zagheni, G. (2006), *La Croce e il Fascio: I cattolici italiani e la dittatura*, Milan

Zanini, L. (1971), *Bibliografia Analitica di S. Caterina da Siena, 1901–1950*, Rome

Zanini, L. (1985), *Bibliografia Analitica di S. Caterina da Siena, 1951–1975, a cura di M. Carlotta Paterna*, Rome

Zetti, M. (1999), 'Sena Vetus Civitas Virginis. Evoluzione dell'iconografia mariana nei drappelloni del Palio di Siena (1930–1996). Annalisi e confronti' in S. Bruschelli (ed.), *Ianua Coeli: Leggere l'arte della Chiesa, Quaderni dell'Opera, 3*, Siena

Internet Sources

animaeuropae.org (accessed 27/11/2007)

caterinati.org (accessed 8/1/2008)

caterinavonsiena.be/frameset140203.htm (accessed 27/11/2007)

centrostudiocateriniani.it/2/2cenno.html (accessed 27/11/2007)

centrostudicateriniani.it/1/1cronologia (accessed 8/1/2008)

esercito.difesa.it (accessed 27/11/2007)

vatican.va/holy_father/john_paul_ii/apost_letters/documents/hf_jp-ii_apl_29041980_amantissima-providentia_it.html (accessed 27/11/2007)

vatican.va/holy_father/john_paul_ii/speeches/1980/september/index.htm (accessed 27/11/2007)
vatican.va/holy_father/john_paul_ii/apost_letters/documents/hf_jp-ii_apl_31121980_egregiae-virtutis_it.html (accessed 27/11/2007)

Index